D1385243

HBJ SPELLING

SIGNATURE EDITION

GREEN

Thorsten Carlson

Richard Madden

HBJ SPELLING

SIGNATURE EDITION

HBJ **HARCOURT BRACE JOVANOVICH, PUBLISHERS**

Orlando   San Diego   Chicago   Dallas

Acknowledgments

For permission to reprint copyrighted material, grateful acknowledgment is made to the following source:

Harcourt Brace Jovanovich, Inc.: Letter forms from *HBJ Handwriting.* Copyright © 1987 by Harcourt Brace Jovanovich, Inc. Definitions and the pronunciation key in the "Spelling Dictionary" are from the *HBJ School Dictionary.* Copyright © 1985, 1977 by Harcourt Brace Jovanovich, Inc.

COVER DESIGN Graphic Concern, Inc.

ART CREDITS

Key: T, Top; B, Bottom; L, Left, C, Center, R, Right.

Yvette Banek: 38, 47(b) 58, 74, 113, 122, 140, 148; Beth Baum: 128, 129, 130, 131, 132; Kevin Callahan: 8(b), 20, 39, 47(t), 70, 91, 94, 95(t), 110, 135; Randy Chewning: 10(b), 42(b), 86(b), 108; Roberta Collier: 27, 29, 46, 50, 53, 54, 76, 77, 78, 79, 83, 120(b), 125, 156(t), 157, 158; Tom Cooke: 4, 5, 6, 32, 42(t), 44, 68(t), 69, 86(t), 100, 112(t), 150; Carolyn Croll: 26, 35, 62, 63, 80, 81, 95(b); Daniel Del Valle: 51, 104; Len Ebert: 13(t), 43, 60(t), 65(t), 82, 146(t); Arthur Friedman: 16, 111(b), 114, 126; Simon Galkin: 5(t); John Killgrew: 30, 31, 57(t), 64, 98(b), 142; Jared Lee: 8(t), 65(b), 108, 120(t), 121(b), 138, 143, Yee Chea Lin: 7, 15, 23, 25, 33, 37, 45, 49, 59, 60(b), 67, 71, 75, 85, 89, 97, 111(t), 115, 119, 121(t), 123, 127, 141, 146(b), 147(t), 149, 153; Sal Murdocca: 10(t), 17, 21, 61, 72, 90, 134, 147(b), 151; Sue Parnell: 156(b); Blanche Sims: 9, 12, 68(b), 73, 88, 112(b), 124; Pat Stewart: 102, 103, 105, 106; Susan Swan: 13(b), 24, 57(b); George Ulrich: 28, 84; Vantage Art: 11, 19, 41, 93, 101; Jenny Williams: 34, 56(b), 98(t), 116, 139, 152(b).

PHOTO CREDITS

Key: T, Top; B, Bottom; L, Left; C, Center; R, Right.

Cover Photography, Ken Lax; page 56, Ken Lax/The Stock Shop; 72, ZEFA/H. Armstrong Roberts; 87, Phoebe Dunn/DPI; 92, Eric Carle/Shostal Associates; 96, Shostal Associates; 99, Stan Wayman/Photo Researchers; 109(l), G. Trouillet/The Image Bank; 109(c), Rhoda Galyn; 109(r), Runk/Schoenberger/Grant Heilman; 117, HBJ Studio; 136, H. Armstrong Roberts; 144, Ruth Dixon; 163, J. A. Robinson/Photo Researchers; 164, Hans Reinhard/Bruce Coleman; 167, Pat Meyers; 169, Antonio Mendoza/Stock, Boston; 170, Sylvia Johnson/Woodfin Camp & Associates; 171, Stephen Kraseman/Photo Researchers; 172, Halley Ganges; 173, Leonard Rue III/Photo Researchers; 174, M. J. Germana/DPI; 175, George Roos/DPI; 177, Kim Massie/Rainbow; 179, Tana Hoban/DPI; 181, G. Schaller/Bruce Coleman; 182, Walter Chandoha; 184, Joe McDonald/Bruce Coleman; 186, A. B. Joyce/Photo Researchers; 188, Phil Dotson/DPI; 190(l), H. Armstrong Roberts; 190(r), Sepp Seitz/Woodfin Camp & Associates; 191, Frost Publishing Group. Ltd.; 193, Hans Pfletschinger/Peter Arnold; 194, HBJ Photo; 196, Florida Dept. of Commerce; 197(1), G. Bordis/De Wys; 197(r), Halley Ganges; 198(l), George Holton/Photo Researchers; 198(r). Ted Horowitz/The Stock Market; 199(l), Blaine Harrington III/The Stock Market; 199(r), Joe McDonald/Bruce Coleman; 200(l), Hill/Frost Publishing Group. Ltd.; 200(r), Mira Atkeson/DPI; 202, Irene Vandermolen/Bruce Coleman.

PRODUCTION AND LAYOUT Helena Frost Associates. Ltd.

Contents

v

Study Steps to Learn a Word

 **SAY** the word. Listen to each sound. Think about what the word means.

 **LOOK** at the word. See how the letters are made. Try to see the word in your mind.

 **SPELL** the word to yourself. Think about the way each sound is spelled.

 **WRITE** the word. Copy it from your book. Check the way you made your letters. Write the word again.

 **CHECK** your learning. Cover the word and write it. Did you spell it correctly? If not, do these steps until you know how to spell the word.

Skills Check

best score

A. (9)

A. Write a word you know that has each vowel sound.

1. short <u>a</u>

2. short <u>e</u>

3. short <u>i</u>

4. short <u>o</u>

5. short <u>u</u>

6. long <u>a</u>

7. long <u>e</u>

8. long <u>i</u>

9. long <u>o</u>

best score

B. (12)

B. Add beginning letters. Use different letters to write two different words each time.

10. ___op

11. ___an

12. ___ame

13. ___ee

14. ___ide

15. ___ut

best score

C. (4)

C. Two words in each row rhyme. One does not. Write the word that does not rhyme.

16. gave   have   save

17. near   hear   bear

18. hair   there   were

19. what   that   cat

D. Write each list of words in ABC order.

20. please
paint
neck
made

21. why
your
winter
wrong

E. Write the words that mean the opposite.

22. up   **23.** left   **24.** on

25. before   **26.** in   **27.** stop

F. Write an action word to finish each sentence.

28. Robin will ___ us a story.

29. Dennis will ___ dinner with us.

30. Tammy will ___ her bike to school.

31. Brian will ___ the game with us.

32. Wendy will ___ in the pool.

G. Say each word to yourself. Write a word that sounds the same but is not spelled the same.

33. wood   **34.** there

35. hear   **36.** rode

37. right   **38.** no

39. blew   **40.** deer

best score

D. (6)

best score

E. (6)

best score

F. (5)

best score

G. (8)

total 50

3

1 Short Vowel Sounds

THIS WEEK'S WORDS

1. flag
2. fed
3. hid
4. dot
5. hunt
6. apple
7. bring
8. club
9. else
10. happy
11. pen
12. river
13. rock
14. shall
15. sunny

I won't run, will you?

Never!

This Week's Words

All of This Week's Words have short vowel sounds. These are the signs for the short vowel sounds.

/a/ /e/ /i/ /o/ /u/

These sounds are usually spelled with one vowel letter.

You hear all the short vowel sounds in this sentence:

/a/ /e/ /i/ /o/ /u/
Fat hens will not run.

Remember this sentence. It will help you to remember which sounds are usually spelled with only one vowel letter.

4

Spelling Practice

A. Finish the sentences. Use This Week's Words.

1. The vowel sound /a/ is spelled with ____ in <u>fat</u>, ____, ____, ____, and ____.

2. The vowel sound /e/ is spelled with ____ in <u>hens</u>, ____, ____, and ____.

3. The vowel sound /i/ is spelled with ____ in <u>will</u>, ____, ____, and ____.

4. The vowel sound /o/ is spelled with ____ in <u>not</u>, ____, and ____.

5. The vowel sound /u/ is spelled with ____ in <u>run</u>, ____, ____, and ____.

B. Write the words that start with the same sounds as the picture names.

6.    7.

C. Write the words that end with the same sounds as the picture names.

8.    9.

flag
fed
hid
dot
hunt
apple
bring
club
else
happy
pen
river
rock
shall
sunny

Spelling and Language • Plurals

THIS WEEK'S WORDS
flag
fed
hid
dot
hunt
apple
bring
club
else
happy
pen
river
rock
shall
sunny

A **plural** names more than one. Add <u>s</u> to make most words plural.

Finish the sentences. Use the plurals of some of This Week's Words.

hen   **hens**

1. Do you have enough ___ to make a pie?
2. Craig has lots of pencils and ___.
3. Pete and I belong to different book ___.
4. Tina and Jim carried ___ in the parade.

Writing on Your Own

Write a postcard to your friends to tell them about a boat trip. Use the plural forms of these words: <u>rock</u>, <u>river</u>.

WRITER'S GUIDE How did you end each sentence? For help with periods and question marks, turn to page 249.

HANDWRITING

i I t T l L e E

The lowercase letters **i, t, l,** and **e** begin with this undercurve stroke.

1. Practice writing **i I, t T, l L, e E** in cursive.

2. Write this sentence: *I let Eli tell it.*

6

Spelling on Your Own

Words can make you think of other words. For example, leap might make you think of frog. And quiet as a might make you think of mouse. Write This Week's Words to go with these words.

1. treasure ___
2. ___ and ink
3. join the ___
4. ___ the i
5. bright and ___
6. anything ___
7. ___ it here
8. ___ ending
9. cross the ___
10. ___ or will
11. ___ the dog
12. ___ pie
13. hard as a ___
14. wave a ___
15. ran and ___

MASTERY WORDS

Follow the directions. Use the Mastery words.

1. Write the two words that begin with a vowel letter.
2. Write the two words that have short a.

Write the Mastery word that rhymes with each word.
3. beg
4. hit
5. hop
6. fast

and
last
leg
sit
top
until

BONUS WORDS

Add the missing letters to write Bonus words.

1. ___ift
2. ___ock
3. ___elt
4. ___ash
5. ___rap
6. ___op
7. ___ruck
8. ___ell

Now add different beginning consonant letters to the word parts above. For example, you can add l to ift to make lift or dr to make drift. See how many different words you can make.

struck
smash
dwell
melt
flock
crop
strap
swift

2 Double Letters

THIS WEEK'S WORDS

1. spill
2. drill
3. ill
4. shell
5. spell
6. smell
7. stuff
8. cliff
9. kiss
10. less
11. mess
12. unless
13. add
14. odd
15. roll

This Week's Words

Most of This Week's Words have a short vowel sound. Most of them end with the consonant sound /l/, /f/, or /s/. These consonant sounds are spelled with two consonant letters.

● /l/ is spelled **ll** in <u>spill</u>
● /f/ is spelled **ff** in <u>stuff</u>
● /s/ is spelled **ss** in <u>kiss</u>

Double consonant letters also spell /d/ in <u>add</u> and <u>odd</u>.

☐ The word <u>roll</u> does not have a short vowel sound. What vowel sound do you hear in <u>roll</u>?

REMEMBER THIS

One <u>d</u> is enough for <u>bad</u> and <u>sad</u>
And <u>lad</u> and <u>had</u> and even <u>mad</u>.
But when it comes to spelling <u>add</u>,
Another <u>d</u> you'll have to add.

One <u>d</u> will do for <u>cod</u> and <u>nod</u>,
And one's enough for <u>rod</u> and <u>pod</u>.
But <u>odd</u> is odd, as you see—
It needs a second letter <u>d</u>.

Spelling Practice

A. Follow the directions. Use This Week's Words.

1. Write the six words that have the vowel sound /e/.

2. Write the five words that have the vowel sound /i/.

3. Write the word that has a long o.

4. Write the word that rhymes with nod.

5. Write the word that rhymes with sad.

B. Finish the story with This Week's Words. The consonant sound that ends each word is given to help you. This will help you get started. The answer for **6** is mess.

My room is a __6__ /s/. Dad says I can't go to Ben's party __7__ /s/ I clean my room today. But cleaning my room makes me feel __8__ /l/. There is so much __9__ /f/ to put away. Here is the __10__ /d/ little __11__ /l/ I found on the beach. I could __12__ /l/ a hole in it and wear it on a chain. But it has a funny __13__ /l/. I guess I should throw it away.

spill
drill
ill
shell
spell
smell
stuff
cliff
kiss
less
mess
unless
add
odd
roll

Spelling and Language • Word Ladders

THIS
WEEK'S
WORDS

spill
drill
ill
shell
spell
smell
stuff
cliff
kiss
less
mess
unless
add
odd
roll

Changing one letter can make a different word. Take add. If you write o in place of a, you spell odd. Change the words below. Put a new letter where the ▲ is. The new letter is the first letter in the picture word. Then make another new word the same way.

1. k i s s

    ▲ _ _ _

    _ _ ▲ _

    _ ▲ _ _

2. s t i l l

    _ _ _ ▲ _

    _ _ _ ▲ _

    _ _ _ ▲ _

Writing on Your Own

Look at the picture on page 8. Write sentences for your classmates about the cat. First tell what is happening in the picture. Then tell what happens next. Use some of This Week's Words.

Using the Dictionary to Spell and Write

A good writer uses the dictionary to check if a word was used correctly. The words in a dictionary are in alphabetical order. **Alphabetical order** is the order of letters from a to z. Write these groups of words in alphabetical order.

1. cliff
   ill
   add
   roll

2. spell
   stuff
   shell
   smell

SPELLING DICTIONARY Remember to use your **Spelling Dictionary** when you write.

a b c d e f g h i j k l m
n o p q r s t u v w x y z

10

Spelling on Your Own

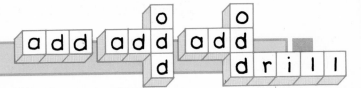

Make a "word chain" with This Week's Words. Write one word. Use a letter in that word to write another word. Then keep going, writing words across and down. Try to link all the words in one chain. You may also make more than one chain.

MASTERY WORDS

egg
fell
grass
off
pull
still

Follow the directions. Use the Mastery words.

1. Write the two words that begin with two consonant letters.
2. Write the two words that begin with a vowel letter.

Write the Mastery word that rhymes with each word below.

3. well   **4.** hill   **5.** pass   **6.** full

Write the Mastery words that go with these words.

7. on and ____   **8.** chicken and ____

BONUS WORDS

foggy
fossils
pillow
pudding
recess
sudden
valley
village

Write the Bonus word that goes with each meaning.

1. play period
2. place to rest your head
3. creamy dessert
4. without warning
5. small town
6. place between mountains
7. full of mist
8. marks of very old plants and animals

Write a short story. Try to use all the Bonus words.

3 Verbs

THIS WEEK'S WORDS

1. bat
2. chop
3. clap
4. drop
5. nap
6. pin
7. step
8. skinned
9. stopped
10. trapped
11. tripped
12. tagging
13. planning
14. wagging
15. tapping

The dogs wag their tails.

This Week's Words

The word wag is a **verb,** or action word. It ends with one vowel letter and one consonant letter. You can add ed to wag to make a word that tells about the past. When you add ed, you must double the last letter.

The dogs wagged their tails.

You can also add ing to wag. When you add ing, you must also double the last letter.

The dogs were wagging their tails.

All of This Week's Words are verbs. They all follow this pattern:

wag   wagged   wagging

Spelling Practice

A. Write the verbs that go with the pictures. Use This Week's Words.

1.

2.

3.

bat
chop
clap
drop
nap
pin
step
skinned
stopped
trapped
tripped
tagging
planning
wagging
tapping

B. Add <u>ed</u> to each of these words.

4. trip   **5.** skin   **6.** stop   **7.** trap

C. Add <u>ing</u> to each of these words.

8. wag   **9.** plan   **10.** tap   **11.** tag

D. Finish the sentences. Use This Week's Words.

12. A ____ of thunder surprised Chee.

13. She was helping her dad ____ wood.

14. The first ____ of rain hit her hand.

15. They decided to watch the rain from the ____.

E. Try this "word math."

16. stopped − ed = ____ + ing = ____

17. planning − ing = ____ + ed = ____

18. tripped − ed = ____ + ing = ____

Spelling and Language • Adding <u>ed</u> and <u>ing</u>

bat
chop
clap
drop
nap
pin
step
skinned
stopped
trapped
tripped
tagging
planning
wagging
tapping

You add <u>ed</u> to a word to tell what has already happened. You add <u>ing</u> to a word to tell what <u>is</u> or <u>was</u> happening.

Finish the sentences. Add <u>ed</u> to the words in dark print.

1. pin Mom ___ Tom's blue ribbon to his shirt.
2. clap We ___ until our hands were red.

Finish the sentences. Add <u>ing</u> to the words in dark print.

3. chop Jeff is ___ mushrooms for the pizza.
4. tag Sam's dog was ___ along after us.

Writing on Your Own

Write a paragraph for a friend telling how to play your favorite game. Be sure to give all the steps in the game. Use some of This Week's Words. Use the <u>ed</u> and <u>ing</u> endings.

 WRITER'S GUIDE For a sample how-to paragraph, turn to page 250.

HANDWRITING

r R   s S   p P

r   s   p

Notice where the beginning undercurve stroke stops in each lowercase letter.

1. Practice writing **r R, s S, p P** in cursive.

2. Write this sentence: *Peter sells pies.*

Spelling on Your Own

BAT

All of This Week's Words are **verbs.** But they can also be used as **nouns,** or naming words. <u>Bat</u> is a verb when you say "<u>Bat</u> the ball." But it is a noun when you say "Use my <u>bat</u>."

Write sentences using This Week's Words as nouns. You will have to take <u>ed</u> and <u>ing</u> off such words as <u>skinned</u> and <u>planning</u>.

MASTERY WORDS

hop
pat
rub
pet
spot
pop

Follow the directions. Use the Mastery words.
1. Write the three words that begin like <u>paw</u>.
2. Write the three words that end like <u>cat</u>.

Finish each sentence pair. Use a Mastery word.

3. Rabbits are hopping.
   Rabbits ___.

4. I am petting the dog.
   I ___ the dog.

5. Balloons are popping.
   Balloons ___.

6. I am rubbing my eyes.
   I ___ my eyes.

BONUS WORDS

scrub
swap
prop
plot
grabbed
shopped
wrapping
stirring

Write the Bonus word that rhymes with each word.
1. clapping   2. club   3. purring   4. hot

Follow the directions. Use the Bonus words.
5. Write the word that rhymes with <u>pop</u> but isn't spelled with <u>o</u>.
6. Make all the words end in <u>ed</u>. You will have to take <u>ing</u> off two words before you add <u>ed</u>. Then use each word in a sentence.

4 Consonant Clusters

THIS WEEK'S WORDS

1. clear
2. close
3. drawer
4. drive
5. flat
6. floor
7. print
8. snow
9. star
10. state
11. stick
12. trick
13. string
14. spray
15. spring

This Week's Words

Say the word <u>clear</u> to yourself. You hear two consonant sounds at the beginning of <u>clear</u>—/k/ and /l/. These sounds are spelled with **c** and **l**.

The letters **cl** in <u>clear</u> are called a **consonant cluster.** The letters are written together. You hear both consonant sounds.

Sometimes three consonant letters make up a consonant cluster. The letters **spr** in <u>spray</u> are a consonant cluster. You hear all three consonant sounds at the beginning of <u>spray</u>.

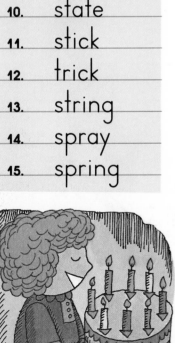

REMEMBER THIS

The word <u>close</u> can be said two ways. You say it one way when you say "<u>Close</u> your eyes." You say it another way when you say "Stand <u>close</u> to the table." But either way you say it, it is spelled the same: <u>close</u>.

Spelling Practice

A. Follow the directions. Use This Week's Words.

1. Write the four words that have <u>l</u> in the consonant cluster.

2. Write the seven words that have <u>r</u> in the consonant cluster.

3. Write the three words that begin with the same cluster as <u>stop</u>.

4. Write the three words that have a three-letter cluster.

5. Write the word that ends with <u>er</u>.

B. Finish the story with This Week's Words. The consonant clusters in ( ) will help you.

Jake was cold. He got up to (cl) **6** the window. The (fl) **7** felt icy under his feet. He looked out. There was fresh (sn) **8** on the ground. The sky was (cl) **9** . He saw a falling (st) **10** . It made a (str) **11** of light in the sky.

clear
close
drawer
drive
flat
floor
print
snow
star
state
stick
trick
string
spray
spring

Spelling and Language • Nouns and Verbs

A **noun** names a person, a place, or a thing. A **verb** shows action or being. Finish each pair of sentences with one of This Week's Words. The word will be a verb in the first sentence and a noun in the second sentence.

1. Tomorrow we will ___ to the mountains.
2. It is a beautiful ___ in the fall.
3. Let's ___ Mimi into thinking we're not going.
4. Mimi will laugh about our ___.

Writing on Your Own

Write a mystery story for your teacher. Tell about two people who are cleaning a house. Suddenly they find a note. Tell what the note says and what the two people do. Use some of This Week's Words.

Using the Dictionary to Spell and Write

On a dictionary page, an **entry word** is a word in dark print that is followed by its meaning. Entry words appear in alphabetical order. This helps you find a word quickly to check its spelling or meaning.

> ▶ **bus·y** /biz'ē/ *adj.* **1** Doing things: I'm *busy* making lunch. **2** Full of things to do: I had a *busy* day.
> ▶ **but·ter** /but'ər/ *n.* A yellow spread made from cream, used on bread.
> —*v.* To spread butter on.
> ▶ **but·ter·fly** /but'ər·flī'/ *n., pl.* **butterflies** An insect with four brightly colored wings.

Look up each word below in the **Spelling Dictionary**. Then write the entry word that follows it.

1. start   2. princess   3. draw   4. spread

 SPELLING DICTIONARY Remember to use your **Spelling Dictionary** when you write.

18

Spelling on Your Own

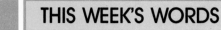

THIS WEEK'S WORDS

Use all of This Week's Words to make a word search puzzle. You can write the words across or down. Fill in the empty spaces with other letters. Let someone else solve the puzzle.

MASTERY WORDS

from
glad
small
start
stay
swim

Write the Mastery word that begins with the same two letters as each word.

1. smile   **2.** free

3. sweet   **4.** glass

Write Mastery words that mean the opposite.

5. stop   **6.** go

7. large   **8.** sad

Put the words in order to make two sentences.

9. from   beginning.   Start   the

10. stay   some   Let's   and   swim   more.

BONUS WORDS

blast
flash
frame
planet
scratch
space
split
spread

1. Combine the beginning consonant clusters at the left with the word endings at the right. Spell as many words as you can.

spr	scr	sp	pl
fr	bl	fl	spl

ead	atch	ace	ame
	ast	ash	it

2. Write the Bonus word you could not make in **1.**

3. Write sentences about outer space with Bonus words.

19

More Consonant Clusters

THIS WEEK'S WORDS

1. act
2. dust
3. east
4. test
5. west
6. lift
7. bend
8. grand
9. ground
10. wind
11. build
12. child
13. wild
14. milk
15. bump

This Week's Words

The letters **cl** in <u>clear</u> are called a consonant cluster. Consonant clusters do not always come at the beginning of words. Often they come at the end of words.

Say the word <u>act</u> to yourself. Listen carefully for the consonant sounds /k/ and /t/ at the end of <u>act</u>. The letters **ct** in <u>act</u> are a consonant cluster.

I spell it with **i.** You spell it with **u.** Then **you** and **I will** spell it with **ui!**

REMEMBER THIS

The vowel sound /i/ in <u>build</u> is spelled <u>ui</u>. Here is the reason why. Hundreds of years ago, the word was sometimes spelled with <u>u</u>, <u>buld</u>, and sometimes spelled with <u>i</u>, <u>bild</u>. No one could decide which was right — <u>u</u> or <u>i</u>. So they decided to use them both!

20

Spelling Practice

A. Follow the directions. Use This Week's Words.

1. Write the two words that begin with the same consonant cluster and end with the same cluster.

2. Write the three words that end with <u>ld</u>.

B. Write the word that rhymes with each word.

3. jump

4. drift

5. fact

6. silk

C. Finish the sentences. Use This Week's Words.

7. I forgot to ___ my watch.

8. The ___ blew the leaves around.

Circle the word you wrote that rhymes with <u>kind</u>.

D. Write the words that end with the same cluster as each picture word does.

band   last

9.   **10.**

act
dust
east
test
west
lift
bend
grand
ground
wind
build
child
wild
milk
bump

Spelling and Language • Adding ed

THIS WEEK'S WORDS
act
dust
east
test
west
lift
bend
grand
ground
wind
build
child
wild
milk
bump

You just add ed to most verbs to tell what already happened. Add ed to the words in parentheses ( ). Make the sentences tell about the past.

1. Carlos and Hilda (milk) ＿＿ cows every day.

2. Then they (lift) ＿＿ the pails onto a shelf.

3. They (bump) ＿＿ into the cows.

4. Laughing, they (dust) ＿＿ themselves off.

Writing on Your Own

Write a paragraph for your classmates about a book you have read. Tell a little about the story. Tell if you think your classmates would like the book. Use some of This Week's Words.

 WRITER'S GUIDE For help editing and proofreading, use the marks on page 248.

HANDWRITING

h H   k K   b B   f F

The lowercase letters **h, k, b,** and **f** all begin with the same undercurve stroke.

1. Practice writing **h H, k K, b B, f F** in cursive.

2. Write this sentence: *Help Beth lift her bike.*

Spelling on Your Own

THIS WEEK'S WORDS

Change the underlined letter in each word. Write one of This Week's Words.

1. b<u>a</u>nd
2. buil<u>t</u>
3. li<u>s</u>t
4. du<u>s</u>k
5. a<u>n</u>t
6. te<u>n</u>t
7. gran<u>t</u>
8. win<u>k</u>
9. we<u>n</u>t
10. <u>m</u>ild
11. <u>h</u>ump
12. <u>a</u>round
13. eas<u>y</u>
14. mil<u>l</u>

Use the word you haven't written yet in a sentence.

MASTERY WORDS

1. Write the three Mastery words that have <u>t</u> in the consonant cluster.
2. Write the two words that have <u>d</u> in the consonant cluster.
3. Write the three words that have short <u>e</u>.
4. Add <u>ed</u> to <u>help</u>. Use the word in a sentence.

felt
hand
help
hold
left
want

BONUS WORDS

1. Write the four Bonus words that begin and end with consonant clusters.
2. Write the three words that have two vowel sounds.
3. Write the word that rhymes with <u>first</u> and <u>worst</u>.
4. The words <u>stamp</u> and <u>tramp</u> both end with <u>amp</u>. Add different beginning consonants to <u>amp</u>. Spell as many words as you can. Then do the same thing with <u>end</u> in <u>blend</u>.

adult
blend
burst
insect
prompt
pumpkin
stamp
tramp

Review

Do these steps if you are not sure how to spell a word.

- **Say** the word. Listen to each sound. Think about what the word means.
- **Look** at the word. See how the letters are made. Try to see the word in your mind.
- **Spell** the word to yourself. Think about the way each sound is spelled.
- **Write** the word. Copy it from your book. Check the way you made your letters. Write the word again.
- **Check** your learning. Cover the word and write it. Did you spell it correctly? If not, do these steps until you know how to spell the word.

UNIT 1
apple
bring
else
flag
shall
hunt
river
happy

UNIT 1 Follow the directions. Use words from Unit 1.

1. Write the two words that begin with a short vowel sound.
2. Write the four words that have /a/.
3. Write the two words that have /i/.
4. Write the word that has /u/.

Finish these sentences.

5. We decided to ___ for treasure today.
6. We started our search on the banks of the ___ that flows past my house.
7. Under an ___ tree we saw a watch.

24

8. I was ___ we had found at least one treasure.

9. I asked my friend to ___ it to me.

10. We wondered what ___ we would find that day.

UNIT 2 Follow the directions. Use words from Unit 2. Write the words that end with these sounds.

11. /f/ **12.** /d/ **13.** /l/ (three words) **14.** /s/ (three words)

Finish these sentences.

15. Another word for <u>sick</u> is ___.

16. You ___ <u>un</u> to <u>less</u> to spell ___.

UNIT 2

add
ill
spell
stuff
unless
mess
roll
less

UNIT 3 Finish this story with words from Unit 3.

Meg's dad was **17** to build a fire. He began to **18** the wood. Meg helped by carrying logs. She was careful not to **19** any on the ground. Then Meg's puppy Pokey ran up. It **20** right in Meg's path, barking and **21** its tail. Meg did not want to **22** on Pokey. She could not see where she was going. She **23** over a rock and almost fell. Meg said, "Pokey, I wish you would go into the house and take a **24** when I work."

UNIT 3

chop
nap
step
tripped
wagging
drop
planning
stopped

WORDS IN TIME

The word <u>spell</u> came from the old word <u>spellen</u>. <u>Spellen</u> meant "to read out." Why do you think <u>spellen</u> became <u>spell</u>?

25

close
drawer
floor
print
spring
drive
state
spray

UNIT 4 Add consonant clusters to these word parts to make words from Unit 4.

25. ___oor

26. ___ose

27. ___awer

28. ___ing

29. ___ive

30. ___ate

31. ___ay

32. ___int

UNIT 5 Follow the directions. Use words from Unit 5.

UNIT 5

act
build
ground
milk
test
east
west
lift

33. Write the word that has /a/.

34. Write the three words that have /i/.

35. Write the two words that have /e/.

36. Write the word that begins with a consonant cluster.

Finish these sentences. Use words from Unit 5.

37. There are lots of sticks lying on the ___.

38. Let's use them to ___ some toy boats.

39. Then we'll go to the pond and ___ them.

40. A good wind is blowing from ___ to west.

41. The wind will ___ the sails and move the boats.

42. We can ___ like sailors sailing off to sea.

Spelling and Reading

Sentences About Actions

Read the following story. Look for all the action verbs.

After a long drive, the Romero family came to the river. They were planning to camp on the west bank. They put up a tent and unloaded food. Then they stopped and decided to take a nap.

Some strange sounds woke them up. They rushed out of the tent. Their stuff was scattered everywhere. Apples and milk had spilled onto the ground. Everything was a mess!

"Watch your step," warned Mr. Romero. "Act calmly and stay close together. Can someone bring me a light?"

"I have a flashlight," said Mrs. Romero. "Let's take a look around."

"Paw prints," whispered Maria. Then everyone shouted, "Raccoons!"

"We should have left our food in the car," Yolanda sighed. "I guess we flunked the raccoon test!" laughed Maria.

Write the answers to the questions.

1. What did the Romeros decide after they unloaded food?
2. What did Mr. Romero tell everyone to do after they found the mess?
3. How did the Romeros know raccoons took the food?
4. Do you think the Romeros will still have a good time camping? Why or why not?

Underline the review words in your answers.
Check to see that you spelled the words correctly.

Spelling and Writing
Sentences About Actions

Think and Discuss

Words that show actions are called action verbs. Look at the pictures.

They put up the tent.

They unloaded the food.

The pictures show some of the actions described in the story on page 27. Read the sentence that goes with each picture.
What verb describes the action in the first picture? What verb describes the action in the second picture?

The story is filled with action. The characters in the story do many different things. The writer uses action verbs to tell what they do. Read the second paragraph on page 27. What verb describes what the Romeros did when strange sounds woke them up? Look at the third paragraph. What verbs does Mr. Romero use when he tells his family what to do?

Sometimes several verbs can describe one action. A good writer will choose the verb that best describes what is happening. For example, there are many verbs that describe how a person can speak. Look at the fifth paragraph of the story. What action verb does the writer use to describe how Maria spoke?

Apply

Write **sentences that tell about actions** for your classmates. Use the guidelines on the next page.

Words to Help You Write

bring
~~roll~~
~~spring~~
~~tripped~~
~~drop~~
~~hunt~~

Prewriting

- Think of something that moves. The pictures may help you.
- Make a list of your subject's actions. Start each idea with a clear and different verb.

 THESAURUS For help finding action verbs, turn to page 203.

Composing

Use your list to write the first draft of your action sentences.

- Make each idea on your list a complete sentence.
- Write at least six sentences telling how your subject moves.

Revising

Read your action sentences and show them to a classmate. Follow these guidelines to improve your work. Use the editing and proofreading marks to show changes.

Editing

- Make sure your sentences use clear and interesting verbs.
- Change the verbs that do not describe actions clearly.

Proofreading

- Look over your spelling and correct any mistakes.
- Check your capitalization and punctuation.

 WRITER'S GUIDE For help with capitalization and punctuation, turn to pages 255-257.

- Copy your action sentences onto a clean paper. Write carefully and neatly.

Publishing

Read your sentences aloud to the class. Ask your classmates what verbs helped them <u>see</u> the action best.

	Editing and Proofreading Marks
☰	capitalize
⊙	make a period
∧	add something
⋏	add a comma
⊸	take something away
◯	spell correctly
⊓	indent the paragraph
/	make a lowercase letter

7 More Letters Than Sounds

THIS WEEK'S WORDS

1. another
2. together
3. weather
4. chin
5. reach
6. which
7. teacher
8. catch
9. kitchen
10. shine
11. shout
12. crash
13. strong
14. angry
15. hungry

That child should sing.

This Week's Words

The words this week have consonant sounds that are spelled with more than one letter. You hear those sounds in this sentence.

/th/   /ch/   /sh/   /ng/
That   child   should   sing.

- The first sound in <u>th</u>at is spelled **th.**

  ano<u>th</u>er

- The first sound in <u>ch</u>ild is spelled **ch** or **tch.**

  <u>ch</u>in   rea<u>ch</u>   ca<u>tch</u>

- The first sound in <u>sh</u>ould is spelled **sh.**

  <u>sh</u>ine   cra<u>sh</u>

- The last sound in si<u>ng</u> is spelled **ng** or **n.**

  stro<u>ng</u>   a<u>ng</u>ry

Spelling Practice

A. Finish the sentences. Use This Week's Words that have /ch/.

1. Nicole ran to the ___ to get a snack.

2. She had to ___ her bus in five minutes.

3. She didn't know ___ fruit to take.

4. She remembered her ___ said apples were a good snack.

5. She stood on her tiptoes to ___ the fruit.

6. An apple fell, hitting her nose and ___.

B. Follow the directions. Use This Week's Words.

7. Write the two words that begin with consonant clusters.

8. Write the four words that end with er. Then draw a line under the two consonant letters that stand for one sound in each word.

9. Write the two words that end with the long e sound.

10. Write the word that sounds like witch.

C. Write This Week's Words that go with these words. Use words that start with /sh/.

11. Don't ___!   **12.** Rise and ___!

another
together
weather
chin
reach
which
teacher
catch
kitchen
shine
shout
crash
strong
angry
hungry

31

Spelling and Language • Writing Sentences

<table>
<tr><td rowspan="99">

THIS WEEK'S WORDS

another
together
weather
chin
reach
which
teacher
catch
kitchen
shine
shout
crash
strong
angry
hungry
</td></tr>
</table>

Write the words in order so they make a sentence. Remember that a sentence begins with a capital letter and ends with a period.

1. kitchen   went   for   I   the   sandwich.   to   a

2. peanut   could   the   butter   reach   jar.   I   not

Writing on Your Own

Write a paragraph for your teacher telling about the picture on page 30. Use as many of This Week's Words as you can.

 THESAURUS For help finding descriptive words, turn to page 203.

Using the Dictionary to Spell and Write

Guide words help you find a word quickly if you need to check its spelling or meaning. There are two **guide words** at the top of each dictionary page. The word on the left is the first word on the page. The word on the right is the last word. All the other words on the page are in alphabetical order between those words.

ear	everyday
ear[1] /ir/ *n.* What people and animals use for hearing. **ear**[2] /ir/ *n.* Where grain grows on	—*v.* **emptied, emptying** To make empty: Ben *emptied* his pockets. **en·e·my** /en′ə·mē/ *n., pl.* **enemies** A

Here are two pairs of guide words. Write two of This Week's Words that would be on each page.

1. all   apple

2. cent   day

Spelling on Your Own

THIS WEEK'S WORDS

Letters that spell a consonant sound are missing from each of This Week's Words. Add the missing letters. Write the whole word.

1. stro___
2. whi___
3. toge___er
4. cra___
5. ___ine
6. rea___
7. hu___gry
8. ki___en
9. ___out
10. a___gry
11. ___in
12. wea___er
13. ano___er
14. tea___er
15. ca___

MASTERY WORDS

Follow the directions. Use the Mastery words.

1. Write the two words that end with /ch/.
2. Write two words. One ends the way the other begins.

Write Mastery words to go with these words.

3. ___ and dinner
4. mother and ___
5. ___ and dance
6. ___ and every

father
each
lunch
shut
push
sing

BONUS WORDS

1. Write the Bonus word that sounds like <u>weather</u>.
2. Write the two words that rhyme.
3. Write the two words that begin with a consonant cluster.
4. Write the word that can name someone who throws a ball or something that holds milk. Write a sentence that uses both meanings.
5. Write sentences about a farm. Try to use all the Bonus words.

clothing
fresh
gather
pitcher
porch
rather
shack
whether

8 Plurals

THIS WEEK'S WORDS

1. paths
2. desks
3. lists
4. fingers
5. robins
6. pictures
7. uncles
8. circuses
9. guesses
10. classes
11. bushes
12. churches
13. inches
14. ranches
15. beaches

paths

path

This Week's Words

A word that names just one thing is **singular.** A word that names more than one thing is **plural.** Here are two ways to make a word plural.

1. Add <u>s</u> to most words.

> path   paths

2. Add <u>es</u> to words that end with <u>s</u>, <u>ss</u>, <u>sh</u>, or <u>ch</u>.

circus	circuses
class	classes
bush	bushes
beach	beaches

REMEMBER THIS

Say <u>beach</u>. Now say <u>beaches</u>. Listen to the extra vowel sound before the <u>s</u> in <u>beaches</u>. That extra vowel sound tells you to add <u>es</u>. But this doesn't work with a word like <u>faces</u>. The <u>e</u> is already there in <u>face</u>.

Spelling Practice

A. Write the plural of each word.

1. church   **2.** beach   **3.** inch

4. ranch   **5.** guess   **6.** class

B. Finish the sentences. Write the plural of each word in dark print.

7. desk   We sat at our ___ and waited.

8. finger   We couldn't keep our ___ still.

9. robin   Even the ___ outside seemed excited.

10. uncle   Today, my ___ invited the class for a field trip to their horse ranch.

11. path   The students would get to ride horses on ___ all through the ranch.

12. list   The teacher checked her ___ for the names of the students signed up to go.

C. Write the word that goes with each picture. Then write the plural.

13.   **14.**   **15.**

paths
desks
lists
fingers
robins
pictures
uncles
circuses
guesses
classes
bushes
churches
inches
ranches
beaches

Spelling and Language • One or More

THIS WEEK'S WORDS

paths
desks
lists
fingers
robins
pictures
uncles
circuses
guesses
classes
bushes
churches
inches
ranches
beaches

Write one of This Week's Words to finish each sentence. Decide if the singular or the plural fits. For example, you would use the plural of <u>path</u> to finish the sentence "These ___ lead to the woods." You would use the singular to finish the sentence "This ___ leads to the woods."

1. Adam built a sand castle at the ___.

2. He took a ___ of it with his camera.

3. Can you tell how many ___ tall it was?

Writing on Your Own

Pretend you have a pen pal. Write a letter to your friend describing your school. Use some of This Week's Words.

 WRITER'S GUIDE For help with the parts of a friendly letter, turn to page 251.

HANDWRITING

Join **o** to other letters at the midline. Join **a** to other letters at the bottom line.

1. Practice writing **c C, o O, a A** in cursive.

2. Practice writing **os, as, co, ca** in cursive.

3. Write this sentence: *Carlos spoke to the class.*

Spelling on Your Own

THIS WEEK'S WORDS

Write sentences using all of This Week's Words. Try to use as many of the words as you can in each sentence. You may use the singular or the plural. Here is an example: "I have lots of <u>pictures</u> of <u>circuses</u> in my <u>desk</u>."

MASTERY WORDS

Write the plural of each word. Draw a line under the letters you added to spell the plural.

1. glass   **2.** wish   **3.** dish   **4.** duck

Finish the sentences. Use the Mastery words.

5. Please turn off the ___.

6. That dog has muddy ___.

7. Do ___ ever come true?

8. Jesse drank three ___ of milk.

9. Sara fed bread to the ___ at the pond.

10. Joan and Chet will wash the ___.

dishes
ducks
glasses
lights
paws
wishes

BONUS WORDS

1. Write the singular of each Bonus word. Circle each singular word that ends with <u>e</u>.

2. Write the names of three things you might take on a picnic.

3. Write the word that means mother and father.

4. Write sentences about a picnic. Try to use the singular or plural of each Bonus word.

bandages
branches
headaches
parents
patches
peaches
pickles
sandwiches

9 The Sound /j/

1. giraffe
2. danger
3. jam
4. jug
5. juice
6. gentle
7. giant
8. magic
9. age
10. cage
11. large
12. page
13. bridge
14. edge
15. judge

This Week's Words

All the words this week have the sound /j/. Here are four ways to spell /j/.

- with **j**

    jam

- with **g** before **e** or **i**

    gentle   magic

- with **ge** at the end of a word

    age

- with **dge** after a short vowel sound

    edge

REMEMBER THIS

There is an e at the tail end of giraffe.

38

Spelling Practice

A. Follow the directions. Use This Week's Words.

1. Write the three words that start with /j/ spelled <u>g</u>.

2. Write the three words that end with /j/ and have long <u>a</u>.

3. Write the word that ends with /j/ and means the opposite of <u>small</u>.

4. Write the three words that end with /j/ and have short vowel sounds.

B. Add the letter that spells /j/ in each word. Write the words.

5. dan__er   **6.** ma__ic

C. Tell what the giant uses when he makes breakfast. Write sentences. Use the three words that start with /j/ spelled <u>j</u> and end with another consonant sound. Then circle all the words you used that have the sound /j/.

giraffe
danger
jam
jug
juice
gentle
giant
magic
age
cage
large
page
bridge
edge
judge

Spelling and Language • Writing Sentences

THIS WEEK'S WORDS

giraffe
danger
jam
jug
juice
gentle
giant
magic
age
cage
large
page
bridge
edge
judge

Put the words in order to write two sentences. Remember that a sentence starts with a capital letter and ends with a period.

1. judge   The   went   zoo.   to   gentle   the

2. giant   saw   there.   He   a   giraffe

Writing on Your Own

Write a story for a young friend. Tell about a magic land where gentle giants live. Use as many of This Week's Words as you can.

WRITER'S GUIDE Can your friend read your story? If you need help writing any letters, turn to page 261.

HANDWRITING

j J   u U   w W

Notice how the letters **u** and **w** are alike.   *u   w*

1. Practice writing **j J, u U, w W** in cursive.

2. Write this sentence: *We sip fruit juice.*

40

Spelling on Your Own

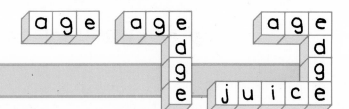

Make a "word chain" with This Week's Words. Write one word. Use a letter in that word to write another word. Keep going, writing words across and down. Try to link all the words in one chain. You may also make more than one chain.

MASTERY WORDS

Follow the directions. Use the Mastery words.

1. Write the word that does not begin with /j/.
2. Write the two words that end with consonant clusters.

Write the Mastery words with these vowel sounds.

3. /e/   4. /o/   5. /i/

Write the Mastery word that goes with each word.

6. ___ rope   7. ___ plane   8. ___ right   9. pickle ___

jar
jet
job
jump
just
give

BONUS WORDS

1. Write the Bonus word that sounds the same as <u>Jim</u>.
2. Write the Bonus words that start with /j/ spelled j.
3. Rewrite these questions. Use Bonus words in place of the underlined words.
    What is in the <u>odd</u> box on the shelf? Is it <u>spicy cake</u>? Is it <u>chocolate candy</u>?
4. Write the names of other things that might be in the box. Use words that have /j/.

join
jungle
gingerbread
gym
package
strange
fudge
ledge

41

10 The Sound /k/

THIS WEEK'S WORDS

1. kick
2. camp
3. candy
4. cane
5. cost
6. kept
7. key
8. kindness
9. kitten
10. speak
11. back
12. lucky
13. neck
14. pack
15. quick

This Week's Words

All the words this week have the sound /k/. Here are the ways /k/ is spelled.

● with **c** or **k** at the beginning of a word

       <u>c</u>amp   <u>k</u>ey

● with **k** after a long vowel sound

       spea<u>k</u>

● with **ck** after a short vowel sound

       ba<u>ck</u>

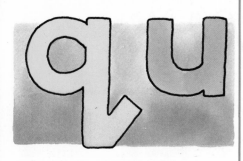

REMEMBER THIS

The consonant sounds that begin <u>quick</u> are spelled **qu.**

That queer old letter q
Would be quite quiet without a <u>u</u>.
It cannot question or quarrel or quack
Unless a <u>u</u> is right at its back.

Spelling Practice

A. Follow the directions. Use This Week's Words.

1. Write the four words that begin with /k/ spelled <u>c</u>.

2. What vowel letters come after <u>c</u> in these words?

3. Write the five words that begin with /k/ spelled <u>k</u>.

4. What vowel letters come after <u>k</u> in these words?

5. Write the six words that end with /k/. Circle the word that has a long vowel sound.

6. What letter spells /k/ in the word you circled?

kick
camp
candy
cane
cost
kept
key
kindness
kitten
speak
back
lucky
neck
pack
quick

B. Finish the sentences. Use This Week's Words. The underlined name shows how /k/ is spelled in the missing word.

7. <u>Kevin</u> dropped the ___ to his house.

8. <u>Carol</u> saw him drop it near the fire in the ___.

9. <u>Vicky</u> was ___ to pick it up and give it back.

10. <u>Chuck</u> said it was ___ Kevin didn't lose it.

Spelling and Language • Adding <u>ed</u>

THIS WEEK'S WORDS

kick
camp
candy
cane
cost
kept
key
kindness
kitten
speak
back
lucky
neck
pack
quick

You add <u>ed</u> to most verbs to tell what already happened. Add <u>ed</u> to the words in dark print. Finish the sentences.

1. camp   We ___ near the river last night.

2. back   Mom ___ the car up to our tent.

3. pack   Dad and I unloaded the ___ car.

4. kick   Then Angela and I ___ rocks into the water.

Writing on Your Own

Write a paragraph telling your classmates how you cooked dinner. Remember to add <u>ed</u> to most verbs to tell what already happened.

WRITER'S GUIDE For help with the past tense, turn to page 240.

Using the Dictionary to Spell and Write

A dictionary gives you information that will help you when you write. The words in a dictionary are in alphabetical order. If the first letters of words are the same, look at the next letter. <u>Cat</u>, <u>come</u>, <u>cut</u> are in order by the second letter—<u>a</u>, <u>o</u>, <u>u</u>.

Write each group of words in alphabetical order.

1. candy
   kick
   back
   cost
   key

2. lucky
   kindness
   quick
   kept
   speak

Spelling on Your Own

camp · stamp

THIS WEEK'S WORDS

Write each of This Week's Words. Think of a word that rhymes with that word. Then write the rhyming word.

MASTERY WORDS

sick
cold
cup
keep
cat
pick

Follow the directions. Use the Mastery words.

1. Write the two words that have the sound /i/.
2. Write the two words that end with the sound /k/.
3. Write the four words that begin with the sound /k/.

Change the first letter of each word. Write a Mastery word.

4. hold   **5.** hat   **6.** deep   **7.** pup

BONUS WORDS

cabin
camera
creek
jacket
kettle
pocket
smoke
tickle

1. Write the six Bonus words that have two or more vowel sounds.
2. Write the two words that begin with consonant clusters.
3. Write the two words that end the way <u>pickle</u> does.
4. Write the two words that end the way <u>ticket</u> does.
5. Write the word that begins and ends with /k/.
6. Write sentences using all the Bonus words. Try to make them tell a story. Your story could be about camping.

11 The Sound /s/

THIS WEEK'S WORDS

1. six
2. city
3. police
4. suit
5. ask
6. listen
7. decide
8. ice
9. pencil
10. price
11. princess
12. fence
13. once
14. piece
15. sentence

This Week's Words

All the words this week have the sound /s/. Here are some ways to spell /s/.

● You can spell /s/ with **s**.

　　six　　　　　　a<u>s</u>k

● You can spell /s/ with **c**.

　　<u>c</u>ity　　　　　de<u>c</u>ide

● You can spell /s/ with **ce** at the end of a word.
　　poli<u>ce</u>

One of the words has /s/ spelled another way.
Which word is it?

REMEMBER THIS
There's a <u>t</u> in <u>listen</u>. That you can see. But when you say <u>listen</u>, You don't hear the <u>t</u>.

46

Spelling Practice

A. Follow the directions. Use This Week's Words.

1. Write the seven words that end with /s/ spelled <u>ce</u>.

2. Write the word that ends with /s/ spelled <u>ss</u>.

3. Write the two words that tell about the picture. Add <u>s</u> to the end of one of the words.

4. Write the word that ends with a consonant cluster.

5. Write the two words that start with <u>p</u> and have the vowel sound in <u>see</u>.

6. Write the word that has a "silent" letter <u>t</u>.

7. Write the three words that have <u>c</u> before <u>i</u>.

six
city
police
suit
ask
listen
decide
ice
pencil
price
princess
fence
once
piece
sentence

B. Write the verbs that go with these words. Use three different verbs.

8. ___ a question

9. ___ what to do

10. ___ to the music

Spelling and Language • Plurals

THIS WEEK'S WORDS

six
city
police
suit
ask
listen
decide
ice
pencil
price
princess
fence
once
piece
sentence

To make most words mean more than one, you add s. You add es to words that end with s, ss, sh, ch, or x.

Finish the sentences. Use the plurals of This Week's Words.

1. Mrs. Fong gave Herb a box of colored ____.

2. Mom and Dad both wear ____ to work.

3. Two ____ make twelve.

4. Are the ____ really lower at this store?

Writing on Your Own

Draw a picture of a city of the future. Write a paragraph for your teacher describing your city. Use some of This Week's Words and as many plurals as you can.

WRITER'S GUIDE For a sample of a descriptive paragraph, turn to page 250.

HANDWRITING

d D g G q Q

Look at the tails on the lowercase **g** and **q**.

The loop stroke on the **g** turns to the left.

g

The loop stroke on the **q** turns to the right.

q

1. Practice writing **d D, g G, q Q** in cursive.

2. Write this sentence: *Did Doug quit?*

48

Spelling on Your Own

THIS WEEK'S WORDS

Write some funny story titles. Use This Week's Words. Try to use more than one of the words in each title. Here is an example: "The Princess and the Pencil."

MASTERY WORDS

face
seed
nice
sent
place
soft

Follow the directions. Use the Mastery words.

1. Write the three words that begin with /s/.
2. Write the three words that end with /s/.
3. Write the three words that have consonant clusters.

Finish the sentences. Use the Mastery words.

4. Mr. Witter is a ____ person.
5. He always has a smile on his ____.

BONUS WORDS

bicycle
certain
notice
peace
recite
secret
silver
since

Follow the directions. Use the Bonus words.

1. Write the word that sounds just like <u>piece</u>. Then use the two words in sentences.
2. Write the word that begins and ends with /s/.
3. Rewrite this sentence: "Are you <u>sure</u> you didn't <u>see</u> anything odd?" Use Bonus words in place of the underlined words.

Write the Bonus words that go with these words.

4. ____ a poem   5. ride a ____   6. keep a ____   7. ____ spoon

12 Review

Do these steps if you are not sure how to spell a word.

- **Say** the word. Listen to each sound. Think about what the word means.
- **Look** at the word. See how the letters are made. Try to see the word in your mind.
- **Spell** the word to yourself. Think about the way each sound is spelled.
- **Write** the word. Copy it from your book. Check the way you made your letters. Write the word again.
- **Check** your learning. Cover the word and write it. Did you spell it correctly? If not, do these steps until you know how to spell the word.

UNIT 7

hungry
kitchen
shine
shout
teacher
together
weather
strong

UNIT 7   Follow the directions. Use words from Unit 7.

1. Write the two words that begin with /sh/.

2. Write the two words that have /ch/.

3. Write the two words that have /th/.

4. Write the two words that have /ng/.

Circle the letters that spell /sh/, /ch/, /th/, and /ng/ in the words you wrote for 1 through 4 above.

WORDS IN TIME

Many of our words come from other languages. The word <u>kitchen</u> came from the old word <u>coquere</u>. <u>Coquere</u> meant "to cook." People began to use <u>coquere</u> to mean kitchen. Why do you think this happened?

50

UNIT 8 Follow the directions. Use words from Unit 8. Finish the sentences in the paragraph.

      We painted __5__ in my art class today. We wanted to hang them in all our __6__ for other students to see. Then we could look at them as we sat at our __7__. One picture was ten __8__ high. It was a drawing of Danielle's favorite aunts and __9__. Another showed sand castles built at nearby __10__. Some students had even used their __11__ to paint with. It took several __12__ to figure out what they had drawn.

UNIT 8
classes
inches
pictures
guesses
uncles
desks
fingers
beaches

Circle the letters in your answers that make the words plural.

UNIT 9 Follow the directions. Use words from Unit 9.

13. Write the three words that start with /j/.

14. Write the four words that end with /j/. Then underline the letters in each word that spell /j/.

UNIT 9
juice
giant
danger
large
bridge
gentle
age
edge

Finish the sentences that tell about the picture.

15. The ___ giraffe came to drink at the river.

16. The giraffe saw a lion at the ___ of the grass.

17. So the giraffe ran from ___.

kept
key
speak
quick
lucky
back
kindness
cost

UNIT 10 **Finish the sentences with words from Unit 10. Then draw a line under all the letters in each sentence that spell /k/.**

18. I don't feel too ___ today.

19. I lost the ___ that unlocks my bike.

20. I should have ___ it in a safer place.

21. I hope the ___ of a new one won't be much.

22. I will ___ to Mom about a small loan.

23. I can repay her ___ by cleaning the house.

Write the word from Unit 10 that rhymes with each word below.

24. tack

25. slept

26. sneak

27. trick

listen
city
pencil
piece
ask
decide
sentence
police

UNIT 11 **Follow the directions. Use words from Unit 11. Remember that nouns are words that name a person, place, or thing. Verbs are words that show action.**

28. Write the three nouns that end with /s/ spelled ce. Circle the word that has short vowel sounds.

29. Write the two verbs that have /s/ spelled s. Circle the silent letter in one word.

30. Write the verb that has /s/ spelled c.

Write the two nouns that go with these words.

31. sharpen a ___

32. live in a ___

Spelling and Reading
A Story

Read the following story. Look for the beginning, middle, and ending.

Long ago, a gentle giant lived in a large house by a river. He had built a strong bridge over the river so that travelers could cross without danger.

One day the giant looked out and frowned at the weather. Thick, heavy storm clouds filled the black sky. Soon, a wild wind tore the giant's bridge apart.

When the storm was over, the giant heard a girl shouting to him from across the river.

"Can you help me?" the girl asked. "I'm in danger. I must reach the other side!"

The giant jumped over the river in one long leap.

"We must be quick," the giant said. "Hold on!" They leaped back just as a hungry bear came out of the bushes.

The girl wanted to thank the giant for his kindness. She gave him a shining gold key. She had found it long ago but never knew its owner.

The giant needed no guesses to name the key's owner. The key to his long-locked chest had finally come back to him. Now he could share the chest's wealth of treasures and jewels.

Write the answers to the questions.

1. In this story, why did the giant build the bridge over the river?

2. What did a wild wind do?

3. Why was the girl in danger?

4. What kind of person is the giant? How do you know?

Underline the review words in your answers. Check to see that you spelled the words correctly.

Spelling and Writing
A Story

Words to Help You Write

shout
together
strong
giant
danger
large
gentle
quick
lucky
kindness
city

Think and Discuss

A story beginning tells about the main character or characters in the story. It also tells when and where the story takes place. Look at the beginning of the story on page 53. Who is the main character? When does the story take place? Where does the main character live?

The middle of the story is the main part of the story. It tells about a problem. It also tells how the character or characters try to solve the problem. What other character is introduced in the middle of the story on page 53? What problem does this character have? What does she ask the giant to do?

The ending tells how the characters solve their problem. It finishes the story. What does the giant do to rescue the girl? What else happens at the end of the story?

Apply

Write a **story** for your classmates to read. Follow the writing guidelines on the next page.

Prewriting

Plan your story. Make a chart with four headings: **Main character, Where, When,** and **Problem.**

● Fill in the chart.
● Make a list of the ways the character could solve the problem. Choose the one you like best.

Composing

Use your chart to help you write the first draft of your story.
● Write the beginning of your story. Tell whom your story is about. Write where and when the story takes place.
● Write the middle of your story. Describe the problem the character has. Tell how he or she solves the problem.
● Write the ending. Tell how everything works out.

Revising

Read your story and show it to a classmate. Follow these guidelines to improve your work. Use the editing and proofreading marks to show changes.

 WRITER'S GUIDE For help revising your story, use the checklist on page 247.

Editing
● Be sure your story has a beginning, middle, and ending.

Proofreading
● Check your spelling and correct any mistakes.
● Check your capitalization and punctuation.
Copy your story onto a clean paper. Write carefully and neatly.

Publishing

Put your story in a class notebook with those of your classmates. Then you can read each other's stories.

Editing and Proofreading Marks	
$\equiv$	capitalize
$\odot$	make a period
$\wedge$	add something
$\wedge$	add a comma
⌐	take something away
$\bigcirc$	spell correctly
⌐⌐	indent the paragraph
/	make a lowercase letter

13 Verbs That End with <u>e</u>

THIS WEEK'S WORDS

1. *invite*
2. *paste*
3. *skate*
4. *stare*
5. *tape*
6. *taste*
7. *wipe*
8. *cared*
9. *hiked*
10. *loved*
11. *moved*
12. *dancing*
13. *hoping*
14. *living*
15. *smiling*

These happy people <u>smile</u>.

This Week's Words

The word <u>smile</u> is a verb in the sentence above. It ends with the letter <u>e</u>. You can add <u>ed</u> to <u>smile</u> to make a word that tells about the past. When you add <u>ed</u>, you must drop the final <u>e</u>.

These happy people <u>smiled</u>.

You can also add <u>ing</u> to smile. When you add <u>ing</u>, you must also drop the final e.

These happy people are <u>smiling</u>.

All of This Week's Words are verbs. They all follow this pattern.

smile   smiled   smiling

Spelling Practice

A. Write the verbs that go with the pictures. Use This Week's Words.

1. _____

2. _____

3. _____

invite
paste
skate
stare
tape
taste
wipe
cared
hiked
loved
moved
dancing
hoping
living
smiling

B. Add <u>ed</u> to each of these words.

4. love   5. care   6. wipe   7. move

C. Add <u>ing</u> to each of these words.

8. smile   9. hope   10. dance   11. live

D. Finish the sentences. Use This Week's Words.

12. Did José ___ Beth to his party?

13. It is not polite to ___ at people.

14. Do you want to ___ this soup?

15. I watched Mom ___ a bandage on Eva's knee.

E. Try this "word math."

16. dancing − ing = ___ + ed = ___

17. hiked − ed = ___ + ing = ___

18. hoping − ing = ___ + ed = ___

57

Spelling and Language •
Adding ed and ing

THIS WEEK'S WORDS

invite
paste
skate
stare
tape
taste
wipe
cared
hiked
loved
moved
dancing
hoping
living
smiling

You add ed to a word to tell what already happened. You add ing to a word to tell what is or was happening. Finish the sentences. Add ed or ing to each word in dark print. Remember to drop the e before adding ed or ing.

1. **paste** Danielle was ____ stars on blue paper.

2. **skate** Then she ____ to the corner store.

3. **tape** She was ____ her notes up all over.

4. **invite** Danielle ____ everyone to her party.

Writing on Your Own

Pretend you are going to have a birthday party at a skating rink. Write an invitation to send to your grandmother, grandfather, or other relative. Use as many of This Week's Words as you can. Try to use ed or ing with some of the words.

 WRITER'S GUIDE For help with the parts of a letter, turn to page 251.

Using the Dictionary to Spell and Write

Look at this dictionary sample. The entry word is stare. The word with ed and ing comes after stare. To find stared or staring in the dictionary, you must look up stare.

> **stare** /stâr/ *v.* **stared, staring** To look hard, often without blinking: The dog *stared* at the cat.
> —*n.* A long, hard look.

Suppose you want to check the spelling of these words in the dictionary. Write each word you would look up.

1. dancing   2. moved   3. hoping   4. cared

58

Spelling on Your Own

This Week's Words are all verbs, but some of them can also be nouns. Choose words that can be nouns. Use them to finish these sentences.

1. David broke the shoestring on his ___.
2. He tried to use ___ to hold it together.

Now write a sentence for each of the rest of This Week's Words.

MASTERY WORDS

bake
name
race
save
use
wave

Write these words without <u>ed</u> to make Mastery words.

1. waved   **2.** raced
3. named   **4.** used

Write these words without <u>ing</u> to make Mastery words.

5. baking   **6.** using
7. saving   **8.** racing

When Leo doesn't listen, he must ask questions. Finish his questions with Mastery words.

9. Al: I baked a cake.   Leo: What did you ___?
10. Al: I saved some for you.   Leo: What did you ___?

BONUS WORDS

manage
prepare
suppose
surprise
divided
promised
behaving
chasing

1. Add <u>ed</u> and <u>ing</u> to the first four Bonus words.
2. Write the last four words without <u>ed</u> or <u>ing</u>.
3. Write the two words that have long <u>i</u>.
4. Write a letter to a friend about a birthday party. Try to use all the Bonus words in your letter.

THIS WEEK'S WORDS

1. awake
2. brave
3. clay
4. gate
5. hay
6. lake
7. lay
8. mail
9. paid
10. safe
11. snake
12. today
13. trail
14. obey
15. eight

This Week's Words

All the words this week have the vowel sound /ā/. Here are three ways to spell /ā/.

- with **a**-consonant-**e**, as in <u>lake</u>
- with **ai,** as in <u>trail</u>
- with **ay** at the end of a word, as in <u>today</u>

☐ The words <u>obey</u> and <u>eight</u> also have the vowel sound /ā/. How is /ā/ spelled in each of these words?

REMEMBER THIS

In <u>clay</u> and <u>hay</u> and <u>lay</u> and <u>day</u>,
The letters <u>a-y</u> spell long <u>a</u>.
But <u>obey</u> is spelled another way.
It ends with <u>e-y</u>, just like they.
Then there's <u>gate</u> and <u>late</u>, you see,
Both spelled the same with <u>a-t-e</u>.
So who would expect <u>8</u> to be
Spelled with <u>e-i-g-h-t</u>?

Spelling Practice

A. Follow the directions. Use This Week's Words.

1. Write the six words that have /ā/ spelled as it is in <u>same</u>.

2. Write the five words that end with /ā/.

3. Circle the word you wrote for **2** that does not end with <u>ay</u>.

4. Write the word that sounds just like <u>ate</u>.

B. Write the words that begin and end with these letters.

5. m____l

6. p____d

7. tr____l

C. Finish the story. Use This Week's Words. The last sound in each word is given to help you. Write one word twice.

Eric and Ed hiked to the __8__ /k/. Next to the __9__ /l/ they saw a __10__ /k/. Ed was afraid, but Eric was __11__ /v/.

"We will be perfectly __12__ /f/. But you must __13__ /ā/ me. Do not make a sound. That __14__ /k/ is not __15__ /k/!"

awake
brave
clay
gate
hay
lake
lay
mail
paid
safe
snake
today
trail
obey
eight

Spelling and Language • Word Ladders

THIS
WEEK'S
WORDS

awake
brave
clay
gate
hay
lake
lay
mail
paid
safe
snake
today
trail
obey
eight

Many of This Week's Words have the same endings. If you change a letter or letters at the beginning of a word, you make a new word. Take gate. If you write l in place of g, you spell late. Start with the words below. Change the underlined letters to make new words. Use the pictures to help you.

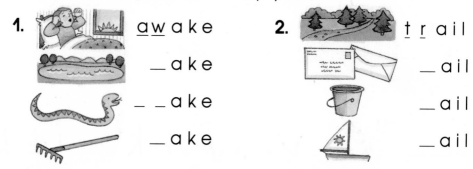

1. a w a k e

    _ a k e

    _ _ a k e

    _ a k e

2. t r a i l

    _ a i l

    _ a i l

    _ a i l

Writing on Your Own

Write a paragraph for a young friend. Tell how to play safely on the playground. Use some of This Week's Words.

WRITER'S GUIDE Did you write neatly? If you need help writing any letters, turn to page 261.

HANDWRITING

v V   x X   z Z

The lowercase letters **v, x,** and **z** begin with this overcurve stroke.

1. Practice writing **v V, x X, z Z** in cursive.

2. Write this sentence: *Val saw six zebras.*

Spelling on Your Own

THIS WEEK'S WORDS

Add <u>a-e</u>, <u>ai</u>, or <u>ay</u> to each group of letters. Write This Week's Words.

1. tr l   **2.** aw k   **3.** cl   **4.** m l   **5.** h
6. sn k   **7.** g t   **8.** p d   **9.** l k   **10.** l
11. br v   **12.** s f   **13.** tod

Now write the words that aren't spelled with <u>a-e</u>, <u>ai</u>, or <u>ay</u>.

MASTERY WORDS

Follow the directions. Use the Mastery words.

1. Write the two words that rhyme with <u>day</u>.
2. Circle the word that is not spelled with <u>ay</u>.
3. Name two things you could use to make a doghouse.

Read each word. Then write two Mastery words that have /ā/ spelled the same way.

4. make   **5.** train

late
may
nail
paint
same
they

BONUS WORDS

Follow the directions. Use the Bonus words.

1. Write the three Bonus words that begin with consonant clusters.
2. Write the words that start with <u>de</u> and <u>mis</u>.
3. Write the four words that have /ā/ spelled as it is in train.
4. Write two words that name things that can be purple.
5. Write four sentences. Use two Bonus words in each sentence.

crayon
delay
faint
grape
mistake
railroad
raisin
snail

THIS WEEK'S WORDS

1. dream
2. asleep
3. any
4. between
5. busy
6. cheek
7. even
8. every
9. meal
10. meat
11. only
12. really
13. seen
14. team
15. weak

This Week's Words

All the words this week have the vowel sound /ē/. Here are four ways to spell /ē/.

- with **ea,** as in dream
- with **ee,** as in asleep
- with **e,** as in even
- with **y** at the end of a word, as in any

REMEMBER THIS

You don't always hear the sound of the second e in every. Here's something that can help you remember to put it in.

ever + y = every

Spelling Practice

A. First write the words that go with the pictures. Then follow the directions. Use This Week's Words.

1. _____

2. _____

3. How is /ē/ spelled in the word you wrote for **1**?

4. Write the other five words that have /ē/ spelled this way.

5. How is /ē/ spelled in the word you wrote for **2**?

6. Write the other three words that have /ē/ spelled this way.

7. Write the word that begins with /ē/.

8. Write the five words that end with /ē/. Circle the word that has /ē/ twice.

B. Finish the sentences. Use This Week's Words.

9. Jean's six cats keep her very ____.

10. She must feed them each and ____ day.

11. Just ____ you and me, Jean has too many cats.

dream
asleep
any
between
busy
cheek
even
every
meal
meat
only
really
seen
team
weak

Spelling and Language • Homophones

THIS WEEK'S WORDS
dream
asleep
any
between
busy
cheek
even
every
meal
meat
only
really
seen
team
weak

<u>Sea</u> and <u>see</u> are **homophones.** They sound alike, but they are not spelled alike. They also have different meanings.

Write the homophones for these words.

1. meet   **2.** week

Finish the sentence. Use one pair of homophones.

3. I will ___ you at the ___ market.

Writing on Your Own

Start keeping a daily journal to help you remember things you do each day. Write the day and date each time you write in your journal. Begin by writing about what you did yesterday. Use some of This Week's Words.

 WRITER'S GUIDE For a sample of a journal entry, turn to page 252.

Using the Dictionary to Spell and Write

A **pronunciation** is given after each entry word in a dictionary. A pronunciation is a special way of writing a word. It shows you how to say the word. Knowing how to pronounce a word can help you remember how to spell it.

> **an•y** /en′ē/ *adj.* No special one: *Any* coat will do.

A **pronunciation key** helps you read the pronunciation. It gives all the special signs and the sounds they stand for.

act, āte, câre, ärt;	egg, ēven;	if, īce;	on, ōver, ôr;	book, food;	up, tûrn;
ə = a in *ago*, e in *listen*, i in *giraffe*, o in *pilot*, u in *circus*;		yoo = u in *music*;		oil;	out;
chair; sing; shop; thank; that; zh in *treasure*.					

Write the word that goes with each pronunciation.

1. /rē′lē/   **2.** /ōn′lē/   **3.** /ev′rē/   **4.** /mēl/

Spelling on Your Own

THIS WEEK'S WORDS

Divide This Week's Words into groups by the way /ē/ is spelled. You will have four groups: ea, ee, e, and y. Then write as many other words as you can that fit into each group. Remember that one of the words fits into two groups.

MASTERY WORDS

Add ea or ee. Write the Mastery words.

1. fr_ _   **2.** _ _ sy   **3.** m_ _ n
4. d_ _ p   **5.** n_ _ t   **6.** f_ _ l

Write Mastery words that mean the opposite of the underlined words.

7. My room is <u>messy</u>, but Jo's is ___.
8. Cleaning is <u>hard</u> for me but ___ for her.

Write the Mastery words that rhyme with these words.

9. tree   **10.** keep   **11.** heel

> deep
> easy
> feel
> free
> mean
> neat

BONUS WORDS

Follow the directions. Use the Bonus words.

1. Write the word that begins with /ē/.
2. Write the two words that end with /ē/.
3. Write the three words that have consonant clusters.
4. Write the two words that are plurals.

Find the Bonus word that rhymes with each word. Then write a sentence using each rhyming pair.

5. beast   **6.** breeze   **7.** crazy   **8.** peace

> cozy
> daisy
> evening
> feast
> freedom
> geese
> measles
> sneeze

16 The Vowel Sound /ī/

THIS WEEK'S WORDS

1. nine
2. lion
3. bite
4. bright
5. fight
6. hide
7. life
8. line
9. myself
10. prize
11. shy
12. sight
13. tiger
14. wise
15. buy

This Week's Words

All the words this week have the vowel sound /ī/. Here are four ways to spell /ī/.

● with **i**-consonant-**e**, as in <u>nine</u>

● with **igh**, as in <u>bright</u>

● with **i**, as in <u>lion</u>

● with **y** at the end of a word or word part, as in <u>myself</u>

☐ The word <u>buy</u> also has the vowel sound /ī/. What letter are you surprised to find in <u>buy</u>?

REMEMBER THIS

<u>By</u> is a very useful word. It helps you tell where and how. You can sit <u>by</u> the fire. You can win <u>by</u> one point. But if you want to talk about what you'll get at the store, remember: you need <u>buy</u> and <u>buy</u> needs <u>u</u>.

Spelling Practice

A. Follow the directions. Use This Week's Words.

1. Write the word for the number 9.

2. Write the six other words that have /ī/ spelled this way.

3. Write the two words that name animals.

4. There are three words you can use to talk about yourself. Write the missing one.

   me, ____, and I

5. Write the two words that rhyme with <u>try</u>. Then circle the word that sounds just like <u>by</u>.

6. Finish the answer to the riddle. Use a word that sounds almost like the word <u>lying</u>.

What do you call a big cat that tells fibs?

   A lying ____.

nine
lion
bite
bright
fight
hide
life
line
myself
prize
shy
sight
tiger
wise
buy

B. Write This Week's Words that end with /t/ and begin with these letters.

7. f   **8.** br   **9.** s

C. Write the words that go with these words. Use This Week's Words.

10. ____ and seek   **11.** pillow ____

12. all by ____   **13.** ____ and sell

Spelling and Language • Rhyming Words

<table>
</table>

THIS WEEK'S WORDS

nine
lion
bite
bright
fight
hide
life
line
myself
prize
shy
sight
tiger
wise
buy

Finish the poem with words that rhyme with the words in dark print. Use This Week's Words.

On a night so warm and **fine,**
As the clock was striking __1__,
I met a frog, quite by **surprise,**
That looked so very old and __2__.
As it chewed upon a **fly,**
It asked me why I was so __3__.

Writing on Your Own

Write two rhyming sentences that end with bright and sight. Then write some more rhyming sentences using This Week's Words.

WRITER'S GUIDE For an example of a rhyming poem, turn to page 254.

HANDWRITING

m N m M

The lowercase letter **n** touches the midline two times.

n

The lowercase letter **m** touches the midline three times.

m

1. Practice writing **n N, m M** in cursive.

2. Write this sentence: *I went to Maine.*

Spelling on Your Own

Write sentences using all of This Week's Words. Try to use more than one of the words in each sentence. Here is an example: "The shy tiger tried to hide."

Write the Mastery words that mean the opposite of the underlined words.

1. When I <u>lose</u> something, I try to ___ it.
2. Sometimes I must look <u>low</u> and ___.

Finish each sentence. Use a Mastery word. Then find the other word in the sentence that has /ī/ spelled the same way. Write that word.

3. Maria rides her ___ to school.
4. Tell me ___ you need my help.
5. Is it all ___ if I turn on the light?
6. The sun is bright and ___ in the sky.
7. Kind people helped us ___ our lost dog.
8. The rug is nine feet long and six feet ___.

bike
find
high
right
why
wide

BONUS WORDS

1. Write the three Bonus words that have /ī/ spelled with <u>i-e</u>. Use each word in a sentence.
2. Write the two Bonus words that have /ī/ spelled with <u>i</u>. Use each word in a sentence.
3. Add a word with /ī/ to each of these word parts. Write four Bonus words.

| a | way | de | mid |

awhile
delight
highway
midnight
pirate
polite
quite
title

THIS WEEK'S WORDS

1. both
2. float
3. blow
4. fold
5. follow
6. hello
7. joke
8. load
9. old
10. rose
11. sold
12. spoke
13. stove
14. window
15. bow

This Week's Words

All the words this week have the vowel sound /ō/. Here are four ways to spell /ō/.

● with **o**-consonant-**e**, as in <u>joke</u>

● with **oa**, as in <u>float</u>

● with **o**, as in <u>both</u> and <u>fold</u>

● with **ow**, as in <u>blow</u>

REMEMBER THIS

The word <u>bow</u> can be said two ways. <u>Bow</u> has /ō/ when you say "Tie the ribbon in a <u>bow</u>." <u>Bow</u> has the vowel sound heard in <u>cow</u> when you say "Take a <u>bow</u>." But either way, it is spelled the same: <u>bow</u>.

Spelling Practice

A. Follow the directions. Use This Week's Words.

1. Write the four words that have /ō/ spelled as it is in <u>nose</u>.

2. Write the five words that end with /ō/.

3. Circle the word you wrote for **2** that does not end with <u>ow</u>.

4. Write the three words that end with the cluster <u>ld</u>.

5. Write the word that means "two."

B. Write This Week's Words that rhyme with these words.

6. boat ____   7. toad ____

C. Finish the sentences. Use This Week's Words. You will use one word twice.

8. Pablo called me on the phone to say ____.

9. He told me a funny ____.

10. He said, "What's big and gray and has a trunk and a rear ____?"

11. I said, "An ____ gray car."

12. He said, "No, an elephant. I made up the part about the ____."

13. We ____ laughed a lot.

both
float
blow
fold
follow
hello
joke
load
old
rose
sold
spoke
stove
window
bow

73

Spelling and Language • Using Verbs

THIS WEEK'S WORDS

both
float
blow
fold
follow
hello
joke
load
old
rose
sold
spoke
stove
window
bow

Finish the answers to these questions. Use This Week's Words. You will write verbs that tell what already happened.

1. When did Lucy rise today?

She _____ at 7:00 this morning.

2. Did she go out to sell juice?

Yes, she _____ twenty glasses of juice.

3. Did you speak to Lucy when she got home?

Yes, I _____ with her when she returned.

Writing on Your Own

Do you help your parents around the house? Write a paragraph which tells how you do one home job. Give all the steps and helpful tips. Use some of This Week's Words.

Proofreading

Doug wrote this secret message. He misspelled six words.

Stand under the front windo. Take six steps toward the roze garden. Point boath feet east. Follo your nose to the old tree. Look for a yellow boe. This is no joak.

1. Find each of Doug's mistakes.

2. Write the six misspelled words correctly.

 WRITER'S GUIDE See the editing and proofreading marks on page 248.

Spelling on Your Own

THIS WEEK'S WORDS

1. Write NOUN, VERB, and OTHER at the top of your paper.
2. Write each of This Week's Words under the right word. A word like <u>load</u> can be a noun or a verb, but write it in just one place. Three of This Week's Words are not nouns or verbs. Write them under OTHER.
3. Think of a describing word that goes with each noun. Write the two words. Here's an example: <u>funny joke</u>.
4. Then think of a noun that goes with each verb. Write the words. Here is an example: <u>corks float</u>.

MASTERY WORDS

also
grow
low
oak
own
those

1. Write the three Mastery words that end with /ō/.
2. Write the two Mastery words that begin with /ō/.
3. Write the Mastery word that rhymes with <u>nose</u>.
4. Use the word you just wrote in a sentence.

BONUS WORDS

slope
vote
boast
throat
narrow
shadow
scold
stroll

Follow the directions. Use the Bonus words.
1. Write all the words in alphabetical order.
2. After each word, write how /ō/ is spelled in that word.

Try this "word math."
3. <u>three</u> − /ē/ + /ō/ + <u>t</u> = ___
4. <u>say</u> − /ā/ + <u>tea</u> − /ē/ + <u>roll</u> = ___
5. <u>show</u> − /ō/ + <u>ad</u> + /ō/ = ___

Now make up your own "word math" problems.
Use the Bonus words.

18 Review

UNIT 13

invite
skate
taste
cared
smiling
loved
living
paste

UNIT 13 **Follow the directions. Use words from Unit 13. Add ed or ing to these words.**

1. care + ed
2. love + ed
3. live + ing
4. smile + ing

Write the words that rhyme with these words.

5. kite
6. plate
7. waste
8. piling

Finish each sentence. Use a word that begins with the same sound as the person's name used in the sentence.

9. Ingrid and her friends will ___ us to a party.

10. Peter will make invitations with paper and ___.

11. Tony will cook a new dish for us to ___.

UNIT 14   Follow the directions. Use words from Unit 14.

12. Write the three words that spell /ā/ with a-consonant-e.

13. Write the two words that end with /ā/.

Add letters that spell /ā/ to finish these words.

14. _ _ _ _ t

15. g _ t _

16. m _ _ l

17. p _ _ d

UNIT 14

brave
mail
today
eight
obey
lake
gate
paid

UNIT 15   Follow the directions. Use words from Unit 15.

18. Write the four words that end with /ē/.

Add letters that spell /ē/ to finish these words.

19. t_ _m

20. betw_ _n

21. _ven

22. ever_

Finish these sentences.

23. My room is ___ a mess!

24. I can't even walk ___ the bed and the desk.

UNIT 15

team
weak
between
busy
every
even
only
really

WORDS IN TIME

The word <u>mail</u> started out as the old word <u>male</u>. <u>Male</u> meant "bag" or "pouch." Why do you think the word <u>male</u> became <u>mail</u>?

77

life
hide
bright
myself
buy
prize
nine
sight

UNIT 16 Change the underlined letter or letters in each word to make a word from Unit 16.

25. li<u>n</u>e

26. <u>i</u>tself

27. <u>w</u>ide

28. <u>l</u>ight

29. <u>f</u>ine

30. b<u>o</u>y

Finish these sentences with words from Unit 16. Then circle the letters that spell /ī/ in the words.

31. I won a ___.

32. I was so proud of ___.

33. I had a ___ smile on my face.

UNIT 17

both
hello
joke
float
follow
sold
window
fold

UNIT 17 Follow the directions. Use words from Unit 17. Write the words that are the opposite of these words.

34. lead

35. good-bye

36. sink

37. bought

Write the words that complete the paragraph.

Just __38__ these directions. Hold this stick with __39__ hands. Stamp your foot and cough. What's the matter? Can't you get your motorcycle started?
Isn't that a funny __40__ ?

Write the words that finish these sentences.

41. Please ___ the leader.

42. Simon says open the ___.

43. Simon says ___ the paper in half.

Spelling and Reading
A Description

Read the following description. Look for the colorful words.

The painter sat in a small blue boat in the middle of the lake. A cool breeze was blowing, but she was warm in her bright red sweater and cap. The painter ate a fresh, juicy orange. Then she placed a clean, white canvas between her paint and her brushes.

The painter felt the weak rays of the sun turn warm. She watched a family of ducks swim into sight. The painter loved little ducks. She wanted to paint them.

Soon the painter saw two tall boats. They seemed to skate across the lake. Their white sails were floating on the wind, like clouds in the sky. The boats seemed to invite her to paint them. The painter grabbed a brush and started to paint.

Write the answers to the questions.

1. In this description, where does the writer say the boat is?

2. What verb does the writer use to describe how the two tall boats moved across the lake?

3. What does the writer mean by saying that the boats seemed to <u>invite</u> the painter to paint them?

4. How does the painter feel about being on the lake? Why do you think as you do?

Underline the review words in your answers. Check to see that you spelled the words correctly.

Spelling and Writing
A Description
Think and Discuss

In a description, a writer uses describing words. These words tell the reader what the writer has seen, heard, smelled, felt, or tasted.

Words to Help You Write

taste
paste
eight
weak
even
really
bright
sight
float
fold

Look at the pictures on this page. Do they show what you saw in your mind as you read the story on page 79? Read the first paragraph of the story. What describing words does the writer use to tell about the boat? What words does the writer use to describe the canvas? These words help the reader see what the writer saw. What sentence in the first paragraph tells the reader about taste?

Read the second paragraph on page 79. How does the writer describe the sun's rays? This description helps the reader feel the weather.

In a description, a writer can use verbs to help the reader see actions. What verbs in the last sentence of the story describe what the painter did?

Apply

Write a description of your favorite food to share with your classmates. Follow the writing guidelines on the next page.

Prewriting

- Think of your favorite food. The pictures on this page might help you.
- Make a chart with these five columns: <u>See</u>, <u>Hear</u>, <u>Touch</u>, <u>Smell</u>, <u>Taste</u>.
- List colorful words in each column that describe the food.

 THESAURUS For help finding describing words, turn to page 203.

Composing

Use your chart to write the first draft of your description.

- Write a topic sentence that tells what your favorite food is.
- Write detail sentences about the food. Use colorful words from your chart that describe the food.

Revising

Read your paragraph and show it to a classmate. Follow these guidelines to improve your work. Use the editing and proofreading marks to show changes.

Editing

- Make sure your descriptions are clear.
- Make sure you used colorful words.

Proofreading

- Check your spelling and correct any mistakes.
- Check your capitalization and punctuation.

 WRITER'S GUIDE If you need help with capitalization and punctuation, turn to pages 255–257.

Copy your story onto a clean paper. Write carefully and neatly.

Publishing

Share your description. Ask your classmates to tell which words make them want to taste your favorite food.

Editing and Proofreading Marks

≡	capitalize
⊙	make a period
∧	add something
⌃,	add a comma
℈	take something away
◯	spell correctly
¶	indent the paragraph
/	make a lowercase letter

THIS WEEK'S WORDS

1. anyone
2. anyway
3. bedroom
4. cannot
5. everybody
6. football
7. grandfather
8. grandmother
9. herself
10. himself
11. maybe
12. outside
13. playground
14. sometimes
15. yourself

This Week's Words

Sometimes two words are put together to make a new word. The new word is called a **compound word.**

All the words this week are compound words. Remember how the smaller words that make up each word are spelled. That will make writing the long word easier.

Spelling Practice

A. Follow the directions. Use This Week's Words.

1. Add a word from the red box to a word in the green box. Write six compound words.

bed	may	play
can	foot	some

ball	not	times
room	be	ground

2. Write two different words made from <u>any</u> and another word.

3. Write three words made from <u>self</u> and another word.

4. Write the two words that name your parent's parents.

5. The first part rhymes with <u>day</u>. The second part rhymes with <u>sound</u>. Write the compound word. Then write the three consonant clusters in the word.

anyone
anyway
bedroom
cannot
everybody
football
grandfather
grandmother
herself
himself
maybe
outside
playground
sometimes
yourself

B. Change one of the smaller words in each compound word. Make a word that means the opposite.

6. inside   7. nobody

C. Finish the sentences. Use This Week's Words.

☐ Hector can ride by __8__. The baby girl can walk by __9__. What can you do by __10__?

Spelling and Language • One Word or Two

THIS WEEK'S WORDS

anyone
anyway
bedroom
cannot
everybody
football
grandfather
grandmother
herself
himself
maybe
outside
playground
sometimes
yourself

In the sentence "Maybe I'll see you tomorrow," you write <u>maybe</u> as one word. But in the sentence "I <u>may be</u> here tomorrow," you write <u>may be</u> as two words. The same thing happens with <u>anyway</u> and <u>any way</u>. It is one word in the sentence "I didn't want it <u>anyway</u>." But it is two words if you write "You may color the picture <u>any way</u> you like."

Finish the sentences with <u>maybe</u> or <u>may be</u>.

1. ____ this path leads to the zoo.

2. This ____ a shorter way to the zoo.

Finish the sentences with <u>anyway</u> or <u>any way</u>.

3. Is there ____ we can help you?

4. We will try to help you ____.

Writing on Your Own

Pretend your school had a spring fair on the playground. Write a news story for the school newspaper. Tell who came and what they did. Use as many of This Week's Words as you can.

 WRITER'S GUIDE For a sample of a news story, turn to page 253.

Using the Dictionary to Spell and Write

A good writer uses the dictionary all the time. The words in a dictionary are listed in alphabetical order. Use This Week's Words. Write the word that would come right after each of these words in a dictionary.

1. grand   **2.** plant   **3.** become   **4.** follow

 SPELLING DICTIONARY Look in the **Spelling Dictionary** to check your answers.

Spelling on Your Own

Add the missing words. Write the compound words that are This Week's Words.

1. can + ____
2. your + ____
3. ____ + way
4. ____ + side
5. foot + ____
6. ____ + room
7. her + ____
8. ____ + times
9. play + ____
10. him + ____
11. ____ + be
12. ____ + one
13. ____ + father
14. every + ____
15. ____ + mother

MASTERY WORDS

into
within
anything
onto
without
inside

1. Write two Mastery words made from <u>with</u> and another word.
2. Write two Mastery words made from <u>to</u> and another word.
3. Match the words. Write three Mastery words.

with   thing   any   side   in   out

BONUS WORDS

everyday
forever
meanwhile
downstairs
everywhere
cupboard
whoever
ourselves

1. Write the Bonus word that does not sound like the two words it is made from.
2. Write the four Bonus words made with <u>ever</u> or <u>every</u>.
3. Replace the underlined words with Bonus words. Then finish the story.

   Jason looked <u>in all places</u> for the lost whistle. <u>At the same time</u> I searched <u>on the floor below</u>. We told <u>our own minds</u> it was lost <u>for the rest of time</u>. But then...

20 Contractions

THIS WEEK'S WORDS

1. can't
2. didn't
3. don't
4. he's
5. I'll
6. I'm
7. isn't
8. it's
9. let's
10. she's
11. that's
12. there's
13. we'll
14. we're
15. won't

This Week's Words

A **contraction** is a short way of writing two words together. Some of the letters are left out. An **apostrophe** takes their place.

<u>Can't</u> is the contraction of <u>can</u> and <u>not</u>. The apostrophe takes the place of <u>n</u> and <u>o</u>.

All the words this week are contractions. What words make up the contractions? What letters are left out?

REMEMBER THIS

How <u>do</u> <u>not</u> becomes <u>don't</u> is easy to tell.
But <u>will</u> <u>not</u> to <u>won't</u>—what happens then?
Why, the <u>i</u> runs away with the double <u>l</u>,
And the <u>o</u> jumps over the <u>n</u>.

Spelling Practice

A. Write the contractions of these words.

1. I will

2. we will

3. let us

4. we are

5. I am

B. Follow the directions. Use This Week's Words.

6. Write the five words that are contractions of <u>not</u> and another word.

7. Write the six words that are contractions of <u>is</u> and another word.

8. Rewrite this sentence twice. **It is not raining now.** Use <u>it's</u> the first time. Use <u>isn't</u> the second time.

C. Rewrite each sentence. Use two contractions each time.

9. Linda will not tell us about the party she is planning.

10. She says we will have more fun if we do not know.

11. I cannot think what it is going to be like.

can't
didn't
don't
he's
I'll
I'm
isn't
it's
let's
she's
that's
there's
we'll
we're
won't

Spelling and Language • *Negative* Sentences

THIS
WEEK'S
WORDS

can't
didn't
don't
he's
I'll
I'm
isn't
it's
let's
she's
that's
there's
we'll
we're
won't

I can't sing means the opposite of I can sing. They didn't sing means the opposite of They sang. I can't sing and They didn't sing are negative sentences.

Write the sentences as negative sentences. Use This Week's Words.

1. Mike and Charles will play in the park.

2. They want to ride on the swings.

Writing on Your Own

Write a letter to your grandmother, grandfather, or other relative. Ask if you can visit. Ask when you can come to visit and what you should bring. Use some of This Week's Words.

 WRITER'S GUIDE How did you end your sentences? For help with periods and question marks, turn to page 238.

Proofreading

1. Read the letter Darin wrote to his grandmother. Find the three spelling mistakes he made.

> Dear Grandma,
> Wer coming to visit you next month. That's what Mom said today. I donn't know when will get there. Dad says his going to call you.
> I'm going to bed now. I'l write again soon.
>   Love,
>   Darin

2. Write the three misspelled words correctly.

 WRITER'S GUIDE Use the editing and proofreading marks on page 248.

Spelling on Your Own

THIS WEEK'S WORDS

Use all of This Week's Words in sentences. Draw a line under the contraction in each sentence. After the sentence, write the two words that make up the contraction. Here is an example.

I <u>can't</u> find my mittens.   can not

MASTERY WORDS

Write the two Mastery words that make up each contraction.

1. isn't   **2.** don't   **3.** there's   **4.** won't

<u>There</u> tells where. <u>Their</u> tells whose. Finish the sentences. Use <u>there</u> or <u>their</u>.

5. Peg and Brian invited me to ___ house.
6. I was ___ all afternoon.
7. I had fun playing with ___ dog.

do
is
not
their
there
will

BONUS WORDS

Follow the directions. Use the Bonus words.

1. Use their, <u>there</u>, and <u>they're</u> in sentences.
2. Use <u>your</u> and <u>you're</u> in sentences.
3. Write the word that is a contraction of <u>is</u> and another word.

Answer these questions. Use a Bonus word contraction made from <u>not</u> and another word in each answer.

4. Have you eaten?   **5.** Were you there?   **6.** Are we next?
7. Does Paul like nuts?   **8.** Were they sad?

aren't
doesn't
haven't
they're
wasn't
weren't
what's
you're

89

21 The Sounds /ô/ and /ôr/

THIS WEEK'S WORDS

1. straw
2. horse
3. born
4. cause
5. corn
6. course
7. four
8. horn
9. jaw
10. north
11. short
12. talk
13. taught
14. walk
15. wash

This Week's Words

The sound /ô/ is heard in <u>straw</u>. It can be spelled with these letters.

● **a,** as in <u>talk</u>

● **aw,** as in <u>straw</u>

● **au,** as in <u>cause</u>

The sounds /ôr/ are heard in <u>horse</u>. The sound /ô/ with <u>r</u> in this word is spelled <u>or</u>.

☐ The words <u>course</u> and <u>four</u> spell the sounds /ôr/ with **our.**

90

Spelling Practice

A. Follow the directions. Use This Week's Words.

1. Write the two words that have /ô/ spelled as it is in <u>paw</u>.

2. Write the word that sounds just like <u>for</u>.

3. Write the six words that have /ôr/ spelled as it is in <u>for</u>.

4. Write the other word that has /ôr/ spelled as it is in <u>four</u>.

5. Write the word that rhymes with <u>caught</u>.

6. Write the three words that have the sound /ô/ spelled with <u>a</u>. Circle the words that have a "silent" letter <u>l</u>.

straw
horse
born
cause
corn
course
four
horn
jaw
north
short
talk
taught
walk
wash

B. Add the letters that spell /ô/ and /ôr/. Write the words that finish the story.

A unicorn looks like a (**7**) h____se. But it has a long, straight (**8**) h____n on its forehead. Unicorns like to (**9**) w____sh their horns in water. This makes the water magic for a (**10**) sh____t time. It can (**11**) c____se people to have good luck. Of (**12**) c____se, there is really no such thing as a unicorn.

Spelling and Language • Nouns and Verbs

THIS WEEK'S WORDS

straw
horse
born
cause
corn
course
four
horn
jaw
north
short
talk
taught
walk
wash

A **noun** names a person, a place, or a thing. A **verb** shows action or being. Finish each pair of sentences with one of This Week's Words. The word will be a verb in the first sentence and a noun in the second.

1. The boys ___ their clothes.
2. When the ___ is done, they have lunch.
3. Aunt Ann always listens when I ___ to her.
4. I feel good after a long ___ with her.

Writing on Your Own

Write a report about your favorite animal for your teacher. Use some of This Week's Words as both nouns and verbs.

 WRITER'S GUIDE For a sample report, turn to page 254.

Using the Dictionary to Spell and Write

A **definition** tells what a word means. Some words have more than one definition. You need to know the different definitions of a word to make sure you used the word correctly in your writing. Read the definitions for the word <u>cause</u>. One is a noun (<u>n.</u>). The other is a verb (<u>v.</u>).

> **cause** /kôz/ *n.* A person or thing that makes something happen; reason: He was the *cause* of the trouble.
> —*v.* **caused, causing** To make something happen: A traffic jam *caused* us to be late.

Write <u>n.</u> or <u>v.</u> to show how <u>cause</u> is used in each sentence.

1. What could have <u>caused</u> Taro to stay at home?
2. No one knows the <u>cause</u> of the fire.
3. You have no <u>cause</u> to be angry.

Spelling on Your Own

THIS WEEK'S WORDS

Make a "word chain" with This Week's Words. Write one word. Use a letter in that word to write another word. Keep going, writing words across and down. Try to link all the words in one chain. You may also make more than one chain.

MASTERY WORDS

Follow the directions. Use the Mastery words.

1. Write the two words that have /ô/ spelled <u>a</u>.
2. Write the two words that have /ô/ spelled <u>aw</u>.
3. Write the two words that have the sounds /ôr/.

Write the Mastery words that are the opposite of these words.

4. less   5. after   6. short

| before |
| crawl |
| draw |
| fall |
| more |
| tall |

BONUS WORDS

Write a Bonus word to go with each definition.

1. girl child   2. place for horses   3. rainstorm
4. baby deer   5. place for a judge   6. seed of oak
                                              trees

Follow the directions. Use the Bonus words.

7. Write the word that sounds just like <u>paws</u>.
8. Write the word with a "silent" letter <u>l</u>.
9. Use the Bonus words in sentences. Try to make your sentences tell a story. Read your story to a friend.

| acorn |
| corral |
| court |
| daughter |
| downpour |
| fawn |
| pause |
| stalk |

22 The Sounds /ûr/

THIS WEEK'S WORDS

1. sir
2. fur
3. learn
4. world
5. birthday
6. bluebird
7. burn
8. circle
9. early
10. earn
11. earth
12. heard
13. return
14. skirt
15. worry

The early bird catches the purple worm.

This Week's Words

The sound /û/ with <u>r</u> is heard in all the words this week. Here are four ways to spell /ûr/.

- with **ir,** as in <u>bird</u> and <u>sir</u>

- with **ur,** as in <u>purple</u> and <u>fur</u>

- with **ear,** as in <u>early</u> and <u>learn</u>

- with **or,** as in <u>worm</u> and <u>world</u>

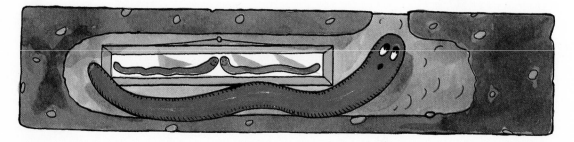

Spelling Practice

A. Follow the directions. Use This Week's Words.

1. Write the words that have /ûr/ spelled the same as it is in these words.

2. Write the compound word made from <u>bird</u> and another word.

3. Write the four other words that have /ûr/ spelled <u>ir</u>.

4. Circle the compound word you wrote for **3**.

5. Write the three words that begin with /ûr/.

6. Put a letter in front of <u>earn</u>. Write another word.

7. Answer this question. Use one of This Week's Words. Did you hear the phone ring?

   Yes, ___.

B. Write the words that have these meanings. Use This Week's Words.

8. find out

9. come back

10. too soon

11. round shape

sir
fur
learn
world
birthday
bluebird
burn
circle
early
earn
earth
heard
return
skirt
worry

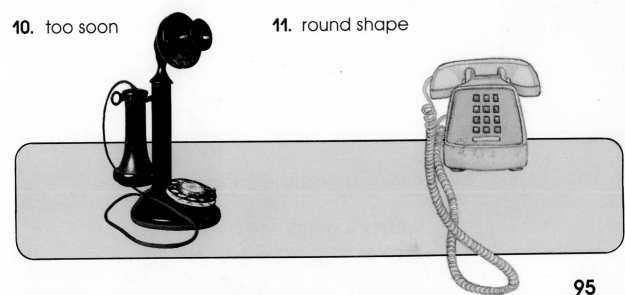

Spelling and Language • Rhyming Words

THIS WEEK'S WORDS

sir
fur
learn
world
birthday
bluebird
burn
circle
early
earn
earth
heard
return
skirt
worry

Finish the poem with words that rhyme with the words in dark print. Use This Week's Words. Remember that /ûr/ can be spelled in different ways.

Late one night, something **stirred.**
What could have made the noise I __1__?

Something was hiding behind a **fern.**
What could it be? I had to __2__.

Then I heard a friendly **purr,**
And touched my cat's soft, silky __3__.

Writing on Your Own

Write a poem for your friends. Begin your poem with the first two lines of the poem above. Use as many of This Week's Words as you can.

Proofreading

Keisha wrote this report. She misspelled five words.

1. Find each mistake.

> Raccoons have thick fir. They have black curcles around their tails. They hunt at night and retearn to their dens erly in the morning. Baby raccoons stay with their mother. They lurn from her how to hunt and climb trees.

2. Write the five misspelled words correctly.

 WRITER'S GUIDE See the editing and proofreading marks on page 248.

Spelling on Your Own

THIS WEEK'S WORDS

In place of <u>ur</u>, write the letters that spell /ûr/. Write each word.

1. sûr
2. retûrn
3. skûrt
4. bûrn
5. bûrthday
6. fûr
7. cûrcle
8. ûrth
9. lûrn
10. bluebûrd
11. ûrn
12. wûrry
13. ûrly
14. hûrd
15. wûrld

MASTERY WORDS

bird
hurt
work
turn
girl
word

1. Write the Mastery word that begins with <u>t</u>. Write the word that ends with <u>t</u>. Then write two other letters that are alike in these two words.
2. Write the two Mastery words that have the letters <u>or</u>.
3. My friend Holly has a parrot named Polly. Write the Mastery words that tell what Holly is and what Polly is.

BONUS WORDS

pearl
purpose
search
thirsty
turtle
whirl
worst
worth

1. Write the Bonus word that goes with <u>hungry</u>.
2. What animal carries its house on its back? Write the name.
3. Write the Bonus word that means "seek, or look for."
4. Write the Bonus word that is the opposite of <u>best</u>.
5. Next to each word you wrote for **1—4,** write another Bonus word that has /ûr/ spelled the same.
6. Write a story you could read to a three- or four-year-old. Your story could be about a baby turtle.

23 The Sounds /är/ and /âr/

THIS WEEK'S WORDS

1. park
2. stairs
3. art
4. bark
5. barn
6. card
7. farm
8. yard
9. air
10. fair
11. hair
12. pair
13. bear
14. pear
15. heart

This Week's Words

The sounds /är/ can be spelled **ar,** as in park.
☐ The sounds /är/ are spelled **ear,** in heart.
The sounds /âr/ can be spelled **air,** as in stairs.
The sounds /âr/ can also be spelled **ear,** as in bear.

REMEMBER THIS

Here's a way to remember the e in heart.
"You can hear your heart." The first four
letters in heart are the letters that spell
hear.

98

Spelling Practice

A. Follow the directions. Use This Week's Words.

1. Write the word for something you cannot see that is all around you.

2. Add one letter at a time to the word you wrote for 1. Write three words.

3. Write the two words that sound alike.

4. Finish this sentence with two of This Week's Words.

   I walked down the ___ to get a juicy ___ from the fruit bowl.

5. Answer this riddle. Use two words that rhyme. What do you call a panda's fur?

B. Write two words that rhyme with each of these words.

6. dark

7. hard

8. part

C. Add one letter to the end of each word. Write some of This Week's Words.

9. car

10. far

11. bar (two words)

park
stairs
art
bark
barn
card
farm
yard
air
fair
hair
pair
bear
pear
heart

99

Spelling and Language • Compound Words

Two words can be put together to make a new word. The new word is called a **compound word.**

THIS
WEEK'S
WORDS

park
stairs
art
bark
barn
card
farm
yard
air
fair
hair
pair
bear
pear
heart

board	plane	up

Put three of This Week's Words together with three words from the box. Make compound words to go with these definitions.

1. It flies in the sky.

2. It is what boxes are made from.

3. You climb the steps to get there.

Writing on Your Own

Tell what your town is like for a friend who does not live there. You may wish to make compound words of some of This Week's Words to use in your description.

Using the Dictionary to Spell and Write

A good place to look for the correct spelling of a word is the dictionary. The words in a dictionary are in alphabetical order. If the first letters of words are the same, look at the second letter. If the second letters are the same, look at the third letter. Back, bad, bag are in order by third letter—c, d, g.

Write each group of words in alphabetical order.

1. stairs
park
straw
pair

2. heart
farm
herself
fair

 SPELLING DICTIONARY Remember to use your **Spelling Dictionary** when you write.

Spelling on Your Own

THIS WEEK'S WORDS

```
M  B  E  A  R
F  A  I  R  E
T  R  H  D  I
N  K  S  T  H
```

Use all the words to make a word search puzzle. You can write the words across or down. Fill in the empty spaces with other letters. Then let someone else solve the puzzle.

MASTERY WORDS

arm
chair
start
far
hard
part

Change one letter in each word. Write Mastery words.

1. park   **2.** card   **3.** car   **4.** art

Add two letters to each word. Write Mastery words.

5. art   **6.** air

Follow the directions. Write the Mastery words.

7. Take away the first letter in <u>farm</u>.

8. Take away the last letter in <u>farm</u>.

Write the Mastery words that mean the opposite of each word.

9. soft   **10.** finish

BONUS WORDS

argue
barber
garden
repair
alarm
haircut
artist
market

Write the Bonus words that go with these words.

1. ___ clock   **2.** ___ shop   **3.** flea ___   **4.** rose ___

Follow the directions. Use the Bonus words.

5. Write the two words that have the sounds /âr/.

6. Write all the words in alphabetical order.

7. Write a story about an artist and a barber. Try to use all the Bonus words in your story.

24 Review

Do these steps if you are not sure how to spell a word.

- **Say** the word. Listen to each sound. Think about what the word means.
- **Look** at the word. See how the letters are made. Try to see the word in your mind.
- **Spell** the word to yourself. Think about the way each sound is spelled.
- **Write** the word. Copy it from your book. Check the way you made your letters. Write the word again.
- **Check** your learning. Cover the word and write it. Did you spell it correctly? If not, do these steps until you know how to spell the word.

UNIT 19

anyway
bedroom
everybody
maybe
sometimes
outside
grandfather
grandmother

UNIT 19 Add one of the words from the box to each word below. Write words from Unit 19.

times side way be father room mother body

1. may   2. every   3. bed   4. some

5. out   6. any   7. grand (two words)

UNIT 20

didn't
I'll
let's
there's
won't
can't
that's
we're

UNIT 20 Follow the directions. Use words from Unit 20. Write the contractions for these words.

8. that is   9. let us

10. did not   11. there is

12. we are   13. can not

14. I will   15. will not

UNIT 21 Follow the directions. Use words from Unit 21. Finish the story. The clues /ô/ and /ôr/ are given. You will use some words twice.

UNIT 21

talk
taught
straw
short
four
born
walk
north

My aunt /ô/ __16__ us a funny

game. You draw straws. There are

/ôr/ __17__ long ones and one that is

/ôr/ __18__. Whoever gets the short

/ô/ __19__ must /ô/ __20__ only in

rhymes. I got the /ôr/ __21__ /ô/ __22__.

So wherever I /ô/ __23__, in rhymes I

must /ô/ __24__.

Write the word that rhymes with each word.

25. horn   **26.** forth

27. caught   **28.** pour

UNIT 22

birthday
heard
learn
return
world
circle
early
worry

UNIT 22 Follow the directions. Use words from Unit 22.

29. Write the three words that have /ûr/ spelled <u>ear</u>.

30. Write the two words that have /ûr/ spelled <u>or</u>.

31. Write the two words that have /ûr/ spelled <u>ir</u>.

32. Write the word that has /ûr/ spelled <u>ur</u>.

UNIT 23

park
yard
heart
stairs
bear
card
hair
air

UNIT 23   **Follow the directions. Use words from Unit 23.**

33. Write the four words that have /är/. Draw a line under the letters that spell /är/ in each word.

34. Write the four words that have /âr/. Draw a line under the letters that spell /âr/ in each word.

35. Write the word from **34** that is a plural word.

Add a word to each word below to make a compound word. Then write the compound word.

36. back + ___ = ___

37. up + ___ = ___

38. Write the two words that rhyme with <u>air</u>.

39. Finish this sentence.

Amanda drew a red ___ on the birthday

___ she gave to her mother.

WORDS IN TIME

The word <u>bear</u> comes from the old word <u>bera</u>. <u>Bera</u> meant "the brown one." Can you guess why people gave this name to a bear?

Spelling and Reading
A Friendly Letter

Read the following friendly letter. Look at the five parts.

387 First Street
Boulder, Colorado 80302
July 15, 19——

Dear Gail,

　　I can't wait for you to come next month. We're going to have a lot of fun.

　　It's going to be my birthday while you're here. Mom is planning a party for me. It will be outside in our yard.

　　I'll talk to my dad about taking us fishing. He just taught me how to fish. I only wish your visit were going to be longer. Four days is such a short time!

　　What is new with you? Write soon and tell me.

Your friend,
Mary

Heading

Greeting

Body

Closing
Signature

Write the answers to the questions.

1. In the letter, where does Mary say her birthday party will take place?
2. How long will Gail's visit be?
3. How does Mary feel about the length of Gail's visit?
4. Why do you think Mary asked Gail what's new with her?

Underline the review words in your answers. Check to see that you spelled the words correctly.

Spelling and Writing
A Friendly Letter

Words to Help You Write

grandmother
grandfather
didn't
I'll
let's
there's
we're
talk
learn
early
park
yard

Think and Discuss

A friendly letter is a letter you write to a friend or a relative. You can tell about things you did, or other news. You can also ask what your friend or relative is doing.

Look at Mary's letter on page 105. To whom did she write? What did she tell Gail about? What question did Mary ask Gail?

Look at the five parts of Mary's letter. Where did she use capital letters? Where did she use commas?

Apply

Now you will write a **friendly letter.** Follow the writing guidelines on the next page.

Prewriting

Get ready to write a friendly letter to a friend or relative who lives in another town.

● Choose someone to receive your letter.
● Make a list of some things you did that might interest the person to whom you are writing.
● Make a list of some things you would like to know about the person.

 THESAURUS If you need more words to tell about things you did, turn to page 203.

Composing

Use your lists to write your letter.

● Write about what you have been doing.
● Ask about news your friend or relative might have.

Revising

Read your letter. Follow these guidelines to improve your work. Use the editing and proofreading marks to show changes.

Editing

● Make sure your letter has all five parts.
● Check that you told something about yourself.
● Be sure you asked about the other person.

Proofreading

● Check your spelling and correct any mistakes.
● Check your capitalization and punctuation.

Copy your letter onto a clean paper. Write carefully and neatly.

Publishing

Send your letter to your friend or relative. Or share your letter with your classmates by posting it on a class bulletin board. See what information other children included in their letters.

Editing and Proofreading Marks	
≡	capitalize
⊙	make a period
∧	add something
⌄	add a comma
ℯ	take something away
○	spell correctly
¶	indent the paragraph
/	make a lowercase letter
tr	transpose

25 More Plurals

THIS WEEK'S WORDS

1. pancakes
2. ears
3. eyes
4. grades
5. lands
6. marbles
7. newspapers
8. shapes
9. wheels
10. buddies
11. butterflies
12. fairies
13. guppies
14. puppies
15. spies

This Week's Words

A **plural noun** names more than one thing. You add <u>s</u> to most nouns to make the plural.

pancake	pancakes
ear	ears

Just <u>s</u> is not enough for words like <u>buddy</u> and <u>spy</u>. These words end with a consonant and <u>y</u>. To make them plural, change <u>y</u> to <u>i</u> and add <u>es</u>.

buddy	buddies
spy	spies

108

Spelling Practice

A. Write the plural of each word.

1. guppy   **2.** fairy   **3.** buddy   **4.** spy

B. Write the plural of the words in dark print. Finish the sentences.

5. newspaper   Mr. Ito reads four ___ every day.

6. land   Some are sent to him from other ___.

C. Write the singular of these words.

7. grades   **8.** pancakes

9. shapes   **10.** marbles

D. Write the singular and plural words for each picture.

11.   **12.**   **13.**

E. Write the plural of the words in dark print. Finish the sentences.

14. eye   He has ___ in the back of his head.

15. ear   Tell me—I'm all ___.

pancakes
ears
eyes
grades
lands
marbles
newspapers
shapes
wheels
buddies
butterflies
fairies
guppies
puppies
spies

Spelling and Language • One or More

THIS
WEEK'S
WORDS

pancakes
ears
eyes
grades
lands
marbles
newspapers
shapes
wheels
buddies
butterflies
fairies
guppies
puppies
spies

One of This Week's Words will finish each sentence. Decide if the singular or plural word fits. For example, puppies fits the sentence "Those ___ wag their tails." But puppy fits the sentence "That ___ wags its tail." Write the words that fit the sentences.

1. A caterpillar becomes a beautiful ___.

2. Jay's ___ get better with each report card.

Writing on Your Own

Write a paragraph for a class booklet called "How We Take Care of Our Pets." Tell how to take care of the pet you have or would like to have. Use some of This Week's Words and some other plurals.

 WRITER'S GUIDE For a sample of a how-to paragraph, turn to page 250.

Proofreading

☐ Jill wrote this in her journal. She misspelled six words and forgot two capital letters.

1. Find each of Jill's mistakes.

> We had panacakes for breakfast. After breakfast I fed my gubbies and counted my marbels. My buddie Todd came over. We decided to paint my old wagon. we put newpapers down on the back porch. now the wagon is purple and the wheals are yellow.

2. Write the six misspelled words correctly.

Spelling on Your Own

 THIS WEEK'S WORDS

Write some funny story titles. Use This Week's Words. Try to use more than one of the words in each title. You may use the singular or the plural. Here are some examples: "Why Wheels Are That Shape" and "Life with Puppies and Guppies."

 MASTERY WORDS

trains
tires
streets
stones
plants
ants

Follow the directions. Use the Mastery words.

1. Write three words that name things in the picture.

2. Write the word that has the sound /ē/.

Finish the sentences. Use the Mastery words.

3. Jenny played with her electric ___.
4. Then she watered the ___ in her room.
5. Next, she pumped up the ___ on her bike.

BONUS WORDS

blueberries
stories
cartwheels
chances
cherries
details
hobbies
puddles

1. Write the singular of each Bonus word. Tell what happens to make the word plural.
2. Write the two Bonus words that are compound words.
3. Write the five Bonus words that have double letters.
4. Write the six Bonus words with long vowel sounds.
5. Write sentences using the Bonus words. Try to use two of the words in each sentence.

26 "Silent" Letters

THIS WEEK'S WORDS

1. knee
2. knew
3. knit
4. knock
5. knot
6. known
7. calf
8. half
9. climb
10. lamb
11. thumb
12. wren
13. written
14. wrote
15. ghost

/knē/

This Week's Words

Say the word <u>knee</u>. Listen to the beginning sound /n/. Hundreds of years ago, people said both /k/ and /n/ at the beginning of <u>knee</u>. Now the sound /k/ is not heard. But the letter <u>k</u> is still written. When the sound of a letter is not heard, we call it a "silent" letter.

Read each of the words to yourself. Decide which letter is a "silent" letter in each word.

Knock, knock. Who's there?

Ellen. Ellen who?

<u>L</u> in <u>calf</u> is silent.

Spelling Practice

A. Follow the directions. Use This Week's Words.

1. Write the three words that begin with the sound /r/.
2. Write the three words that end with the sound /m/.
3. Write the two words that have a "silent" letter <u>l</u>.
4. Write the word that has a "silent" <u>h</u>.

B. Add a "silent" letter and another letter. Write This Week's Words.

5. _ _ it _____   **6.** _ _ ock _____

7. _ _ ee _____   **8.** _ _ ot _____

C. Write This Week's Words that rhyme with these words.

9. jam   **10.** time   **11.** hum

D. Read the first sentence in each group. Find the word that has a "silent" letter. Then finish the next two sentences. Use words that have the same "silent" letter.

12. Luis and Cissy know how to solve the puzzle.

I should have _____ they'd figure it out.

I wish I _____ how they did it so quickly.

13. Debbie writes long letters to Mary Jane.

The one she _____ today was very long.

It may be the longest letter she's ever _____!

knee
knew
knit
knock
knot
known
calf
half
climb
lamb
thumb
wren
written
wrote
ghost

Spelling and Language • Nouns and Verbs

THIS WEEK'S WORDS

knee
knew
knit
knock
knot
known
calf
half
climb
lamb
thumb
wren
written
wrote
ghost

A **noun** names a person, a place, or a thing. A **verb** shows action or being. Finish each pair of sentences with one of This Week's Words. The word will be a verb in the first sentence and a noun in the second.

1. Let's _____ up the mountain on Saturday.

2. It's a rough _____, so wear heavy shoes.

3. Just _____ on the door when you get here.

4. I will come out as soon as I hear your _____.

Writing on Your Own

Write a funny story for your family. Tell about a lamb that knew how to knit.

Using the Dictionary to Spell and Write

Suppose you want to check the spelling of a word in the dictionary. The quickest way to find the word is to use the guide words. Two **guide words** appear at the top of every page. The word on the left is the first word on the page. The word on the right is the last word. All the other words on the page are in alphabetical order between the guide words.

trail	until

trail /trāl/ *n.* **1** A path. **2** The marks left by a person or animal. —*v.* To follow behind: Jacob *trailed* everyone in the race.

Tues. Abbreviation for *Tuesday.*
Tues·day /t(y)o͞oz′dē/ *or* /t(y)o͞oz′dā/ *n.* The third day of the week.

Here are three pairs of guide words. Write two of This Week's Words that would be on each page.

1. cabin color   **2.** game help   **3.** kind knife

Spelling on Your Own

THIS WEEK'S WORDS

What two letters are needed to finish each word?
Add the letters and write This Week's Words.

1. _ _ ost   **2.** thu _ _   **3.** _ _ ock   **4.** _ _ it   **5.** la _ _

6. _ _ en   **7.** ca _ _   **8.** _ _ ot   **9.** _ _ ote   **10.** _ _ ee

11. cli _ _   **12.** _ _ own   **13.** _ _ ew   **14.** ha _ _   **15.** _ _ itten

MASTERY WORDS

know
listen
should
walk
who
write

Follow the directions. Use the Mastery words.

1. Write the three words that start with the letter <u>w</u>.

2. Write the word that starts with the sound /r/.

3. Write a question. Start with the word that rhymes with <u>you</u>.

Add the "silent" letters. Write Mastery words.

4. lis _ en   **5.** _ now   **6.** shou _ d   **7.** wa _ k

BONUS WORDS

crumbs
chalk
knead
kneel
knife
limb
wreck
wrist

Write the Bonus words that rhyme with these words.

1. seal   **2.** peck   **3.** him   **4.** seed

5. comes   **6.** fist   **7.** talk   **8.** life

Follow the directions. Use the Bonus words.

9. Write the word that sounds just like <u>need</u>. Use both words in a sentence.

10. Write a story about Silent Kay, the girl who never talked. Use as many words as you can that start with <u>kn</u>.

115

27 Words That End with y

THIS WEEK'S WORDS

1. family
2. hurry
3. body
4. company
5. lady
6. library
7. party
8. penny
9. pony
10. carry
11. copy
12. cry
13. empty
14. marry
15. study

These families are hurrying.

This Week's Words

All of the words this week end with a consonant and y. Some are nouns. Some are verbs.

To make the nouns plural, change y to i and add es.

    family   families

To make the verbs tell about the past, change y to i and add ed.

    hurry   hurried

The y stays when you add ing.

    hurry   hurrying

REMEMBER THIS

There are two r's in library. They come before and after the a. Think of this. In the library you **reach** **a**nd **read**.

116

Spelling Practice

A. Write the singular of each plural noun.

1. bodies   **2.** ladies   **3.** ponies   **4.** pennies

B. Write these words without <u>ed</u>. Remember to change a letter.

5. emptied   **6.** cried   **7.** studied   **8.** married

C. Add <u>ing</u> to the word in dark print. Finish each sentence.

9. hurry   Melissa is ___ down the street.

10. carry   She is ___ a bag of groceries.

D. Finish the first sentence with <u>copy</u> + <u>ed</u>. Finish the second sentence with <u>copy</u> + <u>es</u>.

11. Steve ___ his paper until it was perfect.

12. He made five ___ before he was done.

E. Finish the sentences. Use This Week's Words.

13. There are three people in Hamad's ___.

14. Hamad's father works for a ___ that makes bikes.

15. Hamad's mother works in a ___ that has many books.

16. I met them both at Hamad's birthday ___.

family
hurry
body
company
lady
library
party
penny
pony
carry
copy
cry
empty
marry
study

Spelling and Language • Verbs and Plurals

THIS WEEK'S WORDS

family
hurry ✓
body ✓
company ✓
lady
library ✓
party
penny
pony ✓
carry ✓
copy ✓
cry ✓
empty
marry
study

You add <u>ed</u> to a verb to tell what already happened. You add <u>ing</u> to make a verb that can be used with <u>am</u>, <u>is</u>, <u>are</u>, <u>was</u>, and <u>were</u>.

Write the verbs. Add <u>ed</u> or <u>ing</u> to the words in dark print.

1. hurry   Lena ____ to her desk.

2. study   She is ____ about animals that work.

A plural noun names more than one thing. Write the plural of the word in dark print.

3. pony   Lena read a book about Shetland ____.

Writing on Your Own

Write a story for your classmates about a pony. Use as many of This Week's Words as you can. Add <u>ed</u> and <u>ing</u> to some of the verbs in your story.

WRITER'S GUIDE Do you need help revising your story? If so, turn to the checklist on page 247.

Using the Dictionary to Spell and Write

A dictionary gives you information that will help you when you write. There are two vowel sounds in <u>pony</u>. So <u>pony</u> has two **syllables.** The pronunciation for <u>pony</u> has this mark: ʹ. It is an **accent mark.** It shows which syllable is said with more force.

> **po·ny** /pōʹnē/ *n., pl.* **ponies** A very small horse.

act, āte, câre, ärt;	egg, ēven;	if, īce;	on, ōver, ôr;	bŏŏk, fōōd;	up, tûrn;
ə = a in *ago*, e in *listen*, i in *giraffe*, o in *pilot*, u in *circus*;		yōō = u in *music*;		oil;	out;
chair; sing; shop; thank; that; zh in *treasure*.					

Find the accent mark in each pronunciation. Write **1, 2,** or **3** to show which syllable the mark follows. Then write the word.

1. /empʹtē/   **2.** /famʹə·lē/

Spelling on Your Own

1. Write **NOUN** and **VERB** at the top of your paper.
2. Write each of This Week's Words under the right word. The words hurry, copy, cry, and study can be nouns or verbs. Write them in both lists.
3. Use one noun and one verb together in a sentence. You can make the noun plural. You can add ed or ing to the verb. Here is an example: "The ladies hurried to the bus stop."
4. Use the nouns and verbs to write two more sentences.

MASTERY WORDS

city ✓
try
baby ✓
sky
dry
candy ✓

Follow the directions. Use the Mastery words.

1. Write the three words that end with /ī/.
2. Write the three words that end with /ē/.

Write the singular of each plural noun. Remember to change a letter.

3. cities   **4.** candies   **5.** skies   **6.** babies

Write these Mastery words without ed.

7. tried   **8.** dried

BONUS WORDS

bury ✓
colony ✓
deny
enemy
envy
factory
memory
supply

1. Write the Bonus word that has two p's. Write two sentences, using it as a noun and as a verb.
2. Write the plurals of the four other nouns.
3. Add ed and ing to the three other verbs.
4. Write a story about hidden treasure. Use the Bonus words.

28 The Sounds /əl/ and /ər/

THIS WEEK'S WORDS

1. purple
2. camel
3. cover
4. able
5. bottle
6. eagle
7. people
8. table
9. level
10. nickel
11. shovel
12. either
13. letter
14. summer
15. sugar

purple camel cover

This Week's Words

All the words this week have two vowel sounds. We say that they have two **syllables.** The first syllable in each word is said with more force. The second syllable has a weak vowel sound called a **schwa.** We use this sign to show the schwa: /ə/.

/əl/ The schwa with /l/ is spelled **le** in <u>purple</u> and **el** in <u>camel</u>.

/ər/ The schwa with /r/ is often spelled **er,** as in <u>cover</u>. But it can be spelled with other vowel letters. It is spelled **ar** in <u>sugar</u>.

REMEMBER THIS

There are two ways to say <u>either</u>. One way begins with long <u>e</u>: /ē'thər/. The other way begins with long <u>i</u>: /ī'thər/. That's good. It helps us remember to put <u>e</u> and <u>i</u> in <u>either</u>.

120

Spelling Practice

A. Follow the directions. Use This Week's Words.

1. Write the three words that name things in the picture.

2. Write three more words that have /əl/ spelled the same way.

3. Write the word for this picture.

4. Write three more words that have /əl/ spelled this way.

5. Write the three words that begin with vowel sounds.

B. Add the letters that stand for /ər/. Write the words.

6. cov___

7. lett___

8. eith___

9. sug___

10. summ___

C. Read the clues. Then write This Week's Words to answer the riddles.

11. I have four legs and a long <u>a</u>.

12. I have the sound /u/ and I dig.

13. I have a head on one side and a short <u>i</u>.

purple
camel
cover
able
bottle
eagle
people
table
level
nickel
shovel
either
letter
summer
sugar

121

Spelling and Language • Plural Nouns

THIS WEEK'S WORDS

purple
camel
cover
able
bottle
eagle
people
table
level
nickel
shovel
either
letter
summer
sugar

A plural noun names more than one thing. You add <u>s</u> to most nouns to make them plural.

Finish the sentences. Use plurals of This Week's Words.

1. Bald ___ have white feathers on their heads.

2. Some ___ have one hump and others have two.

3. There are seven ___ in the word <u>animals</u>.

Writing on Your Own

Write a paragraph for a young child telling about an eagle or a camel. Use plural nouns and some of This Week's Words.

 WRITER'S GUIDE For help revising your paragraph, see the checklist on page 247.

Proofreading

Wendy made up a shopping list. She made three spelling mistakes in her list.

1. Find each mistake.

> *Shopping List*
> *2 pounds of suger*
> *a paper tablecloth*
> *purpel grapes*
> *2 botles of apple juice*

2. Write the three misspelled words correctly.

 WRITER'S GUIDE See the editing and proofreading marks on page 248.

Spelling on Your Own

THIS WEEK'S WORDS

Here are the first syllables of all of This Week's Words.
Add the missing syllable to each one. Write the whole word.

1. sum   **2.** lev   **3.** bot   **4.** pur   **5.** ea
6. cam   **7.** ta   **8.** cov   **9.** shov   **10.** let
11. ei   **12.** nick   **13.** peo   **14.** a   **15.** sug

MASTERY WORDS

after
dollar
ever
other
over
river

Add the vowel letters. Write the Mastery words.

1. d_ll_r   **2.** _th_r   **3.** r_v_r   **4.** _ft_r

Finish the sentences. Use the Mastery words that mean
the opposite of the words in dark print.

5. I went **under** the bridge as she went ___ it.
6. My sister was born **before** me, but ___ my brother.

Write Mastery words to finish the sentence.

7. And they lived happily ___ ___.

BONUS WORDS

answer
clever
collar
paddle
polar
puzzle
travel
tunnel

Write the Bonus words that go with these words.

1. jigsaw ___   **2.** ___ fox   **3.** underground ___
4. ___ the phone   **5.** canoe ___   **6.** ___ bear
7. ___ far   **8.** leash and ___

Use these pairs of Bonus words in sentences.

9. The two words that end with <u>le</u>.
10. The two words that end with <u>el</u>.
11. The two words that end with <u>er</u>.

29 Homophones

THIS WEEK'S WORDS

1. sale
2. sail
3. beat
4. beet
5. break
6. brake
7. main
8. mane
9. read
10. reed
11. meet
12. rode
13. son
14. whose
15. won

This Week's Words

Sale and sail are **homophones.** They sound alike, but they are not spelled alike. They also have different meanings.

Homophones can be tricky. You must pay attention to what the words mean. Then you can write the words that make sense in your sentences.

Spelling Practice

A. Write the homophones for these words. Use This Week's Words.

1. who's
2. sun
3. road
4. one
5. meat

B. A word in each sentence doesn't make sense. Find that word. Then write the right word.

6. The horse has a long, white main.
7. You step on the break to stop a car.
8. The store is having a sail on jeans.
9. Pablo's face is as red as a beat.
10. Gail made a flute out of a read.

C. Finish each sentence. Use the word that has the right meaning.

11. Miko and Chris ____ a book every week.
12. I hope our team can ____ the other team.
13. Children ____ their toy boats on this pond.
14. Dad can ____ open an egg with one hand.
15. What is the ____ street in your town called?

D. Rewrite this sentence. Use road and its homophone.

16. We took a ride down the road.

sale
sail
beat
beet
break
brake
main
mane
read
reed
meet
rode
son
whose
won

125

Spelling and Language • <u>Whose</u> and <u>Who's</u>

**THIS
WEEK'S
WORDS**

sale

sail

beat

beet

break

brake

main

mane

read

reed

meet

rode

son

whose

won

You use <u>whose</u> to ask questions about who owns something: "<u>Whose</u> pencil is this?" The word <u>who's</u> is a contraction for <u>who is</u> or <u>who has</u>. You use <u>who's</u> to ask this kind of question: "<u>Who's</u> using my pencil?"

Start each of these questions with <u>Whose</u> or <u>Who's</u>.

1. ___ going camping with you?

2. ___ tent will you use?

3. ___ doing the cooking?

Writing on Your Own

Write three signs using homophone pairs from This Week's Words. Here is an example: "Sail for Sale." Share your signs with your class.

 WRITER'S GUIDE Can your classmates read your signs? For help writing any letters, turn to page 260.

Using the Dictionary to Spell and Write

Knowing how to pronounce a word can help you remember how to spell it. A **pronunciation** is a special way of writing a word. It shows you how to say the word. As you can see, the pronunciations for <u>who's</u> and <u>whose</u> are the same.

> **who's** /hōōz/ **1** Who is: *Who's* ready for recess?
> **2** Who has: *Who's* got my notebook?
> **whose** /hōōz/ *pron.* Belonging to which person:
> *Whose* book is this?

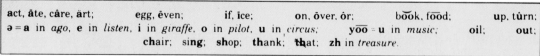

act, āte, câre, ärt;   egg, ēven;   if, īce;   on, ōver, ôr;   bŏŏk, fōōd;   up, tûrn;
ə = a in *ago*, e in *listen*, i in *giraffe*, o in *pilot*, u in *circus*;   yōō = u in *music*;   oil;   out;
     chair; sing; shop; thank; that; zh in *treasure*.

Write the two words for each pronunciation.

1. /brāk/   **2.** /sāl/

Spelling on Your Own

Write sentences using homophone pairs. Use This Week's Words. Use the homophones you know for <u>meet</u>, <u>rode</u>, <u>son</u>, <u>whose</u>, and <u>won</u>, too. Here is an example: "Let's <u>meet</u> at the <u>meat</u> store."

MASTERY WORDS

here
too
would
to
wood
hear

Follow the directions. Use the Mastery words.

1. Write the word that means almost the same as "listen." Then write the word that sounds the same.

2. Write the word that names what comes from trees. Then write the word that sounds the same.

Finish the sentences. Use two Mastery words.

3. Juan walks his little brother ___ school.

4. His brother is ___ little to go alone.

BONUS WORDS

groan
hole
pain
scent
whole
cent
grown
pane

Some homophones are mixed up in this story. Write the story correctly. Then finish the story.

    The night had groan cold. Nan could smell the cent of pine needles. The wind whistled through a whole in the window pain. It sounded like the grown of someone in pane. Nan thought, "For two scents I'd leave this cabin and go home." Still, she knew the hole situation would seem better in the morning.
    Suddenly Nan heard a loud cracking sound.

30 Review

Do these steps if you are not sure how to spell a word.

- **Say** the word. Listen to each sound. Think about what the word means.
- **Look** at the word. See how the letters are made. Try to see the word in your mind.
- **Spell** the word to yourself. Think about the way each sound is spelled.
- **Write** the word. Copy it from your book. Check the way you made your letters. Write the word again.
- **Check** your learning. Cover the word and write it. Did you spell it correctly? If not, do these steps until you know how to spell the word.

UNIT 25

ears
eyes
marbles
butterflies
puppies
grades
wheels
buddies

UNIT 25 Follow the directions. Use words from Unit 25. Write the plurals of these words.

1. puppy
2. marble
3. eye
4. butterfly
5. buddy
6. wheel
7. ear
8. grade

UNIT 26

climb
ghost
half
knock
wrote
knew
thumb
written

UNIT 26 Follow the directions. Use words from Unit 26. Write the words for these pronunciations.

9. /rōt/
10. /nok/
11. /klīm/
12. /haf/
13. /gōst/
14. /thum/
15. /n(y)o͞o/
16. /rit′(ə)n/

SPELLING DICTIONARY If you need help, use the pronunciation key on page 162.

UNIT 27 Follow the directions. Use words from Unit 27. Write the singular of each word.

17. families

18. parties

19. libraries

20. copies

Write each word without <u>ed</u>. Remember to change a letter.

21. studied

22. cried

23. emptied

24. hurried

Finish each sentence by adding <u>ing</u> to a Unit 27 word.

25. No one heard the baby ___ this morning.

26. Dad was ___ to get breakfast ready.

27. Ryan was ___ his story in his room.

UNIT 28 Follow the directions. Use words from Unit 28.

28. Write the four words that end with /ər/.

29. Write the four words that end with /əl/.

30. Write the two words that have /ē/.

Write the word that goes with each meaning.

31. a color

32. a five-cent coin

33. a season

34. one or the other

UNIT 27

family
empty
hurry
library
study
party
cry
copy

UNIT 28

either
nickel
letter
people
sugar
summer
table
purple

UNIT 29
break
read
rode
sale
whose
won
meet
son

UNIT 29 Follow the directions. Use words from Unit 29. Write the homophone for each of these words.

35. sail   **36.** who's

37. road   **38.** brake

39. one   **40.** sun

Write the words that have these vowel sounds.

41. Write the two words that have /ā/.

42. Write the two words that have /ē/.

43. Write the word that has /ō/.

44. Write the word that has /o͞o/.

45. Write the two words that have /u/.

WORDS IN TIME

The word <u>read</u> comes from the old word <u>raeden</u>. <u>Raeden</u> meant "to guess" or "to find the meaning of." Long ago, people did not know why things in nature happened. They thought that when there was a rainbow or a falling star, nature was telling them something. They asked special people to <u>raeden</u>, or guess the meaning of such events. Since most people did not know how to read then, they would also ask special people to <u>raeden</u>, or find the meaning of, words.

Spelling and Reading
A How-to Article

Read the following how-to article. Look for the way the steps are in order.

A good way to make money during the summer is to sell orange juice from a stand. You can do this alone, or you can ask your buddies to help you.

The first step in opening a juice stand is to gather the materials. You will need a <u>table</u>, paper cups, a money box, orange juice, a pitcher, and ice. You will also need heavy paper, crayons, and tacks for your sign.

The second step is to make the sign for your stand. Use brightly colored crayons, such as orange and purple, to catch the eyes of people walking by. Make the letters of your sign large.

Next set up your stand. Place the table on level ground. Put your cups and money box on it. Then tack the sign you have written on or near the stand.

The last step is to get the juice ready. Pour juice into a pitcher and add ice. Now you're ready to sell orange juice from your own stand.

Write the answers to the questions.

1. In this how-to article, who does the writer say you can ask to help you set up an orange juice stand?
2. What materials do you need to set up an orange juice stand?
3. Why should you make the letters of your sign large?
4. Why is summer a good time to sell orange juice?

Underline the review words in your answers. Check to see that you spelled the words correctly.

Spelling and Writing
A How-to Article

Think and Discuss

A how-to article gives directions for making or doing something. What does the article on page 131 tell you how to do?

A how-to article lists the materials and steps needed to do the task. It tells the order in which the steps have to be done. What is the first step in opening an orange juice stand? What materials are needed to do the second step?

A how-to article uses time-clue words, such as <u>first</u>, <u>then</u>, and <u>next</u>. What time-clue words can you find in the how-to article? Why do you think time-clue words are helpful in a how-to article?

Apply

Now it's time for you to write a **how-to article** for a younger friend. Follow the writing guidelines on the next page.

Words to Help You Write

eyes
ears
marbles
butterflies
puppies
ghost
half
thumb
empty
buddies
either
people
table
purple
read

Prewriting

- Think of something you know how to make or do. Choose something that has only a few steps.
- Make a list of the things needed.
- Make a list of steps to follow.

 THESAURUS For help finding more words to tell about the steps, turn to page 203.

Composing

Use your lists to write the first draft of your how-to article.

- Write a sentence that tells what your article will be about.
- Tell what materials are needed.
- Write simple detail sentences to explain each step.
- Use time-clue words to make the order of steps clear.

Revising

Read your article and show it to a classmate. Follow these guidelines to improve your work. Use the editing and proofreading marks to show changes.

 WRITER'S GUIDE For help revising your article, use the checklist on page 247.

Editing

- Make sure your first sentence tells what your article is about.
- Make sure you listed all the materials needed.
- Make sure the steps are in the correct order.
- Check to be sure you used time-clue words.

Proofreading

- Check your spelling and correct any mistakes.
- Check your capitalization and punctuation.

Copy your article onto clean paper. Write carefully and neatly.

Publishing

Show your article to your younger friend. Ask if he or she would like to make or do the thing you tell about.

	Editing and Proofreading Marks
≡	capitalize
⊙	make a period
∧	add something
⋏,	add a comma
ℯ	take something away
◯	spell correctly
¶	indent the paragraph
/	make a lowercase letter
∿ tr	transpose

31 The Sounds /o͝o/ and /o͞o/

THIS WEEK'S WORDS

1. balloon
2. brook
3. shook
4. stood
5. goodness
6. choose
7. noon
8. raccoon
9. roof
10. tooth
11. group
12. soup
13. flew
14. grew
15. lose

This Week's Words

There are two sounds that are spelled with **oo**: /o͝o/, heard in <u>brook</u>, and /o͞o/, heard in <u>noon</u>.

The sound /o͞o/ can also be spelled with these letters.

- ● **ou,** as in <u>group</u>
- ● **ew,** as in <u>flew</u>
- ☐ **o,** as in <u>lose</u>

REMEMBER THIS

<u>Choose</u> and <u>lose</u> rhyme, but they are not spelled alike. Don't mix up the spellings. If you spell <u>lose</u> like <u>choose</u>, you get a word that rhymes with <u>goose</u>.

The goose is loose.

Spelling Practice

A. Follow the directions. Use This Week's Words.

1. Write the four words that have the same vowel sound as <u>look</u>.

2. Write the three words that have double consonant letters.

3. Write the two words that rhyme with <u>new</u>.

4. Write the two words that rhyme but have /o͞o/ spelled in different ways.

5. Write the word that is the same forward and backward.

B. Finish the story. Use This Week's Words.

balloon
brook
shook
stood
goodness
choose
noon
raccoon
roof
tooth
group
soup
flew
grew
lose

One night I dreamed that a dragon __6__ over our house. It landed on the __7__. The whole house __8__ when it landed. A large __9__ of people came to look at the dragon. When it saw all the people, it smiled. It had only one big __10__ in its mouth. The dragon looked hungry. So we fed it some __11__.

Spelling and Language • Using Verbs

THIS WEEK'S WORDS

balloon
brook
shook
stood
goodness
choose
noon
raccoon
roof
tooth
group
soup
flew
grew
lose

Often you add <u>ed</u> to a verb to talk about what already happened. "Dogs <u>bark</u>. Dogs <u>barked</u>." Sometimes the whole word changes. "Dogs <u>eat</u> meat. Dogs <u>ate</u> meat."

Finish the chart. Use This Week's Words.

NOW	BEFORE		BEFORE	NOW
eat	**ate**		**saw**	**see**
1. fly			**3.** lost	
2. shake			**4.** chose	

Writing on Your Own

Write a scary poem for a friend. You can finish this one or you can make up your own.

As I stood beside the brook,
I looked, I saw, and then I shook!

 WRITER'S GUIDE For a sample poem, see page 254.

Proofreading

Pam wrote this story. She made six mistakes in spelling.

1. Find each mistake Pam made.

> Once upon a time a little boy had a red balloon. He was afraid he would loose his balloon. So he tied it to his hand. But the string came loose. The balloon floo away. The boy chased it. The baloon flew over a brook. The boy stod and watched it. It greu smaller and smaller.
>
> Two weeks later the boy saw a racoon. The raccoon was carrying something red. It was the lost red balloon!

2. Write the six misspelled words correctly.

136

Spelling on Your Own

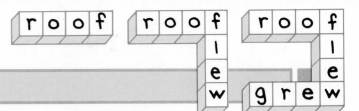

Make a "word chain" with This Week's Words. Write one word. Use a letter in that word to write another word. Keep going, writing words across and down. Try to link all the words in one chain. You may also make more than one chain.

MASTERY WORDS

Follow the directions. Use the Mastery words.

1. Write the two words that have the same vowel sound as <u>book</u>.
2. Write the four words that have the same vowel sound as <u>noon</u>.
3. Write the word that tells when.
4. Write the word that is not spelled with <u>oo</u>.

Write the Mastery words that mean the opposite.

5. old   **6.** gave

took
room
soon
wool
new
school

BONUS WORDS

1. Write the three Bonus words that end with /$\overline{oo}$/.
2. Write the five Bonus words spelled with <u>oo</u>.
3. Write this sentence over. Use three Bonus words that mean the opposite of the underlined words. "The <u>local person</u> drove down a <u>straight</u> but <u>bumpy</u> road."
4. <u>Chew</u> and <u>stew</u> both end with <u>ew</u>. Use other consonants with <u>ew</u>. Spell as many words as you can. Then do the same thing with <u>ook</u>.

chew
crooked
lookout
shampoo
smooth
stew
tourist
wooden

32 The Sounds /ou/ and /oi/

THIS WEEK'S WORDS

1. loud
2. noise
3. cloud
4. mouse
5. mouth
6. sound
7. brown
8. clown
9. crown
10. owl
11. oil
12. point
13. voice
14. joy
15. enjoy

This Week's Words

The vowel sound /ou/ is heard in <u>loud</u>. This sound is spelled two ways.

- /ou/ is spelled **ou** in <u>loud</u>
- /ou/ is spelled **ow** in <u>brown</u>

The vowel sound /oi/ is heard in <u>noise</u>. This sound is also spelled two ways.

- /oi/ is spelled **oi** in <u>noise</u>
- /oi/ is spelled **oy** at the end of <u>joy</u>

138

Spelling Practice

A. Follow the directions. Use This Week's Words.

1. Write the three words that name things in the picture.

2. Write the word for the color of the bird.

3. Write two words that mean about the same thing. Here is a hint. They both name things a horn makes.

4. Write three more words that have /oi/ spelled <u>oi</u>.

5. Write four more words that have /ou/ spelled <u>ou</u>.

6. What should you never use in the library? Write a word with /ou/ and a word with /oi/.

7. Write the word that means about the same thing as <u>happiness</u>. Then add two letters. Spell another one of This Week's Words.

B. Change the underlined letter in each word. Write one of This Week's Words.

8. c<u>l</u>own   9. <u>r</u>ound

10. <u>h</u>ouse   11. <u>s</u>outh

loud
noise
cloud
mouse
mouth
sound
brown
clown
crown
owl
oil
point
voice
joy
enjoy

Spelling and Language • Plural Nouns

THIS WEEK'S WORDS

loud
noise
cloud
mouse
mouth
sound
brown
clown
crown
owl
oil
point
voice
joy
enjoy

A plural noun names more than one thing. You add <u>s</u> to most nouns to make them plural.
Finish the sentences. Write plurals of This Week's Words.

1. There were dark ____ in the sky.

2. Ned could hear the ____ of thunder and wind.

Imagine you are a clown in a circus. Write a paragraph for people who want to learn to be a clown. Tell what you do during a show. Explain how to make people laugh. Use some plurals and some of This Week's Words.

WRITER'S GUIDE For a sample of a how-to paragraph, turn to page 250.

Using the Dictionary to Spell and Write

Knowing the definition of a word can help you check if you used a word correctly in your writing. A **definition** tells what a word means. Read the definitions for <u>noise</u> and <u>sound</u>. <u>Noise</u> has one definition. <u>Sound</u> has more than one.

noise /noiz/ *n.* Sound, especially loud sound: The crowd made a lot of *noise.*

sound /sound/ *n.* Anything that can be heard: Don't make a *sound*!
—*v.* **1** To make a sound: *Sound* the horn. **2** To seem: It *sounds* right to me.

Read each sentence. Can <u>noise</u> take the place of <u>sound</u>? If it can, write <u>noise</u> or <u>noises</u>.

1. The story <u>sounds</u> exciting.

2. The cat was making angry <u>sounds</u>.

3. Shall I <u>sound</u> the dinner bell?

4. Isabel heard a banging <u>sound</u> outside.

Spelling on Your Own

THIS WEEK'S WORDS

Add the letters that spell /ou/. Write This Week's Words.

1. cl_d **2.** cr_n **3.** m_th **4.** _l **5.** br_n
6. m_se **7.** l_d **8.** s_nd **9.** cl_n

Add the letters that spell /oi/. Write This Week's Words.

10. n_se **11.** _l **12.** enj_ **13.** p_nt **14.** v_ce **15.** j_

MASTERY WORDS

> about
> found
> house
> our
> shout
> town

Follow the directions. Use the Mastery words.

1. Write the word that starts with /ou/.
2. Write the two words that have <u>out</u> in them.

Write Mastery words that rhyme with these words.

3. sound **4.** down **5.** mouse **6.** out

Write the Mastery words that mean the opposite.

7. whisper **8.** lost

BONUS WORDS

> spoil
> coins
> loyal
> destroy
> bounce
> proud
> frown
> towel

Follow the directions. Use the Bonus words.

1. Write the four words that have the sound /ou/.
2. Write the four words that have the sound /oi/.
3. Write the two verbs that mean "wreck, or ruin."

Add <u>ed</u> to each of these words. Then use the words with <u>ed</u> in sentences.

4. spoil **5.** destroy **6.** bounce **7.** frown

33 Words with <u>ou</u> and <u>ough</u>

THIS WEEK'S WORDS

1. *double*
2. *country*
3. *cousin*
4. *touch*
5. *count*
6. *flour*
7. *round*
8. *bought*
9. *brought*
10. *thought*
11. *although*
12. *though*
13. *tough*
14. *rough*
15. *enough*

This Week's Words

In double, country, cousin, and touch,
The o-u sounds like the u in much.

In count and flour and also in round,
The o-u has a howling sound.

With g-h in bought, brought, and thought,
The o-u sounds like the end of paw.

The o-u-g-h in although and though
Sounds surprised—scared of a shadow.

These same four letters huff and puff
In tough and rough and in enough.

Spelling Practice

A. Follow the directions. Use This Week's Words.

1. Write a word that means "hard to chew."
   (It rhymes with <u>stuff</u>.)

2. Add an <u>h</u> to make a word that means
   "even if." (It rhymes with <u>go</u>.)

3. Add a <u>t</u> to make a word that means
   "did think." (It rhymes with <u>caught</u>.)

4. Write the three words that end with the sound /f/.

5. Write four more words that have the sound /u/ as
   in <u>up</u>.

6. Write the two words that end with /ō/.

7. Write the three words that have the sound /ou/.

8. Write the three words that rhyme with <u>caught</u>.

B. Use This Week's Words to answer the questions.

9. Did she buy her friend a tie?

   Yes, she ____ her friend a tie.

10. Did she bring it to his birthday party?

    Yes, she ____ it to his birthday party.

11. Did he think the tie was nice?

    Yes, he ____ the tie was nice.

double
country
cousin
touch
count
flour
round
bought
brought
thought
although
though
tough
rough
enough

Spelling and Language • Rhyming Words

THIS WEEK'S WORDS
double
country
cousin
touch
count
flour
round
bought
brought
thought
although
though
tough
rough
enough

Finish the poem with This Week's Words. The words must rhyme with the words in dark print.

Come to my house in about an **hour,**
And help me make bread from yeast and __1__.
Then after all the kneading and **trouble,**
We'll leave it to rise until it is __2__.
After we bake it just as we **ought,**
We'll have fresh bread—quicker than you __3__.

Writing on Your Own

Write a story for your classmates called "The City Cousin." Tell about the funny adventures of a city cousin who comes to visit a country cousin. Use some of This Week's Words.

 WRITER'S GUIDE For a sample of a story, turn to page 252.

Proofreading

David wrote down this phone message for his mother. He made six spelling mistakes.
1. Find David's mistakes.

> Mrs. Logan called at 3:00. She visited her cosin in the contry. She broght back enuff fresh corn for everybody. We can cont on having some for dinner. Please get in tuch with her.

2. Write the six misspelled words correctly.

 WRITER'S GUIDE See the editing and proofreading marks on page 248.

Spelling on Your Own

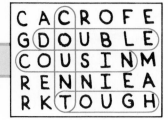

Use all the words to make a word search puzzle. You can write the words across or down. Fill in the empty spaces with other letters. Then let someone else solve the puzzle.

MASTERY WORDS

row
slow
own
bow
how
tower

Follow the directions. Use the Mastery words.

1. Write the four words with /ō/ as in <u>low</u>.
2. Write the three words with /ou/ as in <u>cow</u>.
3. Write the word you wrote for both **1** and **2**.

Use one Mastery word to finish both sentences.

4. Take the oars and ____ the boat.
5. Tall people must stand in the back ____.

BONUS WORDS

couple
southern
south
county
trousers
cough
fought
shoulder

Write the two words in each group that have the same vowel sound.

1. couple	2. cough	3. trousers	4. shoulder
cup	tough	trouble	cold
soup	off	houses	should

Finish these sentences with Bonus words.

5. Think is to <u>thought</u> as <u>fight</u> is to ____.
6. <u>North</u> is to <u>northern</u> as <u>south</u> is to ____.

Write sentences using the Bonus words.

145

34 Syllable Patterns

THIS WEEK'S WORDS

1. butter
2. cattle
3. dinner
4. funny
5. happen
6. lesson
7. matter
8. middle
9. rabbit
10. corner
11. forgot
12. number
13. perhaps
14. problem
15. wonder

This Week's Words

All the words this week have two vowel sounds. We say that they have two **syllables.**

Some of the words have double consonant letters in the middle: bu<u>tt</u>er. These words are divided into syllables between the double consonant letters.

Some of the words have two different consonant letters in the middle: cor<u>n</u>er. These words are divided into syllables between those consonant letters.

Spelling Practice

A. Write This Week's Words that have these double consonant letters. Then draw a line between the two syllables.

1. bb

2. ss

3. pp

4. nn (two words)

5. tt (three words)

6. Now write the word that tells where you divided the words.

B. Add one of the syllables in the box to one of the numbered syllables. Write some of This Week's Words.

lem	ner	der	got	ber	haps

7. num

8. prob

9. per

10. cor

11. for

12. won

C. Copy these words. Write one of This Week's Words that rhymes with each word. Then draw a line between the two syllables in each pair.

13. winner

14. batter

15. sunny

16. riddle

17. mutter

18. battle

butter
cattle
dinner
funny
happen
lesson
matter
middle
rabbit
corner
forgot
number
perhaps
problem
wonder

147

Spelling and Language • Nouns and Verbs

butter
cattle
dinner
funny
happen
lesson
matter
middle
rabbit
corner
forgot
number
perhaps
problem
wonder

A **noun** names a person, a place, or a thing. A **verb** shows action or being. Finish each pair of sentences with one of This Week's Words. The word will be a noun in the first sentence and a verb in the second.

1. Wally chased the dog around the ___.

2. Finally he was able to ___ it.

3. Start with the ___ 1.

4. Then ___ your paper from 1 to 25.

Writing on Your Own

Write a letter to a relative telling about something funny that happened to you. Use some of This Week's Words. Try to use some words both as nouns and as verbs.

Using the Dictionary to Spell and Write

A good speller sometimes uses the pronunciation of a word to remember how to spell the word. The pronunciation for a two-syllable word has an accent mark. It shows which syllable is said with more force. The first syllable in <u>butter</u> is the accented syllable.

but·ter   /but′ər/

act, āte, câre, ärt;	egg, ēven;	if, īce;	on, ōver, ôr;	bŏŏk, fōōd;	up, tûrn;
ə = **a** in *ago*, **e** in *listen*, **i** in *giraffe*, **o** in *pilot*, **u** in *circus*;			yōō = **u** in *music*;	oil;	out;
chair; sing; shop; thank; that; zh in *treasure*.					

Write the words that go with the pronunciations. Then draw a line under the letters in the accented syllable.

1. /prob′ləm/   **2.** /mid′əl/   **3.** /pər·haps′/   **4.** /fər·got′/

SPELLING DICTIONARY Remember to use your **Spelling Dictionary** when you write.

Spelling on Your Own

Write some funny story titles. Use This Week's Words. Try to use more than one of the words in each title. Here are some examples: "The Rabbit Who Forgot How to Hop" and "The Mad Hatter's Funny Dinner."

MASTERY WORDS

follow
happy
hello
pretty
sunny
sister

Follow the directions. Use the Mastery words.

1. Write the two words that have double <u>l</u>.

2. Draw a line under the letters that spell /ō/ in the words you just wrote. Then use both words in a sentence.

Add the letters that spell the second syllable of each Mastery word. Write the whole word.

3. sis **4.** sun **5.** hap **6.** pret **7.** hel **8.** fol

BONUS WORDS

stammer
swallow
hollow
allow
tonsils
seldom
welcome
practice

1. Write all the Bonus words in alphabetical order. Then draw a line between the two syllables in each word.

2. Write the three words that are spelled with double <u>l</u>. Then circle the word that ends with the vowel sound in <u>cow</u>.

3. Use <u>swallow</u> and <u>tonsils</u> in a sentence.

4. Write sentences using <u>welcome</u>, <u>practice</u>, and <u>swallow</u> as nouns. Then write sentences using each word as a verb.

149

Another Syllable Pattern

THIS WEEK'S WORDS

1. pilot
2. above
3. ahead
4. alike
5. alone
6. around
7. become
8. begin
9. behind
10. belong
11. below
12. beside
13. motor
14. paper
15. parade

This Week's Words

All the words this week have two syllables. Each word has one consonant letter between the two vowel sounds.

All of This Week's Words are divided into syllables before the consonant.

Spelling Practice

A. Add <u>a</u> or <u>be</u> to these words. Write This Week's Words.

1. come
2. side
3. head
4. low
5. round
6. like

B. Follow the directions. Use This Week's Words.

7. Add one of the syllables in the circle to each of the syllables in the box. Write five words.

gin	long	hind
bove		lone

8. Write the four words that do not have <u>a</u> or <u>be</u> as the first syllable. Draw a line between the two syllables in each word.

9. Write two pairs of words that are opposites. One word in each pair has the first syllable <u>a</u>. The other one has the first syllable <u>be.</u>

C. The accented syllable is the one you say with more force. Write This Week's Words with these accented syllables.

10. pi
11. mo
12. rade
13. pa

pilot
above
ahead
alike
alone
around
become
begin
behind
belong
below
beside
motor
paper
parade

151

Spelling and Language • Where and How

THIS WEEK'S WORDS

pilot
above
ahead
alike
alone
around
become
begin
behind
belong
below
beside
motor
paper
parade

Many of This Week's Words tell where or how. Look at these shapes. Use This Week's Words to finish the sentences.

1. The purple square is ___ the green square.

2. The blue dot is ___ in the corner.

3. A black line is ___ all the shapes.

4. The green square is ___ the red dots.

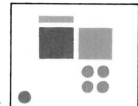

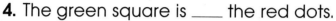

Writing on Your Own

Pretend you have invited friends to your house for a party. You are going to play Treasure Hunt. Write clues to tell your friends where they will find the treasure.

WRITER'S GUIDE Did you write clearly so your friends can read the clues? If you need help writing any letters, turn to page 261.

Proofreading

1. Theo has six spelling mistakes in his sign. Read the sign and find each one.

PET PERADE SATURDAY
Bring all the pets that bilong to you!
The fun will begen arond 2:00.
Meet behined Walker School biside the swings.

2. Write the six misspelled words correctly.

WRITER'S GUIDE See the editing and proofreading marks on page 248.

Spelling on Your Own

First, write the words that go with the pronunciations.

1. /pā′pər/   **2.** /bi·gin′/   **3.** /pə·rād′/   **4.** /bi·lông′/

5. /pī′lət/   **6.** /bi·kum′/   **7.** /mō′tər/

 SPELLING DICTIONARY If you need help, use the pronunciation key on page 162.

Now write the other eight words. Look around your classroom. Use each of these eight words in a sentence. Tell what you see. Here is an example: "The clock is <u>above</u> the chalkboard."

MASTERY WORDS

again
ago
awake
away
because
tiger

Follow the directions. Use the Mastery words.

1. Write the word you use to tell why.
2. Write the word that has the sound /ī/.
3. Write the word with the letters <u>ai</u> but not the sound /ā/.

Add <u>a</u> to each word. Write Mastery words.

4. go   **5.** wake   **6.** way   **7.** gain

BONUS WORDS

broken
final
machine
motel
pretend
reason
spider
total

1. Write all the Bonus words. Then draw a line to divide each word into syllables.
2. You say the second syllable of three of the words with more force. Write these words.
3. Write the six Bonus words that have a long vowel sound in the first syllable.
4. Write the four Bonus words that have /əl/ or /ən/.
5. Write a story for a friend. Use all the Bonus words.

36 Review

Do these steps if you are not sure how to spell a word.

- **Say** the word. Listen to each sound. Think about what the word means.
- **Look** at the word. See how the letters are made. Try to see the word in your mind.
- **Spell** the word to yourself. Think about the way each sound is spelled.
- **Write** the word. Copy it from your book. Check the way you made your letters. Write the word again.
- **Check** your learning. Cover the word and write it. Did you spell it correctly? If not, do these steps until you know how to spell the word.

UNIT 31

choose
noon
group
grew
stood
roof
tooth
flew

UNIT 32

brown
mouth
loud
enjoy
noise
sound
oil
point

UNIT 31 **Follow the directions. Use words from Unit 31.**

1. Write the five words spelled with <u>oo</u>. Circle the word that sounds like <u>chews</u>.

Add the letters to the words below that spell /o͞o/. Write the words.

2. gr__ __p

3. fl__ __

4. gr__ __

UNIT 32 **Follow the directions. Use words from Unit 32.**

5. Write the four words with the vowel sound heard in <u>out</u>.

6. Write the four words with the vowel sound heard in <u>toy</u>.

UNIT 33 Follow the directions. Use words from Unit 33. Write the word that ends with each sound.

7. /ō/

8. /ē/

9. /f/

10. /d/

Write the words that rhyme with these words.

11. amount

12. much

13. puff

14. slow

Finish these sentences.

15. Maria ＿＿ a ticket to the show.

16. She ＿＿ that Elena would go with her.

UNIT 34 Follow the directions. Use words from Unit 34. Write the word that goes with each meaning. Then draw a line between the two syllables of each word you wrote.

17. something you solve

18. maybe

19. It tells how many.

20. did not remember

Write the words that have these double consonant letters. Draw a line between the two syllables.

21. dd

22. tt

23. pp

24. ss

UNIT 33

country
round
though
enough
thought
bought
touch
count

UNIT 34

lesson
matter
number
perhaps
problem
middle
happen
forgot

UNIT 35

ahead
begin
paper
parade
around
below
motor
behind

UNIT 35 Follow the directions. Use words from Unit 35. Write the word that goes with each clue. Draw a line between the two syllables of each word you wrote.

25. I am written on and have /ā/.

26. I mean "in a circle" and have /ou/.

27. I mean "in back of" and have /ī/.

28. I start with /ə/ and mean "out in front."

29. I have marching bands and /ā/.

30. I have /ō/ and help things go.

Finish these sentences.

31. There's going to be a ___ on Saturday.

32. Each float will be run by a ___.

33. Carmen read all about it in the ___.

34. It's going to ___ at noon.

35. It's going to end ___ two o'clock.

36. Let's try to get there ___ of time.

37. Then we won't have to stand ___ any tall people.

WORDS IN TIME

The word <u>motor</u> comes from the old word <u>movere</u>. <u>Movere</u> meant "to move." Think about what things have a motor. Why do you think <u>movere</u> became the name for a motor?

156

Spelling and Reading
A Report

Read the following report. Look for the main idea in each paragraph.

How the Pilgrims Learned About Corn

Corn was first grown in America by American Indians. Hundreds of years ago, a group of American Indians called the Algonquians lived in what is now New England. Every summer, they grew enough corn to feed themselves for the year ahead.

When the Pilgrims first came to this country in 1620, they saw a field where the Algonquians had planted corn. The Pilgrims stood looking in wonder at the strange new food. They thought this food was amazing.

The Pilgrims wanted to learn how to plant corn. The Algonquians gave them lessons. This was very helpful to the Pilgrims. It meant they would not have so many food problems in the years ahead.

Write the answers to the questions.

1. What does the writer of this report say the Algonquians did every summer?
2. How did the Pilgrims learn to plant corn?
3. Why did the Pilgrims have to be taught how to plant corn?
4. How do you think the Algonquians and Pilgrims got along with each other? Give a reason for your answer.

Underline the review words in your answers. Check to see that you spelled the words correctly.

Spelling and Writing
A Report

Words to Help You Write

choose
enjoy
country
though
count
matter
number
problem
begin
below
around
ahead

Think and Discuss

In a report, a writer gives information about a subject. The information may come from books or magazines. A title tells what the report is about. On page 157 is a report one student wrote for a social studies class. What is the title of the report?

How many paragraphs are in the report? Each paragraph in a report has a topic sentence that tells the main idea of the paragraph. What is the topic sentence of the first paragraph? The other sentences in a paragraph are detail sentences. They tell more about the topic sentence. What does the writer tell about in the detail sentences in the first paragraph?

Look at the last paragraph. What is the topic sentence? What does the writer tell about in detail sentences in the third paragraph?

Apply

Write a **report** to share with your classmates. Follow the writing guidelines on the next page.

Prewriting
Choose a subject you find interesting.
- Use books and magazines to find three important ideas about the subject.
- List some facts about each of the three ideas.
- Arrange the three ideas in an order that makes sense.

Composing
Use the facts you listed to write the first draft of your report.
- Write one paragraph about each of the three ideas.
- Write a topic sentence and detail sentences for each paragraph. Use your list to write the detail sentences.
- Write a title that tells what the whole report is about.

Revising
Read your report and show it to a classmate. Follow these guidelines to improve your work. Use the editing and proofreading marks to show changes.

Editing
- Be sure you wrote a topic sentence for each paragraph.
- Be sure the detail sentences in each paragraph tell about the topic sentence.

Proofreading
- Check your spelling and correct any mistakes.
- Check your capitalization and punctuation.

WRITER'S GUIDE If you need help with capital letters and punctuation marks, turn to pages 255-257.
- Copy your report onto clean paper. Write carefully and neatly.

Publishing
Share your report with your classmates. Draw a picture to go with your report, and post it on a class bulletin board.

Editing and Proofreading Marks	
≡	capitalize
⊙	make a period
∧	add something
⌄	add a comma
ℯ	take something away
◯	spell correctly
⌐	indent the paragraph
/	make a lowercase letter
∿ tr	transpose

SPELLING DICTIONARY

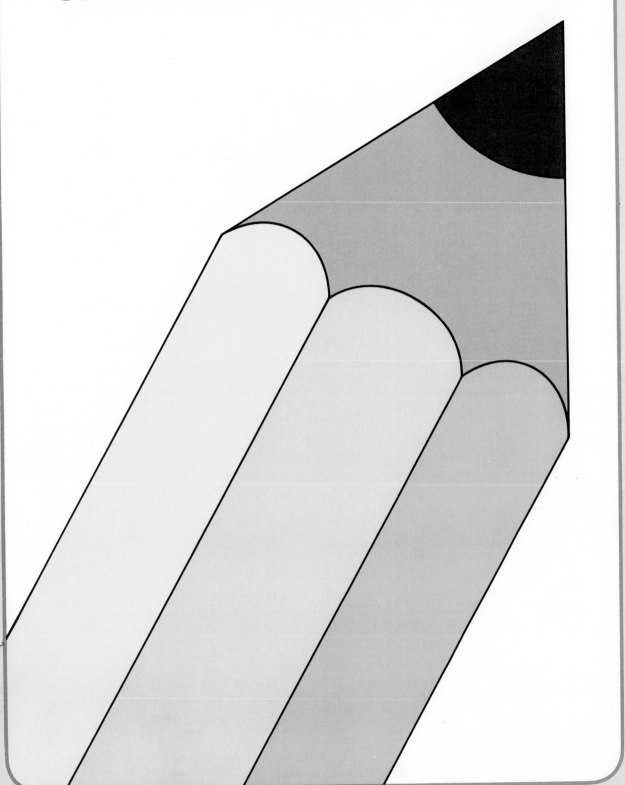

PRONUNCIATION KEY

Remember these things when you read pronunciations:

- When you see ( ) around a sound, it means that sound is not always heard. /gran(d)'chīld'/
- This mark ' comes after the syllable you say with the most force. This lighter mark ' comes after the syllable you say with a little less force. /yes'tər·dā'/

/a/	act, cat	/m/	mother, room	/u/	up, come
/ā/	ate, rain	/n/	new, can	/û/	early, hurt
/â/	care, bear	/ng/	sing, hang	/yōō/	mule, few
/ä/	car, father	/o/	on, stop	/v/	very, five
/b/	bed, rub	/ō/	over, go	/w/	will
/ch/	chair, watch	/ô/	or, saw	/y/	yes
/d/	duck, red	/oi/	oil, toy	/z/	zoo, buzz
/e/	egg, hen	/ou/	out, cow	/zh/	treasure
/ē/	even, see	/ōō/	food, too	/ə/	The schwa
/f/	fish, off	/ŏŏ/	book, pull		is the sound
/g/	go, big	/p/	pig, hop		these letters
/h/	hat, hit	/r/	ran, car		stand for:
/i/	if, sit	/s/	see, miss		a in ago
/ī/	ice, time	/sh/	show, wish		e in listen
/j/	jump, bridge	/t/	take, feet		i in giraffe
/k/	cat, look	/th/	thing, tooth		o in pilot
/l/	lost, ball	/th/	that, weather		u in circus

---

able

A

a·ble /ā'bəl/ *adj.* Having the skill: Jane is *able* to swim.

a·bout /ə·bout'/ *prep.* Having to do with: This story is *about* cats.
—*adv.* Almost: Are you just *about* ready?

---

act

a·bove /ə·buv'/ *prep.* Over: Paul hung the picture *above* his desk.

a·corn /ā'kôrn/ *n.* Seed of an oak tree.

act /akt/ *v.* **1** To do something. **2** To behave in a certain way: Don't *act* silly. **3** To play a part: Tina will *act* in the play.

add

—*n.* **1** Something done: Feeding birds is a kind *act*. **2** Part of a play: The third *act* was funny.

add /ad/ *v.* To put two or more numbers or things together.

a·dult /ə·dult′ *or* ad′ult/ *n.* A grown-up person.

af·ter /af′tər/ *prep.* **1** Later than: We got home *after* dark. **2** Following: Friday comes *after* Thursday.

a·gain /ə·gen′/ *adv.* Once more: Jenny and Scott played in the park *again*.

age /āj/ *n.* **1** The time someone or something has lived: Robin and Tom are the same *age*. **2** A period of time in history: We live in the space *age*.
—*v.* **aged, aging** To grow old.

a·go /ə·gō′/ *adj., adv.* In the past: I got my dog a year *ago*.

a·head /ə·hed′/ *adv.* In front; before: Miguel was *ahead* of me in line.

air /âr/ *n.* **1** What we breathe. **2** The sky: up in the *air*.
—*v.* To let air in: Open the window and *air* out the room.

a·larm /ə·lärm′/ *n.* A signal that warns of danger: fire *alarm*.
—*v.* To frighten: Loud noises *alarm* me.

a·like /ə·līk′/ *adj.* The same: The twins sometimes dress *alike*.

al·low /ə·lou′/ *v.* To permit: Dogs are not *allowed* on the beach.

a·lone /ə·lōn′/ *adj.* Without anyone or anything near.
—*adv.* Without help: Julia baked the cake *alone*.

al·so /ôl′sō/ *adv.* Too: Raymond *also* plays baseball.

argue

al·though /ôl·thō′/ *conj.* Even if: *Although* I'm busy, I'll help you.

and /and/ *conj.* Also; added to.

an·gry /ang′grē/ *adj.* **angrier, angriest** Feeling anger; mad: The *angry* dog growled.

an·oth·er /ə·nuth′ər/ *adj.* **1** One more: May I have *another* apple? **2** A different one: Kurt moved to *another* city.

an·swer /an′sər/ *n.* **1** A reply. **2** A way of solving a problem: What is the *answer* to the riddle?
—*v.* To reply.

ant /ant/ *n.* A small crawling insect.

an·y /en′ē/ *adj.* No special one: *Any* coat will do.

an·y·one /en′i·wun′/ *pron.* No special person: *Anyone* can come.

an·y·thing /en′i·thing′/ *pron.* No special thing: I'll eat *anything*.

an·y·way /en′i·wā′/ *adv.* Anyhow: If it rains, we'll go *anyway*.

ap·ple /ap′əl/ *n.* A round fruit with a thin red, yellow, or green skin.

aren't /ärnt/ Are not.

ar·gue /är′gyoō/ *v.* **argued, arguing** **1** To disagree. **2** To give reasons for or against: Jim *argued* against skipping recess.

---

n = **noun**, a naming word; **pron.** = **pronoun**, a word that takes the place of a noun; **v.** = **verb**, an action word; **adj.** = **adjective**, a describing word; **adv.** = **adverb**, a word that tells when, where, or how; **prep.** = **preposition**, such as *from, by with;* **conj.** = **conjunction**, such as *and, but, because;* **interj.** = **interjection**, such as *hello, oh.*

arm | **bedroom**

arm /ärm/ *n.* **1** The part of your body between your shoulder and hand. **2** A part of a chair.

a·round /ə·round′/ *adv.* Nearby: The cat is *around* here somewhere. —*prep.* On all sides: There is a fence *around* the house.

art /ärt/ *n.* **1** Drawing, painting, or making statues: Ms. Fong teaches *art*. **2** Great paintings or statues.

ar·tist /är′tist/ *n.* A person who draws, paints, or makes statues.

ask /ask/ *v.* To put a question to.

a·sleep /ə·slēp′/ *adj.* **1** Not awake. **2** Numb: My foot is *asleep*.

a·wake /ə·wāk′/ *adj.* Not sleeping.

a·way /ə·wā′/ *adj.* **1** At a distance: My school is a mile *away*. **2** In a different place: My parents are *away* from home.

a·while /ə·(h)wīl′/ *adv.* For a short time.

B

ba·by /bā′bē/ *n., pl.* **babies** A very young child. —*v.* **babied, babying** To treat gently: My brothers *baby* me.

back /bak/ *n.* The rear part of anything: the *back* of the room. —*v.* To cause to go backward: *Back* the car into the garage. —*adv.* **1** To the rear: Sit *back* in your chair. **2** In or to the place you came from: Go *back* home.

bake /bāk/ *v.* **baked, baking** To cook in an oven.

bal·loon /bə·lōōn′/ *n.* **1** A large bag filled with a gas: They floated over the sea in a *balloon*. **2** A small rubber sack filled with air; a toy: We blew up *balloons* for the party.

band·age /ban′dij/ *n.* Something you put over a cut or sore. —*v.* **bandaged, bandaging** To put on a bandage.

bar·ber /bär′bər/ *n.* A person who cuts hair.

bark¹ /bärk/ *n.* The sound a dog makes. —*v.* To make a sound like a dog.

bark² /bärk/ *n.* The outside covering of a tree.

barn /bärn/ *n.* A farm building.

bat¹ /bat/ *n.* A stick or club used for hitting balls. —*v.* **batted, batting** **1** To hit with a bat. **2** To hit as if with a bat: The child *batted* the doll.

bat² /bat/ *n.* A mouselike animal with wings that flies at night.

beach /bēch/ *n., pl.* **beaches** The sandy shore of an ocean or lake.

bear /bâr/ *n.* A furry wild animal.

beat /bēt/ *v.* **1** To hit over and over: *beat* a drum. **2** To win a game. **3** To stir quickly: *Beat* the eggs. —*n.* The accent in music: That song has a good *beat*.

be·cause /bi·kôz′/ *conj.* For the reason that: We stayed home *because* it was snowing.

be·come /bi·kum′/ *v.* To grow to be: You *become* a teenager at thirteen.

bed·room /bed′rōōm′/ *n.* A room for sleeping.

164

beet /bēt/ *n.* A red root vegetable.

be·fore /bi·fôr'/ *prep.* Coming ahead of: We took a walk *before* dinner. Alberto came *before* Loni in line. —*adv.* In the time that is over: Heidi never rode a horse *before*.

be·gin /bi·gin'/ *v.* **began, begun, beginning** To start: School *begins* in September.

be·have /bi·hāv'/ *v.* **behaved, behaving** 1 To act: The children *behaved* like grown-ups. 2 To act properly: Please *behave* yourself.

be·hind /bi·hīnd'/ *prep.* In back of: Kiyo hid *behind* a chair. —*adv.* In, at, or to the back: Luke stayed *behind* to finish his work.

be·long /bi·lông'/ *v.* 1 To be in the right place: Your hat *belongs* on your head. 2 To be someone's: This pencil *belongs* to Luis. 3 To be one of: I *belong* to a club.

be·low /bi·lō'/ *prep.* Lower than or under: A j goes *below* the line.

bend /bend/ *v.* **bent, bending** 1 To make something curve: June *bent* the clay into a C. 2 To stoop: *Bend* down to pick up the dime.

be·side /bi·sīd'/ *prep.* Next to: Ryan's bed is *beside* the wall.

be·tween /bi·twēn'/ *prep.* In the space dividing two things: Kim sat *between* Alice and Todd. Don't eat *between* meals.

bi·cy·cle /bī'sik·əl/ *n.* A vehicle with two wheels, pedals, and handlebars.

bike /bīk/ *n.* Short for *bicycle*.

bird /bûrd/ *n.* An animal with two wings and feathers that flies.

birth·day /bûrth'dā'/ *n.* The day you were born.

bite /bīt/ *v.* **bit, bitten** *or* **bit, biting** To cut with the teeth: Barbara *bit* into the apple. —*n.* 1 A small bit of food: Rita wants a *bite* of your pear. 2 A wound or sting gotten by biting.

blast /blast/ *n.* A loud noise: The horn made a loud *blast*. —*v.* To make a loud noise: The radio was *blasting*.

blend /blend/ *v.* To mix.

blow¹ /blō/ *v.* **blew, blown, blowing** 1 To move with force: The wind is *blowing*. 2 To push by blowing: The wind *blows* leaves around. 3 To send air out: *Blow* out the candles. 4 To make a sound by blowing: *Blow* your horn. 5 To clear by blowing: I *blew* my nose.

blow² /blō/ *n.* A hard hit.

blue·ber·ry /bloo'ber'ē/ *n., pl.* **blueberries** A round, bluish berry.

blue·bird /bloo'bûrd'/ *n.* A small bird with a blue back and wings.

boast /bōst/ *v.* To speak with too much pride; to brag: Jim *boasted* about winning the race.

bod·y /bod'ē/ *n., pl.* **bodies** 1 All of a person or animal: Good food is needed for a healthy *body*. 2 A whole part: a *body* of water.

born /bôrn/ *v.* Brought into the world: Joel was *born* in May.

both /bōth/ *adj., pron.* Two together: *Both* dogs ran. Then *both* stopped.

bot·tle /bot'(ə)l/ *n.* A narrow jar with a small opening at the top.

bought /bôt/ *v.* Past tense of *buy*.

---

act, āte, câre, ärt; egg, ēven; if, īce; on, ōver, ôr; book, food; up, tûrn;
ə = a in *ago*, e in *listen*, i in *giraffe*, o in *pilot*, u in *circus*; yoo = u in *music*; oil; out;
chair; sing; shop; thank; that; zh in *treasure*.

bounce

cage

bounce /bouns/ *v.* **bounced, bouncing** 1 To hit and spring back: The ball *bounced* off the wall. 2 To cause to bounce: Debra *bounced* the ball.

bow[1] /bou/ *v.* To bend your head or body forward.
—*n.* The act of bowing.

bow[2] /bō/ *n.* 1 A knot with loops: Tie the ribbon in a *bow*. 2 A thing used for shooting arrows.

brake /brāk/ *n.* What you use to stop a car or bicycle.

branch /branch/ *n., pl.* **branches** An armlike part of a tree.

brave /brāv/ *adj.* Not afraid.

break /brāk/ *v.* **broke, broken, breaking** To crack into pieces.
—*n.* A rest period: The workers took a ten-minute *break*.

bridge /brij/ *n.* Something built over a river or valley to allow people to get to the other side.

bright /brīt/ *adj.* 1 Giving off a lot of light: *bright* sun. 2 Cheerful: a *bright* smile. 3 Smart; clever.

bring /bring/ *v.* **brought, bringing** To carry to or to take along: I will *bring* Lee to the picnic.

bro·ken /brō′kən/ *v.* Past participle of *break*.
—*adj.* 1 Cracked in pieces: Sweep up the *broken* glass. 2 Not working: Our TV set is *broken*.

brook /brŏŏk/ *n.* A small stream.

brought /brôt/ *v.* Past tense of *bring*.

brown /broun/ *n., adj.* The color of chocolate.

bud·dy /bud′ē/ *n., pl.* **buddies** A close friend.

build /bild/ *v.* **built, building** To put pieces together; to make: Rhonda *built* a model airplane.

bump /bump/ *v.* To knock against: Geraldo *bumped* his head.
—*n.* 1 A swelling caused by bumping. 2 An uneven part: The car hit a *bump* in the road.

burn /bûrn/ *v.* 1 To be on fire. 2 To destroy by fire. 3 To hurt with fire or heat: He *burned* his hand.
—*n.* A wound caused by heat.

burst /bûrst/ *v.* **burst, bursting** 1 To break apart suddenly: The balloon *burst*. 2 To break out: We all *burst* into laughter.
—*n.* Something sudden: Kyle won with a *burst* of speed.

bur·y /ber′ē/ *v.* **buried, burying** 1 To put into the ground. 2 To hide or cover up: Kent *buried* his face in the pillow.

bush /bŏŏsh/ *n., pl.* **bushes** A small treelike plant.

bus·y /biz′ē/ *adj.* 1 Doing things: I'm *busy* making lunch. 2 Full of things to do: I had a *busy* day.

but·ter /but′ər/ *n.* A yellow spread made from cream, used on bread.
—*v.* To spread butter on.

but·ter·fly /but′ər·flī′/ *n., pl.* **butterflies** An insect with four brightly colored wings.

buy /bī/ *v.* **bought, buying** To pay money and get something.
—*n.* Something you get for a low price: A pen for a dime is a *buy*.

C

cab·in /kab′in/ *n.* A small house made of wood.

cage /kāj/ *n.* A box or roomlike place made of wire or iron bars: Clean the bird *cage*.

calf

calf /kaf/ *n., pl.* **calves** A young cow.

cam·el /kam′əl/ *n.* An animal with one or two humps on its back.

cam·er·a /kam′(ə·)rə/ *n.* A small machine used for taking pictures.

camp /kamp/ *n.* A place where people go for vacations: Helen went to summer *camp*.
—*v.* To stay outdoors in a tent or trailer: We *camped* by a pond.

can·dy /kan′dē/ *n., pl.* **candies** A sweet food made with sugar.

cane /kān/ *n.* **1** A stick people use to help them walk. **2** The woody stem of a plant.

can·not /kan′ot *or* ka·not′/ Can not.

can't /kant/ Can not.

card /kärd/ *n.* **1** A piece of stiff paper: a birthday *card*. **2** A card used for playing a game.

care /kâr/ *v.* **cared, caring** **1** To show interest or concern: Mabel *cares* about doing well. **2** To want or like: Would you *care* to come?

car·ry /kar′ē/ *v.* **carried, carrying** To take from one place to another: Flora *carried* her books to school.

cart·wheel /kärt′(h)wēl′/ *n.* Turning sideways to stand on your hands and then on your feet again.

chin

cat /kat/ *n.* A small, furry animal.

catch /kach/ *v.* **caught, catching** **1** To get hold of: *Catch* the ball. **2** To trap: The spider *caught* a fly. **3** To discover or find: Mom *caught* me eating in bed. **4** To get an illness: Eric *caught* a cold.

cat·tle /kat′(ə)l/ *n. pl.* Cows, bulls, and steers.

cause /kôz/ *n.* A person or thing that makes something happen; reason: He was the *cause* of the trouble.
—*v.* **caused, causing** To make something happen: A traffic jam *caused* us to be late.

cent /sent/ *n.* A penny.

cer·tain /sûr′tən/ *adj.* **1** Entirely sure: I'm *certain* that I'm right. **2** Not just any: a *certain* one.

chair /châr/ *n.* A seat with a back.

chalk /chôk/ *n.* A powdery stick for writing on the board.

chance /chans/ *n.* **1** What may happen: There's a *chance* of rain. **2** A good time to do something: Amos has a *chance* to go to camp. **3** A risk: I never take *chances*.

chase /chās/ *v.* **chased, chasing** **1** To run after. **2** To drive away: Lucy *chased* the dog away.

cheek /chēk/ *n.* Either side of your face, below your eyes.

cher·ry /cher′ē/ *n., pl.* **cherries** A small, round, red fruit with a pit.

chew /cho͞o/ *v.* To grind up with your teeth: Always *chew* your food well.

child /chīld/ *n., pl.* **children** A young boy or girl.

chin /chin/ *n.* The part of your face below your mouth.

act, āte, câre, ärt; egg, ēven; if, īce; on, ōver, ôr; bo͝ok, fo͞od; up, tûrn; ə = a in *ago*, e in *listen*, i in *giraffe*, o in *pilot*, u in *circus*; yo͞o = u in *music*; oil; out; chair; sing; shop; thank; that; zh in *treasure*.

choose

choose /chōōz/ *v.* **chose, chosen, choosing** **1** To pick out. **2** To decide to do something: Ronald *chose* to go by himself.

chop /chop/ *v.* **chopped, chopping** **1** To cut with an ax: *Chop* down the tree. **2** To cut into small pieces: Ann is *chopping* onions.

church /chûrch/ *n., pl.* **churches** A building where people worship.

cir·cle /sûr′kəl/ *n.* A round shape.
—*v.* **circled, circling** **1** To draw a circle around. **2** To move in a circle: The plane *circled* the field.

cir·cus /sûr′kəs/ *n., pl.* **circuses** A show with animals and clowns.

cit·y /sit′ē/ *n., pl.* **cities** A large town.

clap /klap/ *v.* **clapped, clapping** To hit your hands together.
—*n.* A loud noise: We heard the *clap* of thunder.

class /klas/ *n., pl.* **classes** **1** A group of students. **2** People or things that are alike in some way: the middle *class*.

clay /klā/ *n.* **1** Mud that is used to make dishes. **2** Something like dough, used for modeling.

clear /klir/ *adj.* **1** Easy to see through. **2** Not cloudy or foggy: a *clear* sky. **3** Easy to understand.
—*adv.* **1** In a clear way: I can hear you loud and *clear*. **2** All the way: *clear* across the room.
—*v.* To take things away: Tomas *cleared* the table.

clev·er /klev′ər/ *adj.* **1** Showing skill: a *clever* idea. **2** Very smart: Seth is a *clever* child.

cliff /klif/ *n.* A high, steep rock.

climb /klīm/ *v.* **1** To go up: Ella *climbed* the stairs. **2** To go down,

colony

over, or into: Jason *climbed* into the car.
—*n.* The act of climbing: It is a long *climb* up the mountain.

close¹ /klōz/ *v.* **closed, closing** **1** To shut: Please *close* the door. **2** To end: Erin *closed* her speech with a poem.

close² /klōs/ *adj.* **closer, closest** **1** Near. **2** Almost equal: a *close* race.
—*adv.* **closer, closest** Near: Alan sat *close* to the window.

cloth·ing /klō′t͟hing/ *n.* The things you wear.

cloud /kloud/ *n.* **1** A mass of tiny water drops that float in the sky. **2** Anything like a cloud: The car raised a *cloud* of dust.

clown /kloun/ *n.* A person in a circus who makes people laugh.
—*v.* To act like a clown.

club /klub/ *n.* **1** A heavy stick. **2** A stick used to hit a ball: a golf *club*. **3** A group of people who join together: a book *club*.

coin /koin/ *n.* A piece of metal used as money.

cold /kōld/ *adj.* **1** Low in temperature. **2** Feeling cold: The children were *cold* and tired.
—*n.* **1** A lack of heat: The *cold* made my face sting. **2** A sickness that makes you sneeze and cough.

col·lar /kol′ər/ *n.* **1** A fold of cloth that goes around your neck: The dress has a lace *collar*. **2** A band put on an animal's neck.

col·o·ny /kol′ə·nē/ *n., pl.* **colonies** **1** A group of people who settle in a new country: The first *colony* in America was in Virginia. **2** Ants living and working together.

company

crooked

com·pa·ny /kum′pə·nē/ *n., pl.* **companies** **1** Guests: We are having *company* for dinner. **2** A business.

cop·y /kop′ē/ *n., pl.* **copies** **1** One thing that looks just like another. **2** One of many things made at one time: I have a *copy* of that book.
—*v.* **copied, copying** **1** To make a copy. **2** To act like someone else: Delia *copies* everything I do.

corn /kôrn/ *n.* A yellow grain that grows on the ears of a tall plant.

cor·ner /kôr′nər/ *n.* Where two walls, streets, or sides meet.
—*v.* To force into a corner; to trap: The cat *cornered* the mouse.

cor·ral /kə·ral′/ *n.* A fenced-in place where animals are kept.

cost /kôst/ *n.* The amount someone charges or pays for something.
—*v.* **cost, costing** To have as its price: The toy *costs* a dollar.

cough /kôf/ *v.* To push air out with a sudden noise.
—*n.* The sound made by coughing.

count /kount/ *v.* **1** To find out how many: *Count* the petals on the daisy. **2** To name numbers in order: *Count* from 1 to 10. **3** To be sure of: You can *count* on me.

coun·try /kun′trē/ *n., pl.* **countries** **1** A nation. **2** The land outside of cities and towns: There are many farms in the *country*.

coun·ty /koun′tē/ *n., pl.* **counties** An area within a state: A *county* has its own local officials.

cou·ple /kup′əl/ *n.* **1** Two or a few: Rosa has a *couple* of things to do. **2** Two people who belong together.

course /kôrs/ *n.* A group of classes: a cooking *course*.
—**of course** Certainly.

court /kôrt/ *n.* **1** Where trials are held. **2** Where tennis or basketball is played.

cous·in /kuz′(ə)n/ *n.* The son or daughter of your uncle or aunt.

cov·er /kuv′ər/ *n.* Anything put over something else: Nilda put a *cover* on the frying pan.
—*v.* To be over or put something over: Snow *covered* the ground.

co·zy /kō′zē/ *adj.* Warm and comfortable: Matt felt *cozy* under his blanket.

crash /krash/ *n.* **1** A loud noise. **2** One thing hitting something else: a car *crash*.
—*v.* To hit with a loud noise: A cup *crashed* on the floor.

crawl /krôl/ *v.* **1** To creep on hands and knees. **2** To move slowly: The cars *crawled* in heavy traffic.

cray·on /krā′on *or* krā′ən/ *n.* A colored wax stick for drawing.

creek /krēk/ *n.* A small stream.

crook·ed /krŏok′id/ *adj.* **1** Not straight. **2** Not honest: Their plan sounds *crooked*.

---

act, āte, câre, ärt;　　egg, ēven;　　if, īce;　　on, ōver, ôr;　　bŏŏk, fōŏd;　　up, tûrn;
ə = **a** in *ago*, **e** in *listen*, **i** in *giraffe*, **o** in *pilot*, **u** in *circus*;　　yŏŏ = **u** in *music*;　　oil;　　out;
chair;　**s**in**g**;　**sh**op;　**th**ank;　**th**at;　**zh** in *treasure*.

crop

crop /krop/ *n.* Something that is grown on a farm: Corn is a *crop.*

crown /kroun/ *n.* A wreath or band worn by a king or queen.
—*v.* To make a person king or queen.

crumb /krum/ *n.* **1** A tiny piece of bread or cake. **2** A tiny bit: There wasn't a *crumb* of food left.

cry /krī/ *v.* **cried, crying** **1** To weep or sob. **2** To call out; to shout: Sam *cried* for help.
—*n., pl.* **cries** A shout.

cup /kup/ *n.* **1** A small, open bowl, usually with a handle, used mainly for drinking: I drink my milk from a *cup.* **2** The amount a cup will hold; cupful.
—*v.* **cupped, cupping** To shape like a cup: He *cupped* his hands to catch the falling water.

cup·board /kub′ərd/ *n.* A cabinet where dishes and food are kept.

D

dai·sy /dā′zē/ *n., pl.* **daisies** A white flower with a yellow center.

dance /dans/ *v.* **danced, dancing** To move in time to music.
—*n.* **1** A set of steps for dancing: The polka is a *dance.* **2** A party or gathering where people dance.

dan·ger /dān′jər/ *n.* Something that can hurt you: Fire is a *danger* to all of us.

daugh·ter /dô′tər/ *n.* What a girl or woman is to her parents.

do

de·cide /di·sīd′/ *v.* **decided, deciding** To make up your mind: Adam *decided* to stay at home.

deep /dēp/ *adj.* **1** Very far from the top: a *deep* hole. **2** Dark in color: Navy is a *deep* blue.
—*adv.* In, at, or to a deep place: Miners work *deep* in the earth.

de·lay /di·lā′/ *v.* **1** To make late: Rain *delayed* the game. **2** To put off: The O'Neals *delayed* their trip.

de·light /di·līt′/ *n.* Great joy.
—*v.* To give joy: Children *delight* their parents.

de·ny /di·nī′/ *v.* **denied, denying** To say that something is not true: He *denied* that he had been there.

desk /desk/ *n.* A table with drawers used for writing or studying.

de·stroy /di·stroi′/ *v.* To break or ruin: Fire can *destroy* a forest.

de·tail /di·tāl′ *or* dē′tāl/ *n.* A small piece of information.

did·n't /did′(ə)nt/ Did not.

din·ner /din′ər/ *n.* The main meal of the day.

dish /dish/ *n., pl.* **dishes** **1** Something used to hold food. **2** A type of food: Spaghetti is my favorite *dish.*

di·vide /di·vīd′/ *v.* **divided, dividing** To make things or numbers into parts: Darin *divided* the clay into three pieces.

do /dōō/ *v.* **did, done, doing** **1** To carry out a task: Alex *did* his homework. **2** To get along: Ginny *does* well at school. **3** To be right: This pencil will *do.* **4** *Do* is used to ask questions: *Do* you like green apples? **5** *Do* can take the place of a verb already used: Helga skates better than I *do.*

does·n't /duz′ənt/ Does not.

dol·lar /dol′ər/ *n.* A unit of money equal to 100 cents.

don't /dōnt/ Do not.

dot /dot/ *n.* A round mark: ·.
—*v.* **dotted, dotting** To mark with a dot: Remember to *dot* your i̱'s.

dou·ble /dub′əl/ *adj.* **1** Twice as much; twice as large: a *double* meat burger. **2** Having two parts: a *double* feature.
—*v.* **doubled, doubling** To make twice as great: If you *double* 2, you get 4.

down·pour /doun′pôr′/ *n.* Heavy rain.

down·stairs /doun′stârz′/ *adv.* **1** Down the stairs. **2** On a lower floor: Tim is *downstairs*.

draw /drô/ *v.* **drew, drawn, drawing** To make a picture with a pencil or crayon.

draw·er /drôr/ *n.* A boxlike container that slides in and out.

dream /drēm/ *n.* **1** What goes through your mind when you are asleep. **2** Something you hope for: Al's *dream* is to be an actor.
—*v.* To have a dream.

drill /dril/ *n.* **1** A tool used for making holes. **2** An exercise: We had a fire *drill* today.
—*v.* **1** To make a hole with a drill. **2** To teach by giving a drill: Ms. Perkins *drilled* us in spelling.

drive /drīv/ *v.* **drove, driven, driving** **1** To run a car, bus, or truck. **2** To go or be carried in a car: Mr. Atkins *drove* me home.
—*n.* A ride: Let's go for a *drive*.

drop /drop/ *v.* **dropped, dropping** **1** To fall or let fall: Don't *drop* crumbs on the rug. **2** To leave out: *Drop* the e̱ in ra̱ce before you add e̱d.
—*n.* A tiny amount of liquid: I felt a *drop* of rain.

dry /drī/ *v.* **dried, drying** To remove water from: Joan *dried* the dishes.
—*adj.* Not wet: Use the *dry* towel.

duck /duk/ *n.* A bird with a flat bill and webbed feet that swims.
—*v.* To lower your head or move quickly: Sara *ducked* when I threw the ball.

dust /dust/ *n.* Tiny pieces of dirt.
—*v.* To wipe away dust: Peggy *dusted* the table.

dwell /dwel/ *v.* To live or make your home: Animals *dwell* in the forest.

E

each /ēch/ *adj., pron.* Every one: *Each* boy sings well. I gave a sandwich to *each*.
—*adv.* Apiece: Mom bought us two books *each*.

ea·gle /ē′gəl/ *n.* A hunting bird with sharp eyes and powerful wings.

---

act, āte, câre, ärt;   egg, ēven;   if, īce;   on, ōver, ôr;   book, fo͞od;   up, tûrn;
ə = a in *ago*, e in *listen*, i in *giraffe*, o in *pilot*, u in *circus*;   yo͞o = u in *music*;   oil;   out;
ch in *chair*; sing; sh in *shop*; thank; th in *that*; zh in *treasure*.

ear[1] /ir/ *n.* What people and animals use for hearing.

ear[2] /ir/ *n.* Where grain grows on some plants: an *ear* of corn.

ear·ly /ûr′lē/ *adv., adj.* **earlier, earliest** 1 Near the beginning: I get up *early* in the morning. 2 Before the regular time: Josh got home *early.*

earn /ûrn/ *v.* 1 To get money for doing work. 2 To get by trying hard: Ellen *earned* the prize.

earth /ûrth/ *n.* 1 The planet we live on. 2 Ground or soil: We planted seeds in the *earth.*

east /ēst/ *n., adj., adv.* A direction; where the sun comes up.

eas·y /ē′zē/ *adj.* **easier, easiest** 1 Not hard to do. 2 Without worry or trouble: an *easy* life.

edge /ej/ *n.* 1 Where something ends: the *edge* of the paper. 2 The cutting side of a knife.

egg /eg/ *n.* 1 An oval body with a hard shell laid by female birds. 2 The food that is inside an egg.

eight /āt/ *n., adj.* The word for *8.*

ei·ther /ē′t͟hər *or* ī′t͟hər/ *adj., pron., conj.* One or the other: *Either* puzzle is fun. You may do *either. Either* do it now or do it later.
—*adv.* Also: Mindy doesn't want to go *either.*

else /els/ *adj.* Other; besides: Do you want anything *else?*

emp·ty /emp′tē/ *adj.* Holding nothing: The box was *empty.*
—*v.* **emptied, emptying** To make empty: Ben *emptied* his pockets.

en·e·my /en′ə·mē/ *n., pl.* **enemies** A person who tries to harm another, or a country that fights another country in war.

en·joy /in·joi′/ *v.* To take pleasure in: Lou *enjoys* playing the piano.

e·nough /i·nuf′/ *adj.* Having the amount needed: There is *enough* turkey for two meals.
—*n.* All that is needed: There is *enough* for everyone.

en·vy /en′vē/ *n.* The desire to have what someone else has: Nadia's coat made me green with *envy.*
—*v.* **envied, envying** To feel envy toward: Pat *envied* his brother.

e·ven /ē′vən/ *adj.* 1 Flat and smooth: The floor is *even.* 2 Steady; regular: She drove at an *even* speed. 3 On the same level: The top of the bush was *even* with my chin. 4 Equal: The score was *even.*
—*adv.* Still: an *even* better idea.
—*v.* 1 To make or become level: The road *evens* out here. 2 To make equal: The touchdown *evened* the score.

eve·ning /ēv′ning/ *n.* The early part of nighttime.

ev·er /ev′ər/ *adv.* At any time: Did you *ever* go to the zoo?

eve·ry /ev′rē *or* ev′ər·ē/ *adj.* Each one: You got *every* answer right.

eve·ry·bod·y /ev′rē·bod′ē/ *pron.* Each person; everyone.

eve·ry·day /ev′rē·dā′/ *adj.* 1 Taking place each day: an *everyday* job. 2 Not special: *everyday* clothes.

everywhere

eve·ry·where /ev′rē·(h)wâr′/ *adv.* In all places; all around.

eye /ī/ *n.* What people and animals use for seeing.
—*v.* **eyed, eying** *or* **eyeing** To watch: The cat *eyed* the bird.

F

face /fās/ *n.* **1** The front part of your head. **2** A look: Miko made a funny *face*.
—*v.* **faced, facing** **1** To turn toward: Everyone should *face* the teacher. **2** To have the front toward: Our house *faces* the road.

fac·to·ry /fak′tər·ē/ *n., pl.* **factories** A place where things are made.

faint /fānt/ *v.* To become weak and pass out.
—*adj.* **1** Dim; slight: There was a *faint* glow in the sky. **2** Weak.

fair[1] /fâr/ *adj.* **1** Following the rules; honest: It was a *fair* game. **2** Not good and not bad: My test mark was *fair*. **3** Clear; bright: The weather will be *fair* tomorrow.
—*adv.* In a fair way: Play *fair*.

fair[2] /fâr/ *n.* **1** A showing of farm animals and farm goods. **2** A sale of things: Our block had a *fair* to raise money.

fair·y /fâr′ē/ *n., pl.* **fairies** A tiny, make-believe being.

fall /fôl/ *v.* **fell, fallen, falling** **1** To drop down: Laura *fell* off the horse. **2** To pass into a state: George *fell* asleep.
—*n.* **1** The season after summer. **2** The act of falling: a bad *fall*.

fence

fam·i·ly /fam′ə·lē *or* fam′lē/ *n., pl.* **families** **1** Parents and their children. **2** Animals or plants that are related in some way: Lions are part of the cat *family*.

far /fär/ *adv., adj.* At a long way away: Our school is *far* from here.

farm /färm/ *n.* Land where crops are grown and animals are raised: My uncle grows corn on his *farm*.
—*v.* To have and run a farm.

fa·ther /fä′thər/ *n.* A male parent.

fawn /fôn/ *n.* A baby deer.

feast /fēst/ *n.* A large, special meal.
—*v.* To eat a feast.

fed /fed/ *v.* Past tense and past participle of *feed*.

feed /fēd/ *v.* **fed, feeding** To give food to: Jerry *fed* the birds.

feel /fēl/ *v.* **felt, feeling** **1** To touch. **2** To be aware of: I *feel* the wind blowing. **3** To be: Hal *feels* sad.

fell /fel/ *v.* Past tense of *fall*: Sandra *fell* and cut her knee yesterday.

felt /felt/ *v.* Past tense and past participle of *feel*.

fence /fens/ *n.* A wall of wood or wire put around a piece of land: He has a *fence* around his yard.

---

act, āte, câre, ärt; egg, ēven; if, īce; on, ōver, ôr; bŏŏk, fŏŏd; up, tûrn;
ə = **a** in *ago*, **e** in *listen*, **i** in *giraffe*, **o** in *pilot*, **u** in *circus*; y͞o͞o = **u** in *music*; oil; out;
chair; sing; shop; thank; that; zh in *treasure*.

fight

fight /fīt/ *n.* **1** A battle. **2** A bad quarrel.
—*v.* **fought, fighting** **1** To make war. **2** To quarrel. **3** To struggle against: Doctors *fight* disease.

fi·nal /fī'nəl/ *adj.* **1** Last: Today is the *final* day of school. **2** Not to be changed: My choice is *final*.

find /fīnd/ *v.* **found, finding** **1** To come upon: I *found* a watch at the beach. **2** To get back something lost: Mark *found* his glasses. **3** To learn: Allison *found* the answer to the math problem.

fin·ger /fing'gər/ *n.* One of the five parts that make up the end of your hand.

flag /flag/ *n.* A piece of cloth with special colors and designs on it.

flash /flash/ *n., pl.* **flashes** **1** A sudden bright light. **2** A short time: Russ finished in a *flash*.
—*v.* **1** To give a quick bright light: Lightning *flashed* in the sky. **2** To move quickly: Diane *flashed* by on her bike.

flat /flat/ *adj.* **flatter, flattest** **1** Smooth and level. **2** Without air: a *flat* tire.
—*adv.* In a flat way: Lie *flat* on your back.

flew /floo/ *v.* Past tense and past participle of *fly*[1].

forget

float /flōt/ *v.* To rest on water or in the air: Eva can *float* on her back. The balloon *floated* away.
—*n.* A display in a parade.

flock /flok/ *n.* **1** A group of birds or animals: I saw a *flock* of geese today. **2** A large crowd: *Flocks* of people came to the park.

floor /flôr/ *n.* **1** The part of a room you stand on. **2** A story of a building: We live on the third *floor*.

flour /flour/ *n.* A fine powder made from wheat or other grain: My mother uses *flour* when she cooks.

fly[1] /flī/ *v.* **flew, flown, flying** **1** To go through the air: Birds can *fly*. **2** To wave in the air: The flags are *flying*. **3** To cause to float in the air: Betsy is *flying* her kite. **4** To go by plane.
—*n., pl.* **flies** In baseball, a ball hit high in the air.

fly[2] /flī/ *n., pl.* **flies** An insect with two wings that flies.

fog·gy /fog'ē/ *adj.* **foggier, foggiest** Full of fog or mist: It was so *foggy* that we could not see.

fold /fōld/ *v.* To bend one part over another: *Fold* the paper in half.

fol·low /fol'ō/ *v.* **1** To go along behind: The dog *followed* me home. **2** To come after: Fall *follows* summer. **3** To obey: Max *follows* orders well.

foot·ball /foot'bôl'/ *n.* **1** An oval ball. **2** A team game played with such a ball.

for·ev·er /fôr·ev'ər/ *adv.* Always: I'll be your friend *forever*.

for·get /fər·get'/ *v.* **forgot, forgotten, forgetting** **1** To fail to remember or think of. **2** To leave behind: Ken *forgot* his book.

forgot

for·got /fər·got′/ v. Past tense and past participle of *forget:* I *forgot* to do my homework last night.

fos·sil /fos′əl/ n. The mark of a very old plant or animal in a rock.

fought /fôt/ v. Past tense and past participle of *fight.*

found /found/ v. Past tense and past participle of *find:* Ben *found* the money he lost.

four /fôr/ n., adj. The word for *4.*

frame /frām/ n. A border around something: a picture *frame.*
—v. **framed, framing** To put something in a frame.

free /frē/ adj. **1** Not costing money. **2** Having liberty: You are *free* to leave when you want to.
—v. **freed, freeing** To let out of: They *freed* the fox from a trap.
—adv. Without paying: Parents may come *free* to the school play.

free·dom /frē′dəm/ n. Being free; liberty: Americans value *freedom.*

fresh /fresh/ adj. **1** Newly made or gotten: *fresh* fruit. **2** Clean and cool: *fresh* air.

from /frum, from, *or* frəm/ prep. **1** Starting at: We drove *from* Ohio to Iowa. **2** Sent or given by: I got a letter *from* my aunt.

give

frown /froun/ v. To look angry or sad.
—n. A sad or angry look.

fudge /fuj/ n. Soft chocolate candy.

fun·ny /fun′ē/ adj. **funnier, funniest** Able to make you laugh: Sue told a *funny* joke.

fur /fûr/ n. The hair on the skin of many animals.
—adj. Made of fur: a *fur* coat.

G

gar·den /gär′dən/ n. A place where flowers or vegetables are grown: We have roses growing in our *garden.*

gate /gāt/ n. The doorlike part of a fence or wall: The *gate* of the fence was open.

gath·er /gath′ər/ v. **1** To bring together: Simon *gathered* up the test papers. **2** To come together: The family *gathered* for dinner.

geese /gēs/ n. Plural of *goose.*

gen·tle /jen′təl/ adj. Kind and tender: Be *gentle* with the baby.

ghost /gōst/ n. A spirit that seems to appear to living people.

gi·ant /jī′ənt/ n. In fairy tales, a very large, strong person.
—adj. Very large; huge: We saw a *giant* elephant at the circus.

gin·ger·bread /jin′jər·bred′/ n. A cake flavored with ginger.

gi·raffe /jə·raf′/ n. An animal with a very long neck and spotted skin.

girl /gûrl/ n. A female child.

give /giv/ v. **gave, given, giving** To hand over; to offer: *Give* me your hand.

---

act, āte, câre, ärt;   egg, ēven;   if, īce;   on, ōver, ôr;   bŏŏk, fōōd;   up, tûrn;
ə = **a** in *ago,* **e** in *listen,* **i** in *giraffe,* **o** in *pilot,* **u** in *circus;*   yōō = **u** in *music;*   oil;   out;
chair; sing; shop; thank; that; zh in *treasure.*

glad /glad/ *adj.* Pleased or happy: I'll be *glad* to come.

glass /glas/ *n., pl.* **glasses** **1** A clear material that breaks easily. **2** A drinking cup. **3** (*pl.*) Two pieces of glass or plastic used to help people see better.

good·ness /gŏŏd′nis/ *n.* The condition of being good: Caring for others is a sign of *goodness*.

goose /gōōs/ *n., pl.* **geese** A bird with a long neck that looks like a duck.

grab /grab/ *v.* **grabbed, grabbing** To take hold of suddenly: Chad *grabbed* my arm to stop me.

grade /grād/ *n.* **1** The school year or level: Mei is in the third *grade*. **2** A mark given in school: Rae gets good *grades* in school.

grand /grand/ *adj.* **1** Large, important: The mayor lives in a *grand* house. **2** Complete: What is the *grand* total? **3** Very good: We had a *grand* time at the zoo.

grand·fa·ther /gran(d)′fä′ᵭ͡hər/ *n.* Your father's or mother's father.

grand·moth·er /gran(d)′muᵭ͡h′ər/ *n.* Your father's or mother's mother.

grape /grāp/ *n.* A fruit that grows in bunches on vines.

grass /gras/ *n.* A plant with green blades that covers the ground.

grew /grōō/ *v.* Past tense of *grow*.

groan /grōn/ *n.* A sound of pain.
—*v.* To make such a sound: Callie *groaned* because her arm hurt.

ground /ground/ *n.* Earth's surface; soil: The *ground* was wet.

group /grōōp/ *n.* Several people or things together.
—*v.* To make a group: Darrel *grouped* his marbles by color.

grow /grō/ *v.* **grew, grown, growing** **1** To become larger or taller: Puppies *grow* very quickly. **2** To plant something: We *grow* tomatoes.

grown /grōn/ *v.* Past participle of *grow*.

guess /ges/ *n., pl.* **guesses** An idea you have without knowing for sure: I think it will rain, but that's just a *guess*.
—*v.* **1** To make a guess. **2** To suppose: I *guess* you are right.

gup·py /gup′ē/ *n., pl.* **guppies** A tiny, colorful fish.

gym /jim/ *n.* Short for *gymnasium*. A large room where people play games and exercise.

H

hair /hâr/ *n.* The threadlike strands that grow on your head.

hair·cut /hâr′kut′/ *n.* The cutting of hair or the way hair is cut.

half /haf/ *n., pl.* **halves** One of two equal parts.
—*adj.* Being half: a *half* hour.
—*adv.* Partly: Don is *half* asleep.

hand /hand/ *n.* **1** The end part of your arm. **2** One of the pointers on a clock or watch.
—*v.* To give or pass: Ken *handed* the money to the clerk.

hap·pen /hap′ən/ *v.* To take place: Nothing *happened* after you left.

hap·py /hap′ē/ *adj.* **happier, happiest** Full of joy; glad.

hard /härd/ *adj.* **1** Solid: *hard* as a rock. **2** Not easy: a *hard* test.
—*adv.* With effort or force: Penny works *hard*.

have·n't /hav′ənt/ Have not.

| hay | house |

hay /hā/ *n.* Grass that is cut and dried to feed animals.

head·ache /hed′āk′/ *n.* A pain in your head.

hear /hir/ *v.* **heard, hearing** To take in sounds through your ears.

heard /hûrd/ *v.* Past tense and past participle of *hear.*

heart /härt/ *n.* **1** The organ in your body that pumps blood. **2** Something that has this shape: ♡.

hel·lo /hə·lō′/ *interj.* A greeting.

help /help/ *v.* To be useful; to do what is needed: Ethel *helps* around the house.
—*n.* A person or thing that helps: Lena is a great *help* to Grandma.

here /hir/ *adv.* In or to this place: Let's sit *here.* Bring it *here.*

her·self /hər·self′/ *pron.* Her own self: She sang to *herself.*

he's /hēz/ **1** He is. **2** He has.

hid /hid/ *v.* Past tense of *hide*[1].

hide[1] /hīd/ *v.* **hid, hidden, hiding 1** To put out of sight: Gene *hid* the gift in the closet. **2** To hide oneself: Keisha *hid* behind a bush.

hide[2] /hīd/ *n.* The skin of an animal.

high /hī/ *adj.* **1** Far up. **2** Great in cost: The price is too *high.*
—*adv.* To a high place: The building reaches *high* in the sky.

high·way /hī′wā′/ *n.* A main road.

hike /hīk/ *n.* A long walk: We went for a *hike* in the woods.
—*v.* **hiked, hiking** To take a hike.

him·self /him·self′/ *pron.* His own self: He taught *himself* to skate.

hob·by /hob′ē/ *n., pl.* **hobbies** A special interest: Steve's *hobby* is collecting stamps.

hold /hōld/ *v.* **held, holding 1** To take and keep: Please *hold* my coat. **2** To keep in place: Glue will *hold* it together. **3** To keep back: *Hold* your breath. **4** To have: We *held* a meeting.

hole /hōl/ *n.* An open space in or through something solid.

hol·low /hol′ō/ *adj.* Empty inside: Squirrels live in that *hollow* tree.

hop /hop/ *v.* **hopped, hopping 1** To move the way a rabbit does. **2** To jump on one foot. **3** To jump over or into: Ted *hopped* into bed.

hope /hōp/ *v.* **hoped, hoping** To wish or expect: I *hope* to do well.
—*n.* **1** Trust that what you wish for will happen. **2** Something hoped for. **3** Cause for hope: Roxie is our team's only *hope.*

horn /hôrn/ *n.* **1** A hard bony growth on an animal's head: Cows have *horns.* **2** Something that makes a warning sound: a car *horn.* **3** A musical instrument.

horse /hôrs/ *n.* A four-legged animal with hoofs and a mane.

house /hous/ *n., pl.* **houses** /hou′zəz/ A building in which people live.

---

act, āte, câre, ärt;   egg, ēven;   if, īce;   on, ōver, ôr;   bo͝ok, fo͞od;   up, tûrn;
ə = a in *ago,* e in *listen,* i in *giraffe,* o in *pilot,* u in *circus;*   yo͞o = u in *music;*   oil;   out;
ch air; sing; shop; thank; that; zh in *treasure.*

how

how /hou/ *adv.* **1** In what way: *How* did you do it? **2** To what degree: *How* tall is Aaron?

hun·gry /hung′grē/ *adj.* Wanting or needing food.

hunt /hunt/ *v.* **1** To kill animals for food. **2** To look for: I *hunted* all over for my lost scarf.
—*n.* A search: a treasure *hunt*.

hur·ry /hûr′ē/ *v.* **hurried, hurrying** **1** To move or act quickly: Pam *hurried* to get home on time. **2** To make someone else move or act quickly: Don't *hurry* me.
—*n.* Eagerness to do something quickly: Grace was in a *hurry*.

hurt /hûrt/ *v.* To feel or cause pain or harm: Troy *hurt* himself.

I

ice /īs/ *n.* Frozen water: The pond turned to *ice* in the winter.
—*v.* **iced, icing** To put frosting on a cake.

ill /il/ *adj.* Feeling sick: I go to the doctor when I feel *ill*.

I'll /īl/ **1** I will. **2** I shall.

I'm /īm/ I am.

inch /inch/ *n., pl.* **inches** A unit of length.

in·sect /in′sekt/ *n.* A very small animal with six legs and often wings: Bees and flies are *insects*.

in·side /in′sīd′ *or* in′sīd′/ *adv.* Indoors.
—*prep.* In or within: Dan put his socks *inside* his shoes.
—*n.* The part that is inside: The *inside* of the house is white.

in·to /in′tŌŌ/ *prep.* **1** To the inside: Walk *into* the room. **2** To the form of: The ice turned *into* water.

juice

in·vite /in·vīt′/ *v.* **invited, inviting** To ask someone to come: Joanne *invited* me to her party.

is /iz/ *v.* Form of the verb *to be*. You use *is* after names, words for one thing, and *he, she,* or *it*.

is·n't /iz′ənt/ Is not.

it's /its/ **1** It is. **2** It has.

J

jack·et /jak′it/ *n.* A short coat.

jam¹ /jam/ **jammed, jamming** *v.* To squeeze into a small space: He *jammed* his books into his bag.

jam² /jam/ *n.* Fruit cooked with sugar until thick: strawberry *jam*.

jar /jär/ *n.* A bottle with a wide top.

jaw /jô/ *n.* The upper or lower bone of a mouth: A whale has huge *jaws*.

jet /jet/ *n.* A kind of airplane.

job /job/ *n.* Work that is done, often for money.

join /join/ *v.* **1** To bring or come together: We all *joined* hands. **2** To become a member of a group.

joke /jōk/ *n.* Something that makes you laugh; a funny story.
—*v.* **joked, joking** To do or say something funny.

joy /joi/ *n.* Great happiness.

judge /juj/ *n.* **1** The person who makes decisions in a court of law. **2** The person who decides who wins a race or contest.
—*v.* **judged, judging** **1** To act as a judge in court. **2** To decide who wins: Liza *judged* the contest.

jug /jug/ *n.* A large bottle with a narrow neck and a handle.

juice /jŌŌs/ *n.* The liquid part of fruits, vegetables, or meat.

jump

jump /jump/ *v.* **1** To leap up or over: The cat *jumped* onto the window sill. **2** To jerk suddenly: Ken *jumped* when the phone rang. —*n.* A leap.

jun·gle /jung′gəl/ *n.* A thick forest where wild animals live.

just /just/ *adv.* **1** A little while ago: We *just* got here. **2** Barely: Alfredo got here *just* in time. **3** Only: I'm *just* tired. **4** Very: This meal is *just* delicious.

K

keep /kēp/ *v.* **kept, keeping** **1** To have and not give up: You may *keep* that pencil. **2** To hold back: *Keep* the dog off the sofa. **3** To continue: Let's *keep* trying.

kept /kept/ *v.* Past tense and past participle of *keep.*

ket·tle /ket′(ə)l/ *n.* **1** A large pot. **2** A pot with a spout; teakettle.

key /kē/ *n.* **1** A small metal thing used to open or close a lock. **2** Something that explains or gives answers: an answer *key* for a test. **3** One of the parts pressed on a piano or typewriter.

kick /kik/ *v.* To hit with your foot. —*n.* A blow with the foot: Lee gave the stone a hard *kick.*

kind·ness /kīnd′nis/ *n.* Being kind and nice: Nicky treats everyone with *kindness.*

kiss /kis/ *v.* To touch someone with your lips as a sign of love. —*n.* The act of kissing: Jake gave Grandma a hug and a *kiss.*

known

kitch·en /kich′ən/ *n.* The room where food is prepared.

kit·ten /kit′(ə)n/ *n.* A young cat.

knead /nēd/ *v.* To mix dough using your hands to push and squeeze.

knee /nē/ *n.* The joint in the middle of your leg and the area around it.

kneel /nēl/ *v.* **knelt** *or* **kneeled, kneeling** To go down on your knees.

knew /n(y)ōō/ *v.* Past tense of *know.*

knife /nīf/ *n.* **knives** A tool with a sharp side for cutting.

knit /nit/ *v.* **knit** *or* **knitted, knitting** To make clothes using yarn and long needles.

knock /nok/ *v.* **1** To hit. **2** To make a pounding noise: *Knock* on the door. —*n.* A pounding noise: We heard a *knock* at the door.

knot /not/ *n.* A fastening made by tying ropes or string. —*v.* **knotted, knotting** To tie in a knot.

know /nō/ *v.* **knew, known, knowing** **1** To be sure: I *know* you are wrong. **2** To understand: Ira *knows* how to do it. **3** To be friends with: We *know* the Wilsons.

known /nōn/ *v.* Past participle of *know.*

---

act, āte, câre, ärt;   egg, ēven;   if, īce;   on, ōver, ôr;   bŏŏk, fōōd;   up, tûrn;
ə = **a** in *ago,* **e** in *listen,* **i** in *giraffe,* **o** in *pilot,* **u** in *circus;*   yōō = **u** in *music;*   oil;   out;
ch**air;** si**ng;** **sh**op; **th**ank; **th**at; **zh** in *treasure.*

lady

L

la·dy /lā′dē/ *n., pl.* **ladies**   **1** A woman.   **2** A woman with good manners.

lake /lāk/ *n.* A body of water.

lamb /lam/ *n.* A young sheep.

land /land/ *n.*   **1** The part of Earth that is not covered by water.   **2** A country.
—*v.* To arrive on land: The airplane *landed* on the runway.

large /lärj/ *adj.* **larger, largest** Big in size or amount.

last¹ /last/ *adj.*   **1** Coming at the end: I ate the *last* piece.   **2** Just before this one: We saw the Itos *last* month.
—*adv.*   **1** Coming at the end: Bob woke up *last*.   **2** Most recently: When were you *last* at the zoo?

last² /last/ *v.* To go on: The picnic *lasted* all day.

late /lāt/ *adj., adv.* After or past a certain time: He came *late*.

lay¹ /lā/ *v.* **laid, laying** To put down: *Lay* your coats on the bed.

lay² /lā/ *v.* Past tense of *lie¹*.

learn /lûrn/ *v.*   **1** To get skill in or knowledge: Diego *learned* to play baseball.   **2** To find out: Janice *learned* why Nina left early.

leave /lēv/ *v.* **left, leaving**   **1** To go away.   **2** To let stay behind: Tad *left* his books at school.   **3** To let someone else do something: Just *leave* everything to me.

ledge /lej/ *n.* A narrow shelf: Put the plant on the window *ledge*.

left¹ /left/ *n.* The opposite of *right*.
—*adj., adv.* On or to the left: Give me your *left* hand. Turn *left*.

left² /left/ *v.* Past tense and past participle of *leave*.

light

leg /leg/ *n.*   **1** One of the parts of the body used to stand and walk.   **2** Something like a leg: a table *leg*.

less /les/ *adj.* Smaller in number or amount: Teddy has *less* money.
—*n.* An amount: I did *less* than I planned to do.
—*adv.* In a smaller amount: This book costs *less* than that one.

les·son /les′(ə)n/ *n.* Something to be learned or taught: Peter did the math *lesson*.

let /let/ *v.* To allow: Will your parents *let* you go to the zoo?

let's /lets/ Let us: *Let's* go now.

let·ter /let′ər/ *n.*   **1** One of the parts of the alphabet.   **2** A written message: I mailed a *letter*.

lev·el /lev′əl/ *adj.* Smooth or even: The ground is *level* over there.

li·brar·y /lī′brer′ē *or* lī′brə·rē/ *n., pl.* **libraries** A place where books are kept.

lie¹ /lī/ *v.* **lay, lain, lying** To rest in a flat position: Sandy is *lying* on the couch.

lie² /lī/ *n.* Something told that is not true: Jessie told me a *lie*.
—*v.* **lied, lying** To tell a lie.

life /līf/ *n., pl.* **lives**   **1** The state of being alive: There are no signs of *life* on Mars.   **2** The period of being alive: I have lived here all my *life*.   **3** A way of living: Firefighters have a dangerous *life*.

lift /lift/ *v.* To pick up and raise: Conchita *lifted* her little sister.
—*n.* A ride: We got a *lift* home.

light¹ /līt/ *n.*   **1** Brightness: We cannot see without *light*. **2** Something that gives light.
—*v.* **lit** *or* **lighted, lighting**   **1** To give light: The lantern *lighted* our

light

path. **2** To set fire to: Mom will *light* the candles.

—*adj.* Pale in color: a *light* color.

light² /līt/ *adj.* Not heavy: as *light* as a feather.

limb /lim/ *n.* A branch of a tree.

line /līn/ *n.* **1** A straight mark. **2** A row: There was a long *line* of people at the checkout counter.

li·on /lī′ən/ *n.* A large, powerful animal of the cat family.

list /list/ *n.* A group of things written down in order: Mom takes a shopping *list* to the market.

—*v.* To make a list.

lis·ten /lis′(ə)n/ *v.* To pay attention; to try to hear: *Listen* carefully.

live¹ /liv/ *v.* **lived, living** **1** To be alive: Grandpa *lived* for eighty years. **2** To make your home: They *live* in Iowa.

live² /līv/ *adj.* Being alive.

load /lōd/ *n.* Something carried: A mule can carry a heavy *load*.

—*v.* To fill or put on: Lisa *loaded* her camera. The movers *loaded* the furniture on the truck.

look·out /look′out′/ *n.* **1** The act of watching out: Be on the *lookout* for a ship with a yellow flag. **2** A person who watches.

manage

lose /lōōz/ *v.* **lost, losing** **1** To be unable to find: Lori *lost* her scarf. **2** To fail to keep: Don't *lose* your temper. **3** To fail to win.

loud /loud/ *adj.* Not quiet; noisy.

love /luv/ *n.* A strong feeling.

—*v.* **loved, loving** **1** To have a deep feeling for: Parents *love* their children. **2** To like very much: Cindy *loves* to swim.

low /lō/ *adj.* **1** Not high: The truck cannot go under the *low* bridge. **2** Not loud: a *low* voice.

loy·al /loi′əl/ *adj.* Faithful: Our dog is very *loyal*.

luck·y /luk′ē/ *adj.* **luckier, luckiest** Having or bringing good luck: You were *lucky* to win.

lunch /lunch/ *n.* The meal eaten in the middle of the day.

M

ma·chine /mə·shēn′/ *n.* Something that does work: a sewing *machine*.

mag·ic /maj′ik/ *n.* The art of pretending to do things that are not possible.

—*adj.* Able to work magic: I will wave my *magic* wand.

mail /māl/ *n.* Letters and packages handled by the post office.

—*v.* To send a letter or package.

main /mān/ *adj.* Most important: Oak Avenue is the *main* street.

man·age /man′ij/ *v.* **managed, managing** **1** To get by: How did you *manage* to do that alone? **2** To be in charge: Ms. Ramos *manages* a store.

---

act, āte, câre, ärt;   egg, ēven;   if, īce;   on, ōver, ôr;   book, food;   up, tûrn;
ə = a in *ago,* e in *listen,* i in *giraffe,* o in *pilot,* u in *circus;*   yoo = u in *music;*   oil;   out;
ch in *chair;* sing; sh in *shop;* th in *thank;* th in *that;* zh in *treasure.*

mane   **more**

mane /mān/ *n.* The long hair on a horse's neck or around a male lion's face.

mar·ble /mär′bəl/ *n.* **1** A small glass ball used for games. **2** A hard stone used for buildings and statues: The floors are of *marble*.

mar·ket /mär′kit/ *n.* **1** A place where things are bought and sold: The farmer brought his fruit to *market*. **2** A store that sells food.

mar·ry /mar′ē/ *v.* **married, marrying** **1** To become husband and wife. **2** To join as husband and wife: The judge *married* my aunt and uncle.

mat·ter /mat′ər/ *n.* Something that troubles you: What is the *matter*?
—*v.* To be of importance: Doing well in school *matters* to me.

may /mā/ *v.* **1** To have permission to: You *may* leave the room. **2** To be possible: It *may* rain today.

may·be /mā′bē/ *adv.* Perhaps; possibly: *Maybe* we'll go tomorrow.

meal /mēl/ *n.* Food eaten at one time: I eat three *meals* a day.

mean[1] /mēn/ *v.* **meant, meaning** **1** To want to: I didn't *mean* to trip you. **2** To have as its sense: What does this word *mean*?

mean[2] /mēn/ *adj.* Cruel.

mean·while /mēn′(h)wīl′/ *adv.* At the same time.

mea·sles /mē′zəlz/ *n.* A disease that makes your skin break out in red spots.

meat /mēt/ *n.* The flesh of animals used as food.

meet /mēt/ *v.* **met, meeting** **1** To come together: Let's *meet* at the corner. **2** To get to know: I *met* Charlie only a year ago.

melt /melt/ *v.* To get soft or become liquid: Butter *melts* on hot toast.

mem·o·ry /mem′ər·ē/ *n., pl.* **memories** **1** The ability to remember: Eliza has a very good *memory* for names. **2** What is remembered: I have happy *memories* of my vacation.

mess /mes/ *n.* A dirty or not neat condition: Your room is a *mess*.
—*v.* To make untidy: Don't *mess* up the living room.

mid·dle /mid′(ə)l/ *n.* The center or halfway point.

mid·night /mid′nīt′/ *n.* Twelve o'clock at night.

milk /milk/ *n.* A white liquid from cows or other female animals.
—*v.* To get milk from: Davey helped the farmer *milk* the cows.

mis·take /mis·tāk′/ *n.* Something that is done wrong: Karen made a *mistake* on the spelling test.

more /môr/ *adj.* **1** Greater in number or amount: Rex has *more* pencils than I have. **2** Additional: I bought *more* pencils today.
—*n.* A greater amount: *More* of my pencils are new.
—*adv.* **1** In a greater amount: I write *more* now. **2** Again: Tell me once *more*.

morning

morn·ing /môr′ning/ *n.* The time of day from sunrise until noon.

mo·tel /mō·tel′/ *n.* A place where travelers can stay overnight.

mo·tor /mō′tər/ *n.* The engine that makes cars and other machines go. —*adj.* Run by a motor: a *motor* boat.

mouse /mous/ *n., pl.* **mice** A small animal with a pointed nose and a long tail: Our cat catches *mice.*

mouth /mouth/ *n.* **1** The opening in your face used for speaking and eating. **2** An opening like a mouth: the *mouth* of a jar.

move /mōōv/ *v.* **moved, moving 1** To go from one place to another: The car *moved* down the street. **2** To change where you live: The Engels *moved* to Grant Street. **3** To change position: The sleeping child didn't *move.*

my·self /mī·self′/ *pron.* My own self: I saw *myself* in the mirror.

N

nail /nāl/ *n.* **1** A thin pointed piece of metal used to hold wood together. **2** The thin, hornlike layer at the end of a finger or toe: Stop biting your *nails.* —*v.* To put something together with nails.

name /nām/ *n.* What someone or something is called. —*v.* **named, naming 1** To give a name: They *named* the baby Inga. **2** To tell the name of: Can you *name* all fifty states?

notice

nap /nap/ *n.* A short sleep. —*v.* **napped, napping** To sleep for a short time: The baby *naps* every afternoon.

nar·row /nar′ō/ *adj.* Not wide: The road was too *narrow* for two cars.

neat /nēt/ *adj.* **1** Clean and tidy. **2** Clever: That's a *neat* trick.

neck /nek/ *n.* The part of your body between your head and shoulders.

new /n(y)ōō/ *adj.* **1** Not old. **2** Started a short time ago: The *new* school year started last week.

news·pa·per /n(y)ōōz′pā′pər/ *n.* Sheets of paper with news stories on them: We read about the parade in the *newspaper.*

nice /nīs/ *adj.* **nicer, nicest** Pleasant; kind.

nick·el /nik′əl/ *n.* A coin worth five cents.

night /nīt/ *n.* The time between sunset and sunrise.

nine /nīn/ *n., adj.* The word for *9.*

nine·teen /nīn′tēn′/ *n., adj.* The word for *19.*

ninth /nīnth/ *n., adj.* Next after eighth.

noise /noiz/ *n.* Sound, especially loud sound: The crowd made a lot of *noise.*

noon /nōōn/ *n.* Twelve o'clock in the daytime.

north /nôrth/ *n., adj., adv.* A direction; the opposite of south.

not /not/ *adv.* In no way: I did *not* go.

no·tice /nō′tis/ *v.* **noticed, noticing** To see; to pay attention to: Do you *notice* anything different?

---

act, āte, câre, ärt;   egg, ēven;   if, īce;   on, ōver, ôr;   bŏŏk, fōōd;   up, tûrn;
ə = a in *ago,* e in *listen,* i in *giraffe,* o in *pilot,* u in *circus;*   yōō = u in *music;*   oil;   out;
chair; sing; shop; thank; that; zh in *treasure.*

number

num·ber /num′bər/ *n.* **1** A unit in math. **2** An amount: I have a *number* of things to do.
—*v.* To give numbers to: Fay *numbered* the pages of her book.

O

oak /ōk/ *n.* **1** A tree that bears acorns. **2** The wood of this tree.
—*adj.* Made of oak.

o·bey /ō·bā′/ *v.* To do as you are told: My dog *obeys* me.

odd /od/ *adj.* **1** Strange; unusual: That is an *odd* house. **2** Not able to be divided by 2: *odd* numbers.

off /ôf *or* of/ *prep.* Away from: The pillow fell *off* the bed.
—*adv.* Not on: Take *off* your coat.

oil /oil/ *n.* A greasy liquid.
—*v.* To put oil on: We *oiled* the gate so it would not squeak.

old /ōld/ *adj.* **1** Having lived for a long time: Grandpa is an *old* man. **2** Of age: Thomas is eight years *old*. **3** Not new: James wore *old* jeans. **4** Known for a long time: Keith and Otis are *old* friends.

once /wuns/ *adv.* **1** One time: We go on a trip *once* a year. **2** At one time (in the past): I *once* saw a purple and red car.

on·ly /ōn′lē/ *adv.* Just: You have *only* one hour to play.
—*adj.* Alone: He is the *only* boy on the team.

on·to /on′too/ *prep.* **1** Upon the top of: The cat jumped *onto* the table. **2** To and upon: The team came *onto* the field.

oth·er /uth′ər/ *adj.* **1** Different: Do you want this crayon or the *other* one? **2** More: Do you want *other* books to read besides this one?
—*pron.* A different person or thing: Ricardo likes to help *others*.

our /our/ *pron.* Belonging to us: *Our* house is yellow.

our·selves /our·selvz′/ *pron.* Us and no one else: We made it *ourselves*.

out·side /out′sīd′ *or* out′sīd′/ *adv.* Outdoors: We played *outside*.
—*n.* The part that is out: We painted the *outside* of the house.
—*prep.* Out of: Put your boots *outside* the door.
—*adj.* On the outside: The *outside* shell of a nut is hard.

o·ver /ō′vər/ *prep.* On top of.
—*adv.* **1** Above. **2** Again: You must write your paper *over* because it is messy. **3** To a certain place: Bring it *over* here.
—*adj.* Finished: School is *over* at three o'clock.

owl /oul/ *n.* A night bird with large eyes and a hooked beak.

own /ōn/ *v.* To have in your possession: I *own* a bicycle.
—*adj.* Belonging to: my *own* room.

P

pack /pak/ *n.* A large bundle to be carried by a person or animal.
—*v.* **1** To put things in a package, box, or suitcase. **2** To crowd or fill up: People *packed* into the bus.

pack

| package | paw |

pack·age /pak′ij/ *n.* **1** Something wrapped up or tied up: We mailed a *package* to my brother at camp. **2** The box that holds something: The directions are on the *package*.

pad·dle /pad′(ə)l/ *n.* A short oar.
—*v.* **paddled, paddling 1** To use a paddle to move a boat. **2** To move your hands and feet in water: The children *paddled* about in the lake.

page /pāj/ *n.* One of the sheets of paper in a book or magazine.

paid /pād/ *v.* Past tense and past participle of *pay*.

pain /pān/ *n.* Ache; soreness.

paint /pānt/ *n.* Colored liquid that is spread on something to make it that color.
—*v.* **1** To spread paint on. **2** To make a picture with paint.

pair /pâr/ *n.* Two people or things that go together: a *pair* of shoes.

pan·cake /pan′kāk′/ *n.* A thin flat cake fried in a pan.

pane /pān/ *n.* A sheet of glass put in the frame of a window: This window has a broken *pane*.

pa·per /pā′pər/ *n.* **1** Material used for writing, printing, and wrapping things. **2** A piece of paper with writing on it: Barney handed in his *paper*. **3** A newspaper.
—*adj.* Made of paper: Joy made a *paper* airplane.

pa·rade /pə·rād′/ *n.* A march of people with bands and floats.
—*v.* **parade, parading** To show off: He *paraded* around in his costume.

par·ent /pâr′ənt/ *n.* A person's mother or father.

park /pärk/ *n.* Land with trees, grass, and playgrounds.
—*v.* To put a car somewhere and leave it: *Park* the car over there.

part /pärt/ *n.* **1** A piece of a whole. **2** Share: We all must do our *part*. **3** A role in a play. **4** Where hair is divided after combing: The *part* in Lynn's hair is crooked.
—*v.* **1** To divide into pieces. **2** To make a part in your hair.

par·ty /pär′tē/ *n., pl.* **parties 1** A group of people gathered together to have fun. **2** A group of people who work to elect government leaders: the Democratic *party*.

paste /pāst/ *n.* A thick, white mixture used to stick things together.
—*v.* **pasted, pasting** To fasten with paste.

pat /pat/ *n.* A light touch.
—*v.* **patted, patting** To touch lightly: *Pat* the dog's head.

patch /pach/ *n., pl.* **patches** A piece of cloth used to cover a hole or weak spot: Mom put *patches* on the knees of my jeans.
—*v.* **1** To put back together: Dad *patched* together the broken bowl. **2** To put a patch on.

path /path/ *n.* A walk or trail.

pause /pôz/ *n.* A short stop.
—*v.* **paused, pausing** To make a pause: The speaker *paused* to drink some water.

paw /pô/ *n.* An animal's foot with nails or claws.

---

act, āte, câre, ärt;   egg, ēven;   if, īce;   on, ōver, ôr;   bŏŏk, fōōd;   up, tûrn;
ə = a in *ago*, e in *listen*, i in *giraffe*, o in *pilot*, u in *circus*;   yōō = u in *music*;   oil;   out;
chair;   sing;   shop;   thank;   that;   zh in *treasure*.

pay /pā/ *v.* **paid, paying** To give money for something: Dad *paid* for my bike.
—*n.* Money you get for doing a job: Mom gets her *pay* on Fridays.

peace /pēs/ *n.* **1** A condition without war. **2** Calmness: Let's have some *peace* and quiet.

peach /pēch/ *n., pl.* **peaches** A round fruit with a fuzzy, yellowish-pink skin and a large seed or pit.

pear /pâr/ *n.* A fruit with a green or yellowish-brown skin. A pear is round at the bottom and smaller near the stem.

pearl /pûrl/ *n.* A small, round white gem formed inside an oyster shell.

pen[1] /pen/ *n.* A writing tool that uses ink.

pen[2] /pen/ *n.* A small, fenced area for animals: Put the pigs in the *pen*.

pen·cil /pen'səl/ *n.* A writing tool that has a stick of graphite inside wood.

pen·ny /pen'ē/ *n., pl.* **pennies** A coin worth one cent.

peo·ple /pē'pəl/ *n.* Plural of *person*.

per·haps /pər·haps'/ *adv.* Maybe; possibly: *Perhaps* I'll go with you.

per·son /pûr'sən/ *n., pl.* **people** *or* **persons** A human being.

pet /pet/ *n.* A tame animal kept in or near the house.

—*v.* **petted, petting** To stroke or pat: Our dog loves to be *petted*.

pick /pik/ *v.* **1** To choose: *Pick* the color you want. **2** To take or pull off with your fingers: I *picked* an apple off the tree.

pick·le /pik'əl/ *n.* A cucumber soaked in salt water or vinegar.

pic·ture /pik'chər/ *n.* **1** A painting, drawing, or photograph. **2** A movie.

piece /pēs/ *n.* **1** A part of a whole thing. **2** An amount of something: a *piece* of cheese.

pil·low /pil'ō/ *n.* A bag filled with feathers or other soft material: I rested my head on the *pillow*.

pi·lot /pī'lət/ *n.* The person who steers or guides an airplane.

pin /pin/ *n.* **1** A thin, pointed piece of wire used to fasten things together: The *pins* are in the sewing box. **2** A piece of jewelry fastened to a pin.
—*v.* **pinned, pinning** To fasten with a pin.

pi·rate /pī'rit/ *n.* A person who attacks and robs ships at sea.

pitch·er[1] /pich'ər/ *n.* A bottle with a spout for pouring.

pitch·er[2] /pich'ər/ *n.* A baseball player who throws the ball for the batter to hit.

place /plās/ *n.* **1** A certain space or area: Put an X in the right *place*. **2** A city, town, or other area: Elmwood is a nice *place* to live.
—*v.* **placed, placing** To put: *Place* your hands on your head.

plan /plan/ *n.* **1** An idea for doing or making something: We have a *plan* for earning money. **2** (*pl.*) Arrangements: vacation *plans*.

planet

—v. planned, planning **1** To make a plan: *plan* a party. **2** To intend: We *plan* to visit Grandma.

plan·et /plan′it/ *n.* Any of the large bodies that move around the sun: Earth is a *planet*.

plant /plant/ *n.* A living thing that grows in soil or water.
—v. To put seeds or plants in the soil: We *planted* vegetables.

play·ground /plā′ground′/ *n.* An outside area for play.

plot /plot/ *n.* **1** A small piece of land: They will use that *plot* for a garden. **2** A secret plan. **3** The events in a story: That book has an exciting *plot*.
—v. plotted, plotting To plan something in secret.

pock·et /pok′it/ *n.* A small pouch sewn into clothing to hold money and other things.

point /point/ *n.* **1** The sharp end of something: The pencil has a sharp *point*. **2** A dot. **3** A unit in scoring: Our team has ten *points*.
—v. **1** To show or indicate: The teacher *pointed* out my mistakes. **2** To aim or direct.

po·lar /pō′lər/ *adj.* Having to do with the North or South Pole: *Polar* bears live in *polar* regions.

po·lice /pə·lēs′/ *n.* A group of people who work to keep order and make people obey the law.

po·lite /pə·līt′/ *adj.* Having good manners; not rude: It is *polite* to say "please."

po·ny /pō′nē/ *n., pl.* **ponies** A very small horse.

problem

pop /pop/ *n.* A sudden sharp noise: The balloon broke with a loud *pop*.
—v. popped, popping To make or cause a sudden noise.

porch /pôrch/ *n., pl.* **porches** A covered opening to a house or building: the front *porch*.

prac·tice /prak′tis/ *v.* **practiced, practicing** To do something over and over so you can do it better.
—n. Doing something over and over to learn it better: Playing the piano well takes lots of *practice*.

pre·pare /pri·pâr′/ *v.* **prepared, preparing** To get or make ready: Dad is *preparing* dinner.

pre·tend /pri·tend′/ *v.* To make believe: Let's *pretend* that we are on a spaceship.

pret·ty /prit′ē/ *adj.* **prettier, prettiest** Attractive; pleasant.

price /prīs/ *n.* The amount of money something costs.

prin·cess /prin′sis/ *n.* The daughter of a king or queen.

print /print/ *n.* **1** Letters and words marked on paper with ink: This book has large *print*. **2** A mark made by pressing: Our feet left *prints* in the snow.
—v. **1** To put letters and words on paper: That machine *prints* newspapers. **2** To write letters as in print: *Print* your name here.

prize /prīz/ *n.* Something won in a contest or game.

prob·lem /prob′ləm/ *n.* Something to be solved: Rabbits in the garden are a *problem*. There were ten *problems* on the test.

---

act, āte, câre, ärt;   egg, ēven;   if, īce;   on, ōver, ôr;   book, food;   up, tûrn;
ə = a in *ago*, e in *listen*, i in *giraffe*, o in *pilot*, u in *circus*;   yoo = u in *music*;   oil;   out;
chair; sing; shop; thank; that; zh in *treasure*.

promise

prom·ise /prom′is/ *n.* Words that show you will or you will not do something: I made a *promise*.
—*v.* **promised, promising** To give a promise.

prompt /prompt/ *adj.* Right on time: A *prompt* person is never late.

prop /prop/ *n.* Something that is used to hold something else up.
—*v.* **propped, propping** To hold something up with a prop: Paula *propped* up the plant with a stick.

proud /proud/ *adj.* Thinking well of: Sonia's parents are *proud* of her.

pud·ding /pŏŏd′ing/ *n.* A soft dessert made with milk and eggs.

pud·dle /pud′(ə)l/ *n.* A small pool of water: There were *puddles* in the street after the rain.

pull /pŏŏl/ *v.* **1** To draw something forward or toward yourself: The dogs *pulled* the sled. **2** To take or tear out: Dad is *pulling* weeds.

pump·kin /pump′kin *or* pung′kin/ *n.* A large, round orange fruit: Did you buy a Halloween *pumpkin*?

pup·py /pup′ē/ *n., pl.* **puppies** A very young dog.

pur·ple /pûr′pəl/ *n., adj.* A color that is a mixture of blue and red.

pur·pose /pûr′pəs/ *n.* A plan or aim: The *purpose* of this book is to teach spelling.

push /pŏŏsh/ *v.* To press against and move something: Polly *pushed* the chair under the table.
—*n.* The act of pushing: That *push* almost knocked Stan over.

puz·zle /puz′əl/ *n.* Something that is confusing or hard to do: Elsa likes to figure out *puzzles*.
—*v.* **puzzled, puzzling** To confuse: The secret message *puzzled* us.

reach

Q

quick /kwik/ *adj.* Done in a short time; fast: a *quick* shower.

quite /kwīt/ *adv.* **1** Completely: I am *quite* happy now. **2** Really: Alvin lives *quite* near me.

R

rab·bit /rab′it/ *n.* A small animal with long ears and a fluffy tail.

rac·coon /ra·kŏŏn′/ *n.* A small, grayish-brown animal with a bushy tail. A raccoon has black marks on its face like a mask.

race[1] /rās/ *n.* A contest of speed: Iris won the swimming *race*.
—*v.* **raced, racing** **1** To take part in a race. **2** To move fast: I *raced* to the door.

race[2] /rās/ *n.* A group of people who are similar in the way they look.

rail·road /rāl′rōd′/ *n.* The track that trains move on.

rai·sin /rā′zən/ *n.* A dried grape.

ranch /ranch/ *n., pl.* **ranches** A large farm where cattle or horses are raised.

rath·er /rath′ər/ *adv.* **1** More willingly: I'd *rather* go tomorrow. **2** Instead: You should ask Philip *rather* than me.

reach /rēch/ *v.* **1** To touch or get hold of: Can you *reach* the top

read

rough

shelf? **2** To arrive at: He *reached* home before dark.

read /rēd/ *v.* **read** /red/, **reading** **1** To get meaning from letters and words. **2** To say aloud something that is written: Please *read* us a story.

re·al·ly /rē′lē *or* rē′ə·lē/ *adv.* **1** In fact: Did that *really* happen? **2** Very; truly: Grandpa was *really* happy to see us.

rea·son /rē′zən/ *n.* **1** Explanation; excuse: What *reason* do you have for being late? **2** Cause: Being sleepy is a *reason* for going to bed.

re·cess /rē′ses/ *n., pl.* **recesses** A short break from work: Let's play hopscotch during *recess*.

re·cite /ri·sīt′/ *v.* **recited, reciting** To repeat something learned by heart: Len can *recite* lots of poems.

reed /rēd/ *n.* The hollow stem of certain kinds of grass.

re·pair /ri·pâr′/ *v.* To fix or mend. —*n. (often pl.)* The act of repairing: Our car needs *repairs*.

re·turn /ri·tûrn′/ *v.* **1** To come or go back. **2** To give back: Ned *returned* his library book.

ride /rīd/ *v.* **rode, ridden, riding** **1** To sit on something and make it move: to *ride* a bike. **2** To be carried along: to *ride* on a bus. —*n.* **1** A trip made when riding. **2** Something such as a merry-go-round that you ride for fun.

right /rīt/ *adj.* **1** Good and just: the *right* thing to do. **2** Correct: the *right* answer. **3** The opposite of *left*: your *right* hand.

—*adv.* **1** According to what is good and just: You did *right* to tell him. **2** Correctly: Ed spelled the word *right*. **3** To the right: Turn *right*. **4** Exactly: Put the books *right* here. **5** With no delay: Go *right* to bed.

rise /rīz/ *v.* **rose, risen, rising** **1** To stand or get up. **2** To move higher: The sun *rises* in the east.

riv·er /riv′ər/ *n.* A large stream of water.

rob·in /rob′in/ *n.* A bird with a reddish-orange breast.

rock¹ /rok/ *n.* A stone; something that is very hard.

rock² /rok/ *v.* To move back and forth: I *rocked* the baby to sleep.

rode /rōd/ *v.* Past tense of *ride*.

roll /rōl/ *v.* **1** To turn over and over: The stone *rolled* down the hill. **2** To move on wheels: The wagon *rolled* down the street. —*n.* **1** Something wrapped around itself: a *roll* of paper towels. **2** A small loaf of bread.

roof /rōof/ *n.* The top of a building.

room /rōom/ *n.* **1** Space: There's *room* for five people in the car. **2** An area within a house separated off by walls.

rose¹ /rōz/ *n.* A sweet-smelling flower that has thorns on its stem.

rose² /rōz/ *v.* Past tense of *rise*.

rough /ruf/ *adj.* **1** Not smooth; uneven: A cat's tongue feels *rough*. **2** Not gentle; rugged: Football can be a *rough* game. —*adv.* Not gently or carefully: Don't play *rough*.

---

act, āte, câre, ärt;   egg, ēven;   if, īce;   on, ōver, ôr;   bŏŏk, fōōd;   up, tûrn;
ə = **a** in *ago*, **e** in *listen*, **i** in *giraffe*, **o** in *pilot*, **u** in *circus*;   yōō = **u** in *music*;   oil;   out;
chair; **s**ing; **sh**op; **th**ank; **th**at; **zh** in *treasure*.

round

round /round/ *adj.* Having a shape like a circle or ball.
—*adv., prep.* **1** To move in a circle: The wheels turned *round*. **2** On all sides; around: The children sat *round* the teacher.
—*v.* To make round: We *rounded* the corners of the paper.

row¹ /rō/ *v.* To move a boat in water using oars.

row² /rō/ *n.* A line of things or people: We all stood in a *row*.

rub /rub/ *v.* **rubbed, rubbing** To press and move one thing against another: *Rub* the cat's back.

S

safe /sāf/ *adj.* **1** Free from danger or harm: Find a *safe* place to hide. **2** Not hurt: Sal was *safe*. **3** Careful: Mrs. Lopez is a *safe* driver.
—*n.* A metal box for keeping money and valuable things.

sail /sāl/ *n.* A piece of strong cloth that catches wind to move a boat.
—*v.* **1** To move on water or in air: The boat *sailed* into the bay. **2** To travel in a boat. **3** To run a sailboat: Brad is learning to *sail*.

sale /sāl/ *n.* **1** The act of selling: The clerk rang up the *sale*. **2** Selling things at low prices: The store is having a *sale* on boots.

search

same /sām/ *adj., pron.* Alike: Tammi and I bought the *same* shoes.

sand·wich /sand'wich *or* san'wich/ *n., pl.* **sandwiches** Two slices of bread with food between them.

save /sāv/ *v.* **saved, saving** **1** To take away from danger: The brave woman *saved* the child. **2** To keep money for a later time: Danny is *saving* for a bike. **3** To avoid waste: *Save* energy.

scent /sent/ *n.* A smell or odor: Flowers have a nice *scent*.

school /skōōl/ *n.* **1** A place where you learn. **2** The time when teaching is done: Let's play soccer after *school*.

scold /skōld/ *v.* To speak in an angry way: Dad *scolded* me for lying.

scratch /skrach/ *v.* **1** To mark with something sharp or rough: The cat *scratched* the table. **2** To scrape something that itches.
—*n., pl.* **scratches** A mark left by scratching.

scrub /skrub/ *v.* **scrubbed, scrubbing** To clean by rubbing very hard: *Scrub* the bathtub.

search /sûrch/ *v.* To look for or through: I'm *searching* for Nan.
—*n., pl.* **searches** The act of searching: We didn't find any shells during our *search*.

se·cret /sē′krit/ *n.* Something you must not tell anyone else.

—*adj.* Known only to a few people: a *secret* meeting place.

see /sē/ *v.* **saw, seen, seeing** **1** What you do with your eyes. **2** To understand: I *see* what you mean. **3** To find out: *See* what he's doing.

seed /sēd/ *n.* The tiny thing from which a plant or tree grows.

seen /sēn/ *v.* Past participle of *see.*

sel·dom /sel′dəm/ *adv.* Not very often: Darrell is *seldom* late.

sell /sel/ *v.* **sold, selling** To give something in return for money: Mr. Roberts *sold* his car for $2,000.

send /send/ *v.* **sent, sending** To cause to go: We *sent* the dog home.

sent /sent/ *v.* Past tense and past participle of *send:* I *sent* my uncle a birthday card.

sen·tence /sen′təns/ *n.* A group of words that makes sense by itself.

shack /shak/ *n.* A small building, usually one in bad condition.

shad·ow /shad′ō/ *n.* The dark image made when a person or thing blocks the light.

shake /shāk/ *v.* **shook, shaken, shaking** **1** To move something back and forth or up and down quickly: *Shake* your head. **2** To tremble: Gerry *shook* with fear.

shall /shal/ *v.* A word used with other verbs to talk about the future: What *shall* I do next?

sham·poo /sham·poo′/ *n.* A soap used to wash hair.

—*v.* To wash hair.

shape /shāp/ *n.* **1** The form of something: The *shape* of a ball is round. **2** The condition of someone or something: He is in good *shape.*

—*v.* **shaped, shaping** To give form to something: I *shaped* the clay into a ball.

she /shē/ *pron.* A word used in place of a girl's or woman's name.

shell /shel/ *n.* A hard outside covering: Turtles have *shells.*

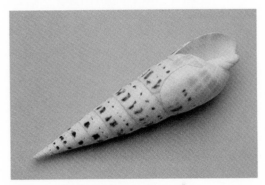

she's /shēz/ She is.

shine /shīn/ *n.* Brightness.

—*v.* **shined, shone, shining** **1** To give off light: The stars *shine* at night. **2** To polish or make bright: *Shine* your shoes.

shook /shook/ *v.* Past tense of *shake.*

shop /shop/ *v.* **shopped, shopping** To look for things and buy them.

—*n.* A place where things are sold.

short /shôrt/ *adj.* **1** Not long: a *short* time. **2** Not tall. **3** Not enough: You are a nickel *short.*

—*n., pl.* **shorts** Pants that come above the knees.

should /shood/ *v.* Past tense of *shall.* Ought to: You *should* go home.

---

act, āte, câre, ärt; egg, ēven; if, īce; on, ōver, ôr; book, food; up, tûrn; ə = a in *ago,* e in *listen,* i in *giraffe,* o in *pilot,* u in *circus;* yoo = u in *music;* oil; out; chair; sing; shop; thank; that; zh in *treasure.*

shoulder

shoul·der /shōl′dər/ *n.* The part of your body where your arm joins your body.

shout /shout/ *n.* A sudden, loud yell: They heard a *shout* for help.
—*v.* **1** To make a sudden, loud yell. **2** To talk loud.

shov·el /shuv′əl/ *n.* A tool used for digging.
—*v.* To use a shovel: Bonnie *shoveled* the snow.

shut /shut/ *v.* **shut, shutting 1** To close: *Shut* the door. **2** To turn off: *Shut* off the light.

shy /shī/ *adj.* Quiet; not at ease with strangers: The *shy* boy was afraid to ask for help.

sick /sik/ *adj.* **1** Having an illness. **2** Tired of something: Oliver is *sick* of playing the same games.

sight /sīt/ *n.* **1** The act of seeing: The *sight* of home made him smile. **2** The ability to see. **3** What is seen: The sunset is a beautiful *sight*. **4** View; area reached by sight: out of *sight*.

sil·ver /sil′vər/ *n.* A shiny, whitish-gray metal.
—*adj.* **1** Made of silver: a *silver* ring. **2** Having the color of silver.

since /sins/ *prep., adv., conj.* From then until now: Rita has been here *since* Monday. I have seen her every day *since*. We have had fun *since* she came.

sing /sing/ *v.* **sang, sung, singing** To make music with your voice.

sir /sûr/ *n.* A title of respect used for a man.

sis·ter /sis′tər/ *n.* A girl who has the same parents as you do.

sit /sit/ *v.* **sat, sitting** To take a seat: Maury *sat* on the floor.

smile

six /siks/ *n., adj.* The word for *6*.

skate /skāt/ *n.* A boot or shoe with a metal blade or four small wheels attached to the bottom.
—*v.* **skated, skating** To move on skates: We *skate* in the park.

skin /skin/ *n.* The outside covering of people, animals, fruits, and vegetables.
—*v.* **skinned, skinning** To scrape off skin: Larry *skinned* his knee.

skirt /skûrt/ *n.* A piece of clothing that hangs from the waist.

sky /skī/ *n., pl.* **skies** The air above Earth: Planes fly in the *sky*.

slope /slōp/ *v.* **sloped, sloping** To be at an angle: That roof *slopes* down almost to the ground.
—*n.* A hillside: The children went down the *slope* on their sleds.

slow /slō/ *adj.* Not fast: A turtle walks at a *slow* pace.
—*v.* To make or become slower: The car *slowed* down.
—*adv.* In a slow or careful way: Cars should go *slow* near schools.

small /smôl/ *adj.* Little; not large: A mouse is a *small* animal.

smash /smash/ *v.* **1** To break into pieces. **2** To crash into.

smell /smel/ *v.* **1** To get the scent of something through your nose: *Smell* the flowers. **2** To give off a scent: Garbage *smells* awful.
—*n.* **1** The sense used to recognize odors: Dogs have a good sense of *smell*. **2** An odor.

smile /smīl/ *v.* **smiled, smiling** To raise the corners of your mouth to show that you are happy: Peter *smiled* when he heard the joke.
—*n.* The act of smiling: Mrs. Gregor gave us a friendly *smile*.

smoke

smoke /smōk/ *n.* The dusty cloud that rises from anything burning.
—*v.* **smoked, smoking** To give off smoke: The fire *smoked.*

smooth /smo͞oth/ *adj.* Without bumps or lumps: New sidewalk is *smooth.*
—*v.* To make something smooth.

snail /snāl/ *n.* A slow-moving animal with a shell on its back.

snake /snāk/ *n.* A reptile with no legs that moves by crawling.

sneeze /snēz/ *v.* **sneezed, sneezing** To blow air out through your nose and mouth: Dust makes me *sneeze.*
—*n.* The act of sneezing: A *sneeze* can be a sign of a cold.

snow /snō/ *n.* Small, white flakes of frozen water.
—*v.* To fall as snow: Does it *snow* here in the winter?

soft /sôft/ *adj.* **1** Not hard. **2** Quiet; not loud: a *soft* voice.

sold /sōld/ *v.* Past tense and past participle of *sell.*

some·times /sum'tīmz'/ *adv.* Now and then: *Sometimes* we eat out.

son /sun/ *n.* What a boy or man is to his parents.

soon /so͞on/ *adv.* **1** In a little while.

split

2 Quickly: We'll be there as *soon* as we can.

sound /sound/ *n.* Anything that can be heard: Don't make a *sound!*
—*v.* **1** To make a sound: *Sound* the horn. **2** To seem: It *sounds* right to me.

soup /so͞op/ *n.* A liquid food made with water or milk, meat or fish, and vegetables.

south /south/ *n., adj., adv.* A direction; the opposite of north.

south·ern /suth'ərn/ *adj.* **1** Of or from the south. **2** Toward the south: the *southern* part of the state.

space /spās/ *n.* **1** The unlimited area that holds the universe: The rocket traveled through *space.* **2** A limited area: a parking *space.*

speak /spēk/ *v.* **spoke, spoken, speaking** **1** To say words; to talk. **2** To make a speech: Our teacher *spoke* at the meeting.

spell¹ /spel/ *v.* **1** To say or write the letters of a word. **2** To stand for sounds: C-a-r *spells* car.

spell² /spel/ *n.* Words that are supposed to have magic power: The wizard cast a *spell* on me.

spi·der /spī'dər/ *n.* An animal that has eight legs and spins a web.

spill /spil/ *v.* **1** To let fall or run out: Lenny *spilled* his milk. **2** To fall or flow: Water *spilled* on the floor.

split /split/ *v.* **split, splitting** **1** To cut lengthwise: We *split* logs for the fire. **2** To share: Let's *split* a cup of yogurt.

act, āte, câre, ärt; egg, ēven; if, īce; on, ōver, ôr; bo͝ok, fo͞od; up, tûrn; ə = a in *ago*, e in *listen*, i in *giraffe*, o in *pilot*, u in *circus;* yo͞o = u in *music;* oil; out; chair; sing; shop; thank; that; zh in *treasure.*

spoil

spoil /spoil/ *v.* **1** To ruin: The rain *spoiled* our day at the beach. **2** To become bad: Milk *spoils* if it is not kept cold. **3** To give someone everything he or she wants: Grandma *spoils* the baby.

spoke[1] /spōk/ *v.* Past tense of *speak*.

spoke[2] /spōk/ *n.* Part of a wheel.

spot /spot/ *n.* **1** A mark or stain: A leopard has *spots*. **2** A place: The park is my favorite *spot*.
—*v.* **spotted, spotting** To notice: Ann *spotted* a deer in the woods.

spray /sprā/ *n.* Water or other liquid in fine drops: Mom uses hair *spray*.
—*v.* To send out liquid in fine drops: *Spray* water on the plants.

spread /spred/ *v.* **spread, spreading** **1** To open completely: The bird *spread* its wings. **2** To smooth on: Zelda *spread* jelly on her toast.

spring /spring/ *v.* **sprang** *or* **sprung, springing** To leap suddenly: The dog *sprang* at me.
—*n.* **1** The season after winter. **2** A flow of water out of the ground.

spy /spī/ *n., pl.* **spies** A person who watches other people secretly.
—*v.* **spied, spying** **1** To keep watch secretly: They *spied* on our club meeting. **2** To catch sight of: I *spied* Morgan in the corner.

step

stair /stâr/ *n.* A step that goes from one level to another: Jack ran up the *stairs*.

stalk /stôk/ *n.* A stem of a plant.

stam·mer /stam′ər/ *v.* To pause while you are talking or repeat sounds without wanting to: When she is nervous, Hilary *stammers*.

stamp /stamp/ *n.* **1** A small piece of paper with glue on the back: Put a *stamp* on the letter. **2** A tool that makes a mark: a rubber *stamp*.
—*v.* **1** To put your foot down hard: The angry boy *stamped* his foot. **2** To mark with a stamp.

stand /stand/ *v.* **stood, standing** **1** To take or keep an upright position. **2** To put up with: I can't *stand* the smell of paint.

star /stär/ *n.* **1** A shining body that appears in the sky at night. **2** A shape with five or six points: ☆ ☆ **3** An actor or actress who plays the main part.
—*v.* **starred, starring** To play the main part.

stare /stâr/ *v.* **stared, staring** To look hard, often without blinking: The dog *stared* at the cat.
—*n.* A long, hard look.

start /stärt/ *v.* **1** To begin. **2** To turn on: Dad *started* the car.

state /stāt/ *n.* **1** The way something is: The dogs were in an excited *state*. **2** An area within a country: There are fifty *states* in the United States.

stay /stā/ *v.* To remain: You can *stay* for one more hour.

step /step/ *n.* **1** A movement made by lifting your foot and putting it down in another place. **2** A stair: We sat on the front *steps*.

—*v.* **stepped, stepping** **1** To move by taking steps: Please *step* over here. **2** To put your foot down on: Don't *step* on the bug.

stew /st(y)o͞o/ *n.* A thick soup made with meat and vegetables.

stick[1] /stik/ *n.* A thin piece of wood.

stick[2] /stik/ *v.* **stuck, sticking** **1** To prick with something sharp: I *stuck* myself with a needle. **2** To fasten with glue or paste. **3** To put: I *stuck* the book in my desk.

still /stil/ *adj.* Quiet: The house is *still* because everyone is asleep.
—*adv.* **1** Not moving: Sit *still* during dinner. **2** To this time: Aaron is *still* sick.

stir /stûr/ *v.* **stirred, stirring** To mix.

stone /stōn/ *n.* A small piece of rock.

stood /sto͝od/ *v.* Past tense and past participle of *stand*.

stop /stop/ *v.* **stopped, stopping** **1** To come or bring to a halt: The cars *stopped* at the light. **2** To leave off doing something: *Stop* talking to Sara. **3** To keep from doing something: I *stopped* Tamara from leaving.
—*n.* **1** The act of stopping: The plane makes a *stop* in Denver. **2** The place where something stops: a bus *stop*.

sto·ry[1] /stôr′ē/ *n., pl.* **stories** **1** An account that tells what happened. **2** A tale: Harvey loves adventure *stories*.

sto·ry[2] /stôr′ē/ *n, pl.* **stories** A floor in a building or house.

stove /stōv/ *n.* Something used for cooking or heating.

strange /strānj/ *adj.* **1** Odd; unusual: You look *strange* in that costume. **2** Not known: There is a *strange* dog in our yard.

strap /strap/ *n.* A thin piece of leather or cloth used to close or hold something.

straw /strô/ *n.* **1** Dried grass or stalks: We put *straw* in the stalls for the horses. **2** A thin tube used for sucking up a drink.

street /strēt/ *n.* A road.

strike /strīk/ *v.* **struck, striking** **1** To hit: The car *struck* a tree. **2** To tell time by sounding a bell: The clock *struck* one.
—*n.* In baseball, a swing that misses the ball.

string /string/ *n.* A thin rope or cord: Rudy tied the box with *string*.
—*v.* **strung, stringing** To put on a string: It's fun to *string* beads.

stroll /strōl/ *v.* To walk in a slow, easy way.
—*n.* A slow walk: Caroline took a *stroll* in the park.

strong /strông/ *adj.* **1** Powerful; not weak: It takes a *strong* person to lift a heavy box. **2** Not easily broken: This rope is *strong*.

struck /struk/ *v.* Past tense and past participle of *strike*.

stud·y /stud′ē/ *v.* **studied, studying** To work to learn something.

stuff /stuf/ *n.* Lots of different things: Put this *stuff* away.
—*v.* To pack in; to fill: Annie *stuffed* the bag with presents.

sud·den /sud′(ə)n/ *adj.* Quick; without warning: a *sudden* stop.

---

act, āte, câre, ärt;   egg, ēven;   if, īce;   on, ōver, ôr;   bo͝ok, fo͞od;   up, tûrn;
ə = a in *ago*, e in *listen*, i in *giraffe*, o in *pilot*, u in *circus*;   yo͞o = u in *music*;   oil;   out;
chair;   sing;   shop;   thank;   that;   zh in *treasure*.

sugar

sug·ar /shŏŏg'ər/ *n.* Something used to make food sweet.

suit /sōōt/ *n.* A set of clothes made up of a jacket and pants or a jacket and skirt.
—*v.* To be right for: Let's meet at a time that *suits* everyone.

sum·mer /sum'ər/ *n.* The season that comes after spring.

sun·ny /sun'ē/ *adj.* **sunnier, sunniest** Filled with sunshine; bright: It was a *sunny* afternoon.

sup·ply /sə·plī'/ *v.* **supplied, supplying** To give what is needed: Dad *supplied* the money.
—*n., pl.* **supplies** Things that are needed to do something: Notebooks and pencils are school *supplies*.

sup·pose /sə·pōz'/ *v.* **supposed, supposing** To think or believe: I *suppose* I can go.

sur·prise /sə(r)·prīz'/ *v.* **surprised, surprising** To do something unexpected: Jo's parents *surprised* her with a puppy.
—*n.* **1** The feeling caused by something unexpected: We all giggled with *surprise*. **2** Something not expected: Mom had a *surprise* for me when I got home.

swal·low /swol'ō/ *v.* To make food or drink go from your mouth into your stomach.

swap /swop/ *v.* **swapped, swapping** To trade or exchange: Clyde *swapped* his yo-yo for a whistle.

tape

swift /swift/ *adj.* Quick; fast: A deer is a *swift* animal.

swim /swim/ *v.* **swam, swimming** To use your arms and legs to move along in water.

T

ta·ble /tā'bəl/ *n.* **1** A piece of furniture that has a flat top and is held up by legs. **2** A list or chart: a *table* of numbers.

tag¹ /tag/ *n.* A small piece of paper or cloth: a price *tag*.
—*v.* **tagged, tagging** To follow closely: Her brother *tagged* along.

tag² /tag/ *n.* A game in which you chase and try to touch others.
—*v.* **tagged, tagging** To touch someone with your hand.

take /tāk/ *v.* **took, taken, taking** **1** To get hold of: *Take* my hand. **2** To use: I *take* the bus to school. **3** To bring: We *took* the clock to the repair shop. **4** To receive: Jon *took* the message.

talk /tôk/ *v.* To say words.
—*n.* A conversation: Dad and I had a *talk* about airplanes.

tall /tôl/ *adj.* The opposite of short: Are you *tall* enough to reach the top shelf?

tap /tap/ *v.* **tapped, tapping** To hit or touch lightly: Lonnie *tapped* his pencil on the desk.
—*n.* A light touch: Ethan felt a *tap* on his shoulder.

tape /tāp/ *n.* **1** A long, narrow strip with one sticky side. **2** A plastic strip used to record sounds.
—*v.* **taped, taping** **1** To put tape on something. **2** To record on tape: We *taped* the school concert.

| taste | thumb |

taste /tāst/ *v.* **tasted, tasting** **1** To get the flavor of something: The cook *tasted* the soup. **2** To have a flavor: The soup *tasted* salty.
—*n.* The flavor of something: Sugar has a sweet *taste*.

taught /tôt/ *v.* Past tense and past participle of *teach:* My mother *taught* me how to tie my shoes.

teach /tēch/ *v.* **taught, teaching** To help someone learn.

teach·er /tē′chər/ *n.* A person who helps others learn: Mr. Collins is my music *teacher*.

team /tēm/ *n.* **1** A group of people who work or play together: Our baseball *team* won the game. **2** Animals that do work together: The sled was pulled by a *team* of dogs.

test /test/ *n.* A way to find out how much someone has learned: I have a spelling *test* tomorrow.
—*v.* To give a test; to try out: I *tested* the watch to see if it worked.

that's /thats *or* thəts/ That is.

their /thâr/ *pron.* Belonging to them.

there /thâr/ *adv.* At or to that place: Let's go *there* for dinner.

there's /thârz/ There is.

they /thā/ *pron.* More than one person or thing: *They* are friends.

they're /thâr/ They are: *They're* going to the park on Saturday.

think /thingk/ *v.* **thought, thinking** **1** To use your mind to remember, to imagine, or to solve a problem: Greg is *thinking* of the answer to the question you asked him. **2** To believe: I *think* you are right.

thirst·y /thûrs′tē/ *adj.* Needing or wanting something to drink.

those /thōz/ *adj., pron.* Plural of *that;* the ones there: *Those* pencils are mine. These pencils are longer than *those*.

though /thō/ *conj.* In spite of the fact that: I like tennis, *though* I don't play it well.
—*adv.* However: Juan took the medicine. He didn't like it, *though*.

thought[1] /thôt/ *n.* An idea: Think happy *thoughts*.

thought[2] /thôt/ *v.* Past tense and past participle of *think*.

thou·sand /thou′zənd/ *adj., n.* The word for *1,000*.

three /thrē/ *n., adj.* The word for *3*.

throat /thrōt/ *n.* The back part of your mouth: a sore *throat*.

thumb /thum/ *n.* The short, thick finger on one side of your hand.

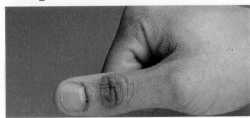

---

act, āte, câre, ärt;　　　egg, ēven;　　　if, īce;　　　on, ōver, ôr;　　　bŏŏk, fōōd;　　　up, tûrn;
ə = **a** in *ago*, **e** in *listen*, **i** in *giraffe*, **o** in *pilot*, **u** in *circus;*　　　yōō = **u** in *music;*　　oil;　　out;
chair; sing; shop; thank; that; zh in *treasure*.

tickle

tick·le /tik′əl/ *v.* **tickled, tickling** To touch someone in a way that makes the person laugh.

ti·ger /tī′gər/ *n.* A large animal of the cat family. A tiger has an orange body with black stripes.

tire¹ /tīr/ *n.* The rubber that goes around a wheel.

tire² /tīr/ *v.* **tired, tiring** To make or become weak or sleepy.

ti·tle /tīt′(ə)l/ *n.* The name of a book, a song, or something else: The *title* of the poem was "The Children's Hour."

to /tōō/ *prep.* **1** In the direction of: Les went *to* his room. **2** Until: We are at school from 9 *to* 3. **3** On: Tape the card *to* the box.

to·day /tə·dā′/ *n.* This day; the present time: *Today* is Friday.
—*adv.* On this day: Susan worked hard *today*.

to·geth·er /tə·geth′ər/ *adv.* **1** With each other: The children played *together*. **2** Into one: Neila knotted the ropes *together*.

ton·sil /ton′səl/ *n.* One of two oval-shaped tissues in the throat: Marcia had her *tonsils* taken out.

too /tōō/ *adv.* **1** Also. **2** More than enough: It is *too* cold to swim.

took /tŏŏk/ *v.* Past tense of *take*.

tooth /tōōth/ *n., pl.* **teeth** **1** One of the hard white parts in your mouth used to bite and chew.

town

2 Anything like a tooth: The comb has a broken *tooth*.

top¹ /top/ *n.* **1** The highest part: Touch the *top* of your head. **2** A cover or lid: a bottle *top*.
—*adj.* Highest; best: The book is on the *top* shelf. Vera is the *top* student in her class.
—*v.* **topped, topping** **1** To put on top: I *topped* my cereal with fruit. **2** To do or be better: Hank's score *topped* mine.

top² /top/ *n.* A toy that spins.

to·tal /tōt′(ə)l/ *n.* The whole amount: Add the numbers to find the *total*.
—*adj.* Complete: The story he told was a *total* lie.
—*v.* To add: You must *total* the numbers to find the answer.

touch /tuch/ *v.* **1** To put your hand or another part of your body on or against something: Don't *touch* the hot stove. **2** To be up against: The sofa *touches* the wall.

tough /tuf/ *adj.* **1** Strong; rugged. **2** Hard to chew. **3** Hard to do: It's *tough* to get up early.

tour·ist /tŏŏr′ist/ *n.* A person who travels and visits other places.

tow·el /toul *or* tou′əl/ *n.* Cloth or paper used to dry something.

tow·er /tou′ər/ *n.* A tall, narrow building or part of a building.

town /toun/ *n.* A small city.

trail		until

trail /trāl/ *n.* **1** A path. **2** The marks left by a person or animal.
—*v.* To follow behind: Jacob *trailed* everyone in the race.

train /trān/ *n.* A line of railroad cars.
—*v.* To teach: I *trained* my dog to roll over.

tramp /tramp/ *v.* **1** To walk with a heavy step: Mino *tramped* down the stairs. **2** To walk or wander: We *tramped* around in the woods.
—*n.* A person who wanders about and has no home.

trap /trap/ *n.* **1** A thing used to catch animals. **2** A trick to catch people off guard: The police set a *trap* for the robbers.
—*v.* **trapped, trapping** To catch and hold: Spider webs *trap* flies.

trav·el /trav'əl/ *v.* To go from one place to another: We *traveled* to Canada.

trick /trik/ *n.* **1** Something done to fool or cheat. **2** Something clever or skillful: magic *tricks*.
—*v.* To fool or cheat: They *tricked* Chet into thinking they had left.

trip /trip/ *n.* A journey or vacation.
—*v.* **tripped, tripping** To stumble or make fall: Andrea *tripped* over a rock. Hal stuck out his foot and *tripped* Anton.

trou·sers /trou'zərz/ *n., pl.* A pair of pants.

try /trī/ *v.* **tried, trying** **1** To make an effort. **2** To test: *Try* the soup to see if it needs salt.
—*n., pl.* **tries** A chance: You have three *tries* to hit the target.

tun·nel /tun'əl/ *n.* A narrow way under a river or a mountain.

turn /tûrn/ *v.* **1** To move around: He *turned* over in his sleep. **2** To change direction: We *turned* right at the corner. **3** To change: The leaves *turned* brown and then fell off the trees.
—*n.* A time or chance: It's your *turn* to do the dishes.

tur·tle /tûr'təl/ *n.* A slow-moving animal with a hard shell.

U

un·cle /ung'kəl/ *n.* **1** Your mother's or father's brother. **2** Your aunt's husband.

un·less /un·les'/ *conj.* Except if: We won't go *unless* you go too.

un·til /un·til'/ *prep., conj.* Up to the time of or when: I slept *until* nine o'clock. We played outside *until* it got dark.

---

act, āte, câre, ärt;   egg, ēven;   if, īce;   on, ōver, ôr;   bŏŏk, fōōd;   up, tûrn;
ə = **a** in *ago*, **e** in *listen*, **i** in *giraffe*, **o** in *pilot*, **u** in *circus*;   yōō = **u** in *music*;   oil;   out;
chair; sing; shop; thank; that; zh in *treasure*.

use

use /yōōz/ *v.* **used, using** **1** To put into action. **2** To finish: Alex *used* up all the paint.
—*n.* /yōōs/ **1** The act of using. **2** Reason: There is no *use* crying.
—**used to** **1** Familiar with: I'm *used to* getting up early. **2** Did in the past: Miro *used to* live here.

V

val·ley /val′ē/ *n.* A low area between mountains or hills.

vil·lage /vil′ij/ *n.* A small town.
voice /vois/ *n.* **1** The sound made through the mouth. **2** The ability to make sounds: Helene lost her *voice* and could not sing.
vote /vōt/ *n.* A formal choice.
—*v.* **voted, voting** To choose by a vote: Americans *vote* for a president every four years.

W

wag /wag/ *v.* **wagged, wagging** To move quickly: Dogs *wag* their tails.
—*n.* A wagging motion: The dog knocked over the lamp with a *wag* of its tail.
walk /wôk/ *v.* **1** To go on foot. **2** To make to walk: *Walk* the dog. **3** To walk with: *Walk* me home.
—*n.* **1** The act of walking: We took a *walk*. **2** The distance walked: It is a long *walk* home.

west

want /wont *or* wônt/ *v.* To wish for: Sheila *wants* a new pair of skates.
wash /wôsh *or* wäsh/ *v.* To clean with soap and water.
—*n.* Clothing washed at one time: Elyse helped me fold the *wash*.
was·n't /wuz′ənt *or* woz′ənt/ Was not.
wave /wāv/ *v.* **waved, waving** **1** To flutter: The flags *waved* in the wind. **2** To move your hand to greet or to signal.
—*n.* **1** A moving ridge of water. **2** The act of waving your hand.

we /wē/ *pron.* I and others: *We* all went camping.
weak /wēk/ *adj.* Not having strength: A cold makes me *weak*.
wea·ther /weth′ər/ *n.* The state of the air: The *weather* has been warm and sunny all week.
wel·come /wel′kəm/ *v.* **welcomed, welcoming** To greet gladly: Our dog *welcomed* us home.
—*n.* A friendly greeting: Aunt Katie gave me a warm *welcome*.
—*adj.* Freely allowed: You are *welcome* to borrow my book.
we'll /wēl/ **1** We will. **2** We shall.
we're /wir/ We are.
weren't /wûrnt *or* wûr′ənt/ Were not.
west /west/ *n., adj., adv.* A direction; where the sun goes down.

what's

what's /(h)wots *or* (h)wuts/ What is.

wheel /(h)wēl/ *n.* A round thing that turns in a circle to move a car, wagon, bicycle, or similar thing.

wheth·er /(h)weth'ər/ *conj.* If: Let me know *whether* you will come or not.

which /(h)wich/ *adj., pron.* What one or ones of several: *Which* book did you read? *Which* do you like best?

whirl /(h)wûrl/ *v.* To spin or make to spin around very fast: The skaters *whirled* around on the ice.

who /hoo/ *pron.* **1** What person: *Who* is ready? **2** That: Anyone *who* came got a prize.

who·ev·er /hoo·ev'ər/ *pron.* Any person who: *Whoever* comes will have a good time.

whole /hōl/ *adj.* Complete; all of: The *whole* class got A's.
—*n.* The entire thing.

who's /hooz/ **1** Who is: *Who's* ready for recess? **2** Who has: *Who's* got my notebook?

whose /hooz/ *pron.* Belonging to which person: *Whose* book is this?

why /(h)wī/ *adv.* For what reason.

wide /wīd/ *adj.* **wider, widest** **1** Far from side to side: The puddle was too *wide* to jump across. **2** Having a distance from side to side: My desk is one meter *wide*.
—*adv.* All the way: *wide* open.

wild /wīld/ *adj.* **1** Living or growing in nature; not tame: a *wild* animal. **2** Crazy or hard to believe: a *wild* story.

will /wil/ *v.* **would** A word used with other verbs to tell what is going to

wood

happen or what can be: Our school *will* be closed tomorrow. The car *will* hold five people.

win /win/ *v.* **won, winning** To do better than all others: Peter *won* the race.

wind¹ /wind/ *n.* **1** Moving air: The *wind* blew my hat off. **2** Breath: I had the *wind* knocked out of me.

wind² /wīnd/ *v.* **wound, winding** **1** To wrap around: Sharon *wound* the yarn into a ball. **2** To make a machine go by turning a part of it: I forgot to *wind* my watch. **3** To turn and twist: The road *winds* through the mountains.

win·dow /win'dō/ *n.* An opening in a wall that lets in air and light.

wipe /wīp/ *v.* **wiped, wiping** To clean or dry by rubbing: Please *wipe* your feet on the mat.

wise /wīz/ *adj.* **wiser, wisest** Having or showing good sense: My parents gave me *wise* advice.

wish /wish/ *n., pl.* **wishes** A hope or desire: My *wish* came true.
—*v.* **1** To hope for something: Mara *wished* for a pony. **2** To make a wish: Have you ever *wished* on a star?

with·out /with·out' *or* with·out'/ *prep.* With no: Mother cooks *without* salt.

won /wun/ *v.* Past tense and past participle of *win*.

won·der /wun'dər/ *v.* To want to know: I *wonder* where he is.

won't /wōnt/ Will not.

wood /wood/ *n.* What makes up the trunk and branches of a tree.

---

act, āte, câre, ärt; egg, ēven; if, īce; on, ōver, ôr; book, food; up, tûrn;
ə = a in *ago*, e in *listen*, i in *giraffe*, o in *pilot*, u in *circus*; yoo = u in *music*; oil; out;
chair; sing; shop; thank; that; zh in *treasure*.

wooden

wood·en /wŏŏd′(ə)n/ *adj.* Made of wood: *wooden* toys.

wool /wŏŏl/ *n.* **1** The hair of sheep: The sheep's *wool* is soft. **2** Yarn or cloth made from sheep's hair: My coat is made of *wool*.
—*adj.* Made of wool: a *wool* scarf.

word /wûrd/ *n.* **1** A sound or group of sounds that has meaning. **2** The letters that stand for a word.

work /wûrk/ *n.* **1** The effort needed to do something: Pulling weeds is hard *work*. **2** A job: My mother goes to *work* every morning.
—*v.* **1** To make an effort: Doug *works* hard. **2** To have a job: Dad *works* for the newspaper. **3** To run: That radio does not *work*.

world /wûrld/ *n.* **1** Earth: Blake would like to travel around the *world*. **2** Everything; the universe.

wor·ry /wûr′ē/ *v.* **worried, worrying** To be or make someone uneasy or upset: Mom will *worry* if I don't go straight home.
—*n., pl.* **worries** Something that makes you worry.

worst /wûrst/ *adj.* Most bad: I made the *worst* mistake of all.

worth /wûrth/ *prep.* **1** Good enough for: The zoo is a place *worth* visiting. **2** Having the same value: A quarter is *worth* twenty-five cents.
—*n.* Value: We got our money's *worth*.

would /wŏŏd/ *v.* Past tense of *will*. *Would* is often used to talk about wants and to ask polite questions: I *would* like another sandwich. *Would* you help me?

yourself

wrap /rap/ *v.* **wrapped, wrapping** To put a cover around something: Theo *wrapped* the present.

wreck /rek/ *v.* To destroy: The storm *wrecked* our tree house.
—*n.* Something that has been ruined: That car is a *wreck*.

wren /ren/ *n.* A small songbird.

wrist /rist/ *n.* The place where your hand joins your arm: Carol wears a watch on her *wrist*.

write /rīt/ *v.* **wrote, written, writing** **1** To make letters and words. **2** To be an author: Diane is *writing* a book.

writ·ten /rit′(ə)n/ *v.* Past participle of *write*.

wrote /rōt/ *v.* Past tense of *write*: George *wrote* a letter to his aunt.

Y

yard¹ /yärd/ *n.* The land around a building: the front *yard*.

yard² /yärd/ *n.* A measure equal to 3 feet or 36 inches.

your /yôr or yŏŏr/ *pron.* Belonging to you: Is this *your* pencil?

you're /yŏŏr or yôr/ You are: *You're* a very nice person.

your·self /yôr·self′ or yŏŏr·self′/ *pron., pl.* **yourselves** Your own self: Help *yourself* to an apple.

SPELLING THESAURUS

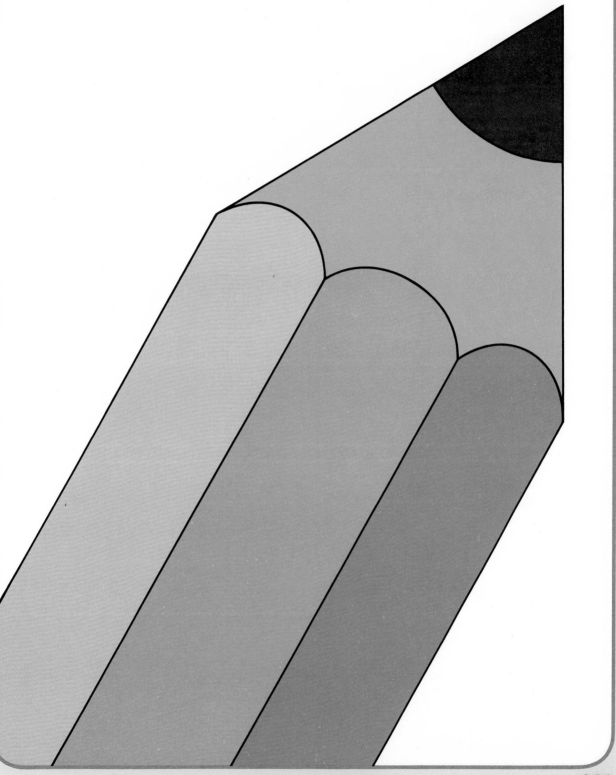

What Is a Thesaurus?

A **thesaurus** lists words and their synonyms. Like a dictionary, a thesaurus lists words in alphabetical order. Each of these words is called an **entry word.** A list of synonyms follows the entry word. Sometimes a thesaurus lists antonyms.

Look at the parts of this thesaurus entry for the word *move.*

The **entry word** is in red letters. It is followed by the part of speech and a definition. An **example sentence** shows how the word can be used.

> move *v.* To go from one place to another. Our family is going to move to another city.

Synonyms for the entry word are in *slanted* letters. Each synonym is followed by a definition and an example sentence.

> *climb* To go up. The men plan to *climb* to the top of the mountain.
> *crawl* To creep on hands and knees. The baby can *crawl* to her blanket.
> *dance* To move in time to music. The students will *dance* at the party.
> *hurry* To move or act quickly. *Hurry* to the exit when the fire alarm sounds.
> *race* To move fast. Some rabbits *race* into the bushes when they are afraid.
> *skate* To move on ice. The children *skate* on the frozen pond.
> *travel* To go from one place to another. I want to *travel* on a train.

If an **antonym** is given, it is printed in dark letters.

> ANTONYMS: stay, stop

How to Use Your Spelling Thesaurus

Suppose you are writing a story that tells about how a runner moves. You read over your work and see you have used the word *move* too many times. You decide to use the Spelling Thesaurus to find some synonyms. Here are the steps you should follow.

1. Look for the word in the Thesaurus Index. The Index lists every word in the Spelling Thesaurus.
2. Find the word in the Index. This is what you will find:
   move *v.*
   The red letters tell you that *move* is an entry word.

3. Turn to the correct page in the Spelling Thesaurus and read the entry carefully. Choose the synonym or synonyms that will make your writing clearer and stronger. Not every synonym will fit in the context of your story.

Remember: Not every synonym will have the meaning you want. Look at the sample entry for *move* on page 206. Which synonyms for *move* would fit best in the paragraph about a runner?

- Sometimes you may find a word listed in the Index like this:
   hurry move *v.*
   This means you will find the word *hurry* listed as a synonym under the entry word *move*. Since *hurry* is not printed in red, you can tell that it is not an entry word. If you look for *hurry* in the Spelling Thesaurus as an entry word under the letter *H,* you will not find it!

- You will also see some lines in the Index that look like this:
   stay move *v.*
   This means that *stay* is listed as an antonym under the entry word *move*.

A

adventurous brave *adj.*
afraid brave *adj.*
agree argue *v.*
aim point *v.*
alarm *n.*
amusing funny *adj.*
ancient old *adj.*
area space *n.*
argue *v.*
ask *v.*
attractive pretty *adj.*
avenue street *n.*
award prize *n.*

B

bang beat *v.*
bare empty *adj.*
bark sound *n.*
bathe swim *v.*
beam shine *v.*
beat *v.*
beautiful pretty *adj.*
begin stop *v.*
bell alarm *n.*
bend *v.*
bent crooked *adj.*
bit part *n.*
bite part *n.*
blank empty *adj.*
blast sound *n.*
blend *v.*
bold brave *adj.*
boulder rock *n.*
brave *adj.*
break *v.*
break repair *v.*
bright *adj.*
bright clever *adj.*
bright dark *adj.*

bright faint *adj.*
bright foggy *adj.*
brisk cold *adj.*
broad narrow *adj.*
brook river *n.*
build *v.*
build destroy *v.*
bumpy rough *adj.*
bundle package *n.*
burst break *v.*
bury cover *v.*
bury find *v.*

C

cabin house *n.*
call shout *v.*
calm still *adj.*
carry fall *v.*
carry hold *v.*
carton package *n.*
catch find *v.*
catch trap *v.*
chant sing *v.*
charming nice *adj.*
chat talk *v.*
cheer shout *v.*
cheerful happy *adj.*
chief main *adj.*
choppy rough *adj.*
clap sound *n.*
class group *n.*
clear *adj.*
clear easy *adj.*
clear foggy *adj.*
clever *adj.*
climb move *v.*
clip trim *v.*
cloudy clear *adj.*
club group *n.*
coach teacher *n.*
cold *adj.*

comfort hurt *v.*
construct build *v.*
cool cold *adj.*
corner trap *v.*
correct repair *v.*
correct right *adj.*
cover *v.*
cover find *v.*
crack break *v.*
crash sound *n.*
crawl move *v.*
creek river *n.*
crooked *adj.*
crop trim *v.*
crowd group *n.*
cruel mean *adj.*
crumb part *n.*
crush destroy *v.*
cry shout *v.*
curl bend *v.*
curve bend *v.*
curved crooked *adj.*
cut hurt *v.*

D

dance move *v.*
daring brave *adj.*
dark *adj.*
dark bright *adj.*
dazzling bright *adj.*
decide *v.*
delight *n.*
delightful happy *adj.*
desire want *v.*
destroy *v.*
destroy build *v.*
destroy repair *v.*
determine decide *v.*
different odd *adj.*
difficult easy *adj.*
dim bright *adj.*

dim dark *adj.*
dim faint *adj.*
direct point *v.*
dirt ground *n.*
disagree argue *v.*
discover find *v.*
discuss talk *v.*
drag pull *v.*
drag push *v.*
drawing picture *n.*
dream plan *v.*
drop fall *v.*
drop hold *v.*
dull bright *adj.*
dull dark *adj.*
dwell live *v.*

E

earth ground *n.*
easy *adj.*
empty *adj.*
end stop *v.*
enormous large *adj.*
even flat *adj.*
exact right *adj.*
explain argue *v.*

F

fable story *n.*
faint *adj.*
fair clear *adj.*
fall *v.*
fall hold *v.*
familiar odd *adj.*
fast quick *adj.*
fearless brave *adj.*
feathery soft *adj.*
filled empty *adj.*
find *v.*
find cover *v.*

fine clear *adj.*
fine narrow *adj.*
firm strong *adj.*
fix break *v.*
fix destroy *v.*
flash shine *v.*
flat *adj.*
float fly *v.*
float swim *v.*
fluffy light *adj.*
fluffy soft *adj.*
flutter fly *v.*
fly *v.*
foggy *adj.*
foggy clear *adj.*
forceful strong *adj.*
form make *v.*
friendly nice *adj.*
frightened brave *adj.*
frosty cold *adj.*
full empty *adj.*
funny *adj.*

G

gentle nice *adj.*
giant large *adj.*
give hold *v.*
glad happy *adj.*
glare shine *v.*
glitter shine *v.*
gloomy dark *adj.*
gloomy foggy *adj.*
glow shine *v.*
glowing bright *adj.*
grab fall *v.*
grab hold *v.*
grand large *adj.*
grasp hold *v.*
gray foggy *adj.*
great large *adj.*
groan sound *n.*

ground *n.*
group *n.*

H

halt stop *v.*
handsome pretty *adj.*
happiness delight *n.*
happy *adj.*
hard easy *adj.*
hard soft *adj.*
harm hurt *v.*
hazy foggy *adj.*
heal hurt *v.*
healthy ill *adj.*
heavy light *adj.*
hide cover *v.*
hide find *v.*
high *adj.*
highway street *n.*
hike walk *v.*
hold *v.*
hold fall *v.*
hollow empty *adj.*
home house *n.*
hooked crooked *adj.*
hop jump *v.*
hope desire *v.*
horn alarm *n.*
hot cold *adj.*
house *n.*
huge large *adj.*
hum sing *v.*
hunt see *v.*
hurried quick *adj.*
hurry move *v.*
hurt *v.*
hut house *n.*

I

idea plan *n.*

| alarm | | blend |

A

alarm *n.* Something that warns of danger. All homes should have a smoke alarm.

bell Something that makes a ringing sound when rung. The school *bell* rang three times at the fire drill.

horn Something that makes a warning sound. Mrs. Lopez honked her car *horn* at the dog in the street.

signal A sign used to send a message. A red light is a *signal* for a car to stop.

siren Something that gives out a loud whistle. A fire truck *siren* tells all cars to stop.

argue *v.* To give reasons for or against. No one on the team will argue with the umpire.

disagree To have a different opinion. Margaret thought the book was funny, but I had to *disagree.*

explain To give reasons for. Dr. Wall can *explain* why an ice pack will help your sore ankle.

ANTONYM: agree

ask *v.* To put a question to. Be sure to ask for help if you need it.

inquire To ask questions to get information. Max should *inquire* about a job at the library.

question To ask a question or questions. Did you *question* the teacher about the homework assignment?

B

beat *v.* To hit over and over. The drummer beat the drum.

bang To beat or hit hard and noisily. Babies love to *bang* on pots and pans.

knock To hit. *Knock* on the front door of my house when you arrive.

slap To hit or strike. Terry watched the waves *slap* the shore.

strike To hit. *Strike* the rug with a stick to shake out the dust.

tap To hit or touch lightly. If the cabin door is locked, *tap* on the window.

bend *v.* To make something curve. Steel is not easy to bend.

curl To become twisted. Amy likes to *curl* her hair.

curve To bend into or take the form of a curve. This road must *curve* around the lake.

twist To curve or bend. The tree branches *twist* around each other.

wind To run or move in a turning way. The runners had to *wind* through the trees.

ANTONYM: straighten

blend *v.* To mix. The artist must blend white paint with blue to make that color.

knead To mix dough using your hands; to push and squeeze. First *knead* the bread dough, and then form it into loaves.

brave

mix To stir in order to blend. *Mix* the muffin batter and pour it into a pan.

stir To mix. *Stir* the orange juice before you drink it.

brave *adj.* Not afraid. The brave scouts hiked to the top of the trail.

adventurous Liking adventure. The *adventurous* sailors began their trip across unknown seas.

bold Having courage. The astronaut Neil Armstrong was a *bold* man.

daring Brave and adventurous. The *daring* swimmer stepped into the river.

fearless Without fear. The *fearless* tigers search the jungle for food.

ANTONYMS: afraid, frightened, scared

break *v.* To crack into pieces. Glass will break easily.

burst To break apart suddenly. A balloon will *burst* when pricked with a pin.

crack To break or split apart. I like to *crack* peanuts open.

smash To break into pieces. Don't drop the plate, or it will *smash*.

split To cut or break lengthwise. We *split* logs for firewood.

tear To pull apart or rip. The thorns on the bushes can *tear* your shirt.

ANTONYMS: fix, mend, repair

bright *adj.* Giving off a lot of light. Do not look directly at the bright sun.

clear

dazzling Blinding because of too much light. There is a *dazzling* light at the top of the lighthouse.

glowing Shining because of great heat. The *glowing* coals mean the fire is not out.

shiny Bright. The *shiny* stones sparkled in the water.

See also **clever.**

ANTONYMS: dark, dim, dull

build *v.* To put pieces together. Beavers build their homes with mud and sticks.

construct To make by putting parts together. The members plan to *construct* a clubhouse.

form To make or shape. Lava will *form* a cone around a volcano's center.

make To put parts together or to shape. Alex can *make* a kite with paper, sticks, and string.

shape To form. The birds *shape* their nests like small bowls.

See also **make.**

ANTONYMS: destroy, ruin, wreck

C

clear *adj.* Not cloudy or foggy. Sue looked for the plane in the clear sky.

fair Clear and bright. The weather report said it will be a *fair* weekend.

fine Not cloudy; clear. We had *fine* weather for our picnic.

ANTONYMS: cloudy, foggy, stormy

clever

clever *adj.* Very smart. A fox is known as a clever animal.

bright Smart; clever. Emma had a *bright* idea.

intelligent Smart; bright. The *intelligent* dog found its way home.

smart Bright; clever. The *smart* dog knows many tricks.

ANTONYM: stupid

cold *adj.* Low in temperature. Winters in the northern United States are cold.

brisk Cool. The *brisk* fall air makes leaves turn many colors.

cool Slightly cold. Bears like to live in *cool* places.

frosty Cold enough to make frost. Victor handed me a *frosty* glass of juice.

ANTONYMS: hot, warm

cover *v.* To be over or put something over. Cover your head with a hat or scarf in cold weather.

bury To hide or cover up. Dogs often *bury* a favorite bone or toy.

hide To put out of sight. Mice *hide* from owls in the tall grass.

wrap To put a cover around something. Please *wrap* the food in foil to keep it fresh.

ANTONYMS: find, open, uncover

crooked *adj.* Not straight. The line you drew is crooked.

bent Made crooked by bending. The tree branches were *bent* toward the sun.

delight

curved Bent in the shape of a curve. The *curved* train track goes around the mountain.

hooked Curved like a hook. A lobster has a *hooked* claw.

ANTONYM: straight

D

dark *adj.* Without light. Bears sleep in dark caves.

dim Without enough light. In *dim* light, the black pupil of the eye grows larger to let light in.

dull Not bright or clear. Many fish live in *dull* water.

gloomy Dark and dismal. We play games inside on a *gloomy* day.

sunless Without sun or sunlight. The plant cannot live in that *sunless* corner.

ANTONYMS: bright, lighted

decide *v.* To make up your mind. You must decide which book to read first.

determine To decide firmly. The umpire must *determine* if the pitch was a strike.

judge To decide who wins. Our teacher will *judge* which is the most interesting science project.

settle To decide or determine. Let's *settle* on a safe place to build a campfire.

delight *n.* Great joy. The children squealed with delight as they played in the swimming pool.

happiness A feeling of joy. I could see the *happiness* on my friend's face when he smiled.

destroy	fall

joy Great happiness. *Joy* spread through the crowd as the firefighter carried a child from the burning house.

pleasure A feeling of enjoyment or delight. I take *pleasure* in doing any job well.

ANTONYMS: sadness, sorrow

destroy *v.* To break or ruin. Too little rain can destroy a farm crop.

crush To press or squeeze out of shape. Squirrels *crush* nuts with their teeth.

ruin To destroy. If you ride over a nail, you may *ruin* your tire.

wreck To destroy. An ocean wave could *wreck* the sand castle.

ANTONYMS: build, fix, mend, repair

E

easy *adj.* Not hard to do. This book is easy to read.

clear Easy to understand. This map shows a *clear* way to the airport.

plain Easy to understand. Always give *plain* turn signals from your bike.

simple Easy to understand or do. A dog can learn *simple* tricks.

smooth Without any difficulties or troubles. Scouts should mark a *smooth* trail to a camp.

ANTONYMS: difficult, hard

empty *adj.* Holding nothing. When the big van drove away, the house was empty.

bare Empty. The room is *bare*.

blank Not completed or filled out. Please write your name in the *blank* space.

hollow Empty on the inside. Chris carved the *hollow* pumpkin.

open Not filled. There is an *open* seat in the front of the train.

ANTONYMS: filled, full

F

faint *adj.* Dim. A faint beam of light showed through the dark forest.

dim Without enough light. Abraham Lincoln read by *dim* firelight.

light Not great. A *light* snow fell.

slight Small in amount. In the quiet house, Pat heard the *slight* creak of the door.

ANTONYMS: bright, sharp, strong

fall *v.* To drop down. A gymnast learns how to fall safely.

drop To fall or let fall. We watched the monkey *drop* the banana to the ground.

sink To go down. Soap with air in it does not *sink* in the bathtub.

spill To fall or flow. The rocks will soon *spill* into the river.

stumble To miss a step in walking or running. Don't *stumble* over the roller skates.

trip To stumble or make fall. Be careful not to *trip* on the stairs.

tumble To fall. A baby may *tumble* when she first tries to walk.

ANTONYMS: carry, grab, hold

find

find *v.* To come upon. Sandra cannot find her book.

catch I try to *catch* words that I spelled wrong.

discover To learn or find out. The sailors hope to *discover* a treasure chest.

locate To find. You can *locate* the pears in the fruit and vegetable section.

uncover To make known. Scientists may *uncover* new facts about the sun.

ANTONYMS: bury, cover, hide

flat *adj.* Smooth and straight. Baseball is played on a flat field.

even Flat and smooth. Greg built a table with an *even* top.

level Smooth or even. Skate on the *level* sidewalk.

smooth Without bumps or lumps. The worker used a board to make the cement *smooth*.

ANTONYMS: rough, uneven

fly *v.* To go through the air. Many airplanes fly higher than birds.

float To rest on water or in the air. The soap bubbles *float* above our heads.

flutter To move quickly. Look at the butterfly *flutter* through the garden.

soar To rise high into the air. The eagle will *soar* over the lake looking for food.

foggy *adj.* Full of fog or mist. Drivers often turn on their car lights on a foggy day.

ground

gloomy Dark; dismal. The ship sailed through the *gloomy* night.

gray Dark or dull. The *gray* skies warned us that a rainstorm was coming.

hazy Full of haze. Clouds filled the *hazy* sky.

misty Of or like mist. Ted couldn't see through the *misty* windows.

ANTONYMS: bright, clear

funny *adj.* Able to make you laugh. Do you think the comic strip is funny?

amusing Causing fun or laughter. Sid looked *amusing* dressed up as a pumpkin.

jolly Full of life and merriment. Everyone laughed at the *jolly* clown.

ANTONYMS: sad, serious

G

ground *n.* Earth's surface; soil. The spaceship is expected to touch ground in January.

dirt Loose earth. The groundhog leaves a mound of *dirt* at the door of its home.

earth The softer, loose part of the land. Flower bulbs must be covered with *earth*.

land The part of Earth that is not covered by water. Our world has more water than *land*.

soil The ground in which plants grow. The farmer pulled a carrot out of the *soil*.

group

group *n.* Several people or things together. A group of fish is called a school.

class A group of persons or things that have something in common. The music *class* is preparing for a concert.

club A group of people who do things together. The students formed a *club* to walk their dogs together.

crowd A large number of people gathered closely together. A *crowd* gathered around the visiting astronauts.

team A group of people who work or play together. The students formed *teams* to make science projects.

H

happy *adj.* Full of joy; glad. The story has a happy ending.

cheerful Happy; joyous. The *cheerful* clown rode around the tent in a wagon.

glad Pleased or happy. The child was *glad* to see his father.

delightful Giving joy or pleasure. Ruthie wrote a *delightful* story about her visit to her aunt's farm in the country.

merry Full of fun and laughter. The Glee Club sings *merry* songs on holidays.

ANTONYMS: sad, unhappy

high *adj.* Far up. Les could hardly reach the high walls with his paintbrush.

house

long Extending quite far between ends. The kite was tied to a *long* string.

tall More than usual height. There are sixty floors in the *tall* building.

towering Like a tower. The coast redwood is a *towering* tree.

ANTONYMS: low, short

hold *v.* To take and keep. That glass pitcher can hold two quarts of water.

carry To take from one place to another. Mother cats *carry* their kittens in their mouths.

grab To grasp suddenly and forcefully. It is not polite to *grab* something from someone else.

grasp To take hold of firmly. A newborn baby can *grasp* onto your finger.

keep To have and not give up. Please *keep* my fish while I am away.

ANTONYMS: drop, fall, give, spill, tumble

house *n.* A building in which people live. Would you like to study at my house after school?

cabin A small house made of wood. This *cabin* was built with logs.

home The place where a person or animal lives. That bird makes its *home* in our tree.

hut A small house or cabin. The children built a *hut* on the beach.

shack A small building. Tony uses the *shack* as a workshop.

hurt	light

hurt *v.* To feel or cause pain or harm. Angela hurt her ankle when she fell.

cut To make an opening in something with a sharp edge. James *cut* his finger on the broken glass.

harm To do damage to. The dentist said that too much sugar will *harm* my teeth.

wound To hurt by cutting through the skin. Did Matt *wound* his chin when he fell off his bike?

ANTONYMS: comfort, heal

I

ill *adj.* Feeling sick. Two third-grade students are ill today.

sick Having an illness. The *sick* child has the mumps.

unwell Not well; sick. Peter has felt *unwell* since he ate.

ANTONYMS: healthy, well

J

jump *v.* To leap up or over. Try to jump over the puddle.

hop To move the way a rabbit does. Some birds *hop* but others walk.

leap To jump or spring. How far can a frog *leap?*

spring To leap suddenly. Watch the basketball player *spring* for the ball.

L

lake *n.* A body of water. The boat is in the lake.

pond A body of still water smaller than a lake. Frogs and tadpoles live in the *pond.*

pool A small body of still water. The swan saw itself in the *pool* of water.

puddle A small pool of water. The car drove through the *puddle* and splashed me.

large *adj.* Big in size or amount. The United States is a large country.

enormous Unusually large or great. People travel across the ocean on *enormous* ships.

giant Very large. Some elephants have *giant* ears.

grand Large; important. The big house looks *grand.*

great Very large. A *great* hot-air balloon passed in the sky.

huge Very large. The Rocky Mountains are *huge.*

wide Far from side to side. Before trains, covered wagons carried people across the *wide* desert.

ANTONYMS: narrow, small, tiny

light *adj.* Not heavy. The mail carrier delivered a light package.

fluffy Light and frothy. *Fluffy* clouds dotted the sky.

weightless Having no weight. The *weightless* astronauts floated through the spaceship.

ANTONYM: heavy

live

live *v.* To make a home. Does Cleo still live nearby?

dwell To live in a home. Tuna fish *dwell* in warm ocean waters.

settle To come to make a home. When did you *settle* in this town?

stay To remain. Maria will *stay* with her aunt for the summer.

M

main *adj.* Most important. The main **reason you are here is to find a book to read.**

chief Most important. The *chief* job for worker ants is to build homes.

important Having much value. Fruits are an *important* part of a healthy diet.

leading Most important. Nebraska is a *leading* farm state.

principal First in rank or importance; chief; main. Judy plays the *principal* part in the school play.

mean *adj.* Cruel. The mean giant scared the little boy.

cruel Eager or willing to give pain to others. Who could ever be *cruel* to a puppy?

unkind Mean or cruel. Valerie does not say *unkind* words about her friends.

ANTONYMS: kind, nice

meet *v.* To come together. The Mississippi River and the Red River meet in Louisiana.

narrow

join To bring or come together. I'm going to *join* my friends at the movie theater.

unite To join together. The families *unite* once a year for a party.

ANTONYM: leave

move *v.* To go from one place to another. Our family is going to move to another city.

climb To go up. The men plan to *climb* to the top of the mountain.

crawl To creep on hands and knees. The baby can *crawl* to her blanket.

dance To move in time to music. The students will *dance* at the party.

hurry To move or act quickly. *Hurry* to the exit when the fire alarm sounds.

race To move fast. Some rabbits *race* into the bushes when they are afraid.

skate To move on ice. The children *skate* on the frozen pond.

travel To go from one place to another. I want to *travel* on a train.

ANTONYMS: stay, stop

N

narrow *adj.* Not wide. Cars must cross the narrow bridge one at a time.

fine Very thin. A *fine* line shows the state borders on a map.

thin Not fat or plump. The *thin* dog looks hungry.

neat	part

tight Fitting closely. The mouse ran into the *tight* space between the walls.
ANTONYMS: broad, wide

neat *adj.* Clean and tidy. I hang up my clothes to keep my room neat.
orderly Neat and tidy. Sean can always find his books because he has an *orderly* desk.
tidy Neat and orderly. My father hangs tools on the wall to keep the garage *tidy*.
trim Neat, smart, or tidy. The gardener clipped the row of *trim* bushes.
ANTONYMS: messy, untidy

nice *adj.* Pleasant; kind. I like going to my dentist because she is a very nice woman.
charming Pleasing or delightful. "Cinderella" is a *charming* fairy tale.
friendly Showing friendship or kindness. We moved to a *friendly* neighborhood.
gentle Kind and tender. A bunny is a *gentle* pet.
kind Gentle or friendly. A *kind* police officer helped me find my new school.
ANTONYMS: mean, rude

O

odd *adj.* Strange; unusual. Many people thought the artist painted odd pictures.

different Unusual. That's a *different* way of dancing.
strange Odd or unusual. An anteater is a *strange* animal that eats ants.
unusual Not usual or ordinary. These flowers have an *unusual* smell.
ANTONYMS: familiar, usual

old *adj.* Not new. The old house on the corner needs repair.
ancient Very old. Some *ancient* buildings were built more than 2000 years ago.
used That has belonged to another. The store sells new and *used* books.
worn Damaged by much use. My *worn* red sweater is still the most comfortable.
ANTONYMS: modern, new, recent

P

package *n.* The box that holds something. Jake opened a package of writing paper.
bundle A package. Lisa's books made a heavy *bundle*.
carton A cardboard container. Please pack the books in a *carton*.

part *n.* A piece of a whole. Which part of the book did you like best?
bit A small part. The girl threw a *bit* of bread to the duck.
bite A small bit of food. Rebecca tried a *bite* of the unusual fish.

| picture | prize |

crumb A tiny piece. My dog ate the *crumb* off the floor.

piece A part of a whole thing. There is one *piece* missing from the puzzle.

scrap A little piece. Please throw away the *scrap* of paper.

section A separate part. Paul reads the news *section* of the newspaper every day.

ANTONYM: whole

picture *n.* A painting, drawing, or photograph. The artist drew my picture

drawing A picture, design, or sketch made by drawing lines and by shading areas. A map is a *drawing* of an actual place in the world.

painting A picture made with paints. The artist did that famous *painting*.

photograph A picture made with a camera. John took my *photograph* with his camera.

sketch An unfinished drawing. The *sketch* seemed to show a man's sad face.

place *v.* To put. Please place the dishes on the table.

lay To put or place. The teacher said to *lay* the books on our desks.

put To set, lay, or place. Harry *put* his letters in the mailbox.

set To put in a certain place. Fred *set* the goldfish bowl on the table.

See also **space**.

ANTONYM: remove

plan *n.* An idea for doing or making something. Carlos had a plan to become a doctor.

dream Something you hope for. Terry's *dream* is to become president.

idea A thought. Henry has an *idea* for the school play.

plot The events of a story. The *plot* of that book is exciting.

thought An idea. Amy wrote down every *thought* in her journal.

point *v.* To show or indicate. The scientist asked us to point to the North Star.

aim To direct at something. You should *aim* the hose at the garden.

direct To tell or show the way. Can you *direct* me to the nurse's office?

pretty *adj.* Attractive; pleasant. Healthy, strong teeth will give you a pretty smile.

attractive Pleasing. Sweet-smelling flowers are *attractive* to bees.

beautiful Very lovely. It was a *beautiful* day at the beach.

handsome Looking pleasing. The *handsome* colt won a prize in the horse show.

lovely Beautiful. Martina has a *lovely* singing voice.

ANTONYMS: plain, ugly

prize *n.* Something won in a contest or game. Otis won first prize in the spelling contest.

pull

right

award A prize. He received an *award* for his painting.

medal An award for an outstanding act. Mary received a *medal* for her school work.

reward A gift given for working hard or doing something special. Cindy will give a *reward* to the person who finds her lost dog.

pull *v.* To draw something forward or toward yourself. Brian had to pull the wagon all the way home.

drag To haul or pull away. A beaver can *drag* small logs to a stream to build a dam.

tow To pull or drag by a rope or chain. A truck will *tow* the car to the garage.

tug To pull at with effort. The cat likes to *tug* at the ball of string.

ANTONYMS: poke, press, push, shove

push *v.* To press against and move something. Please push me on the swing.

poke To push in, out, or through. That bottle might *poke* a hole in the bag.

press To act upon by weight or pressure. Please *press* the first-floor button on the elevator.

shove To move by pushing from behind. We were not able to *shove* the wagon up the hill.

ANTONYMS: drag, pull, tow, tug

Q

quick *adj.* Done in a short time; fast. A shortcut is a quick way home.

fast Moving or acting with speed. Andrew passed everyone on the street. He is a *fast* walker.

hurried Made, done, or acting in haste. A *hurried* job is likely to be poorly done.

speedy Swift; fast; rapid. I would like a *speedy* answer.

swift Moving very fast. The *swift* horses galloped across the field.

ANTONYMS: plodding, slow

R

repair *v.* To fix or mend. She tried to repair the broken watch.

correct To change to make right. The glasses will *correct* your eyesight.

mend To repair. Tom will *mend* the tear in the tent.

patch To put a patch on. Please *patch* the hole in the roof before it rains.

ANTONYMS: break, destroy, ruin, wreck

right *adj.* Correct. Who can give me the right answer?

correct Exact; right. What is your *correct* shoe size?

exact Completely right. I had the *exact* change for the phone.

proper Correct. Set the oven for the *proper* temperature.

ANTONYMS: incorrect, wrong

221

river

river *n.* A large stream of water. The Mississippi is the longest river in the United States.

brook A natural stream. Rosie liked to wade across the *brook*.

creek A stream. We caught some fish in the *creek*.

stream A small body of flowing water. Many goldfish live in the *stream*.

rock *n.* A stone; something that is very hard. The pillow felt as hard as a rock.

boulder A large rock or stone. The sea lion sat on a *boulder* near the edge of the ocean.

pebble A small, smooth stone. Joan filled the bottom of the fishbowl one *pebble* at a time.

stone A small piece of rock. The boy skimmed a *stone* over the water.

See also **shake.**

rough *adj.* Not smooth. Sandpaper can smooth the rough edges of cut wood.

bumpy Having or making bumps. The car bounced along the *bumpy* road.

choppy Full of short, rough waves. The *choppy* sea was not safe for small boats.

lumpy Covered with or having lumps. I couldn't sleep on the *lumpy* bed.

ANTONYM: smooth

shake

S

see *v.* What you do with your eyes. Your eyes have many parts that help you see.

hunt To look carefully. Birds *hunt* for worms in the early morning.

look To turn the eyes to see or try to see something. Will you help me *look* for my book?

notice To see; to pay attention to. Did you *notice* Adam's new jacket?

search To look for. Scientists *search* the sky for new stars.

spot To notice. The park ranger can *spot* a rattlesnake from many feet away.

stare To look hard, often without blinking. Mickey will *stare* at the sky until he sees a shooting star.

shake *v.* To move something back and forth or up and down quickly. A wet dog will shake the water off its fur.

jar To cause to tremble or shake. Strong thunder can *jar* the windows in our house.

rattle To make or cause a series of quick, sharp noises. The monkey likes to *rattle* coins in a can.

rock To move back and forth. I tried to *rock* the baby to sleep.

shiver To shake. Jane started to *shiver* when she went out into the cold.

tremble To shake. I started to *tremble* when I saw Max in his monster mask.

shine

shine *v.* **To give off** light. Does the sun shine **all the time?**

beam **To send out rays of light. The light from the lighthouse will *beam* across the sea.**

flash **To give a quick, bright light. The car's headlights *flash* on and off.**

glare **To give off a bright, blinding light. The baseball player wears a cap to keep the *glare* out of his eyes.**

glitter **To sparkle brightly. Raindrops *glitter* in the sunlight.**

glow **To shine because of great heat. We watched the fire *glow* in the darkness.**

sparkle **To give off sparks or flashes. A diamond will *sparkle* when light shines on it.**

shout *v.* **To make a sudden loud yell. We heard the umpire** shout **"Safe!"**

call **To speak in a loud voice. Please *call* your brother to dinner.**

cheer **To urge or encourage. The fans *cheer* for their favorite team.**

cry **To call out. Some animals *cry* at the full moon.**

scream **To make a long, loud cry. Did the baby *scream* when his toy fell to the floor?**

squeal **To give a long, high cry. Pigs *squeal* in their pens.**

yell **To shout; scream; roar. The children *yell* on the playground.**

ANTONYM: whisper

sound

sing *v.* **To make music with your voice. Jordan likes to** sing **in the shower.**

chant **To sing to a chant. The Glee Club learned to *chant* the poem.**

hum **To sing with closed lips. Many people *hum* while they work.**

whistle **To make a sound by forcing breath through the teeth and lips. Andrea can *whistle* a tune.**

soft *adj.* **Not hard. A pillow is** soft.

feathery **Light as a feather. The sky was filled with *feathery* clouds.**

fluffy **Light and frothy. The whipped cream was *fluffy*.**

ANTONYM: hard

sound *n.* **Anything that can be heard. We heard the** sound **of firecrackers on July Fourth.**

bark **The sound a dog makes. The dog's *bark* is very loud.**

blast **A loud noise. The foghorn sounded a *blast* over the dark ocean.**

clap **A loud noise. Did you hear that *clap* of thunder?**

crash **A loud noise. The trash can fell over with a *crash*.**

groan **A sound of pain. With a *groan*, Manuel rubbed his sore arm.**

noise **Sound; especially loud sound. The three cooks made a lot of *noise* banging the pots.**

pop **A sudden sharp noise. The balloon made a loud *pop* when it broke.**

space

space *n.* A limited area. Patty made a space on her shelf for her award.

area An open space. Many parks have an *area* for camping.

place A city, town, or other area. The people chose a *place* to build a new library.

room Space. The closet has *room* for more boxes.

still *adj.* Quiet. The classroom was still during the test.

calm Quiet; peaceful; still. The sea was *calm* after the storm.

peaceful Quiet; calm. The sky looked *peaceful* after the storm ended.

quiet Having or making no noise. The baby became *quiet* and fell asleep.

ANTONYMS: loud, noisy

stop *v.* To come or bring to a halt. Our teacher told us to stop writing and put our pencils down.

end To come or bring to an end. The show will *end* with our song.

halt To stop. We should *halt* to let our friends catch up.

pause To make a short stop. Paul had to *pause* to catch his breath.

quit To stop. Please *quit* singing that same song over and over.

ANTONYMS: begin, start

strong

story *n.* A tale. I would like to read a story about people or animals.

fable A short story teaching a lesson. In one *fable,* a fox tricks a crow into giving him some cheese.

legend A story handed down from earlier times. People long ago had more than one *legend* about how things in nature happened.

tale A story. Melissa tells a funny *tale* about how she found her turtle.

street *n.* A road. Our street does not have a sidewalk.

avenue A broad street. Ben took a walk down the *avenue.*

highway A main road. Trucks use that *highway* to bring goods to the city.

lane A narrow path or road. My grandfather's house is the last on the *lane.*

path A road or trail. Follow the *path* to the clubhouse.

road An open way which vehicles, persons, or animals travel to get from one place to another. Cars and trucks blocked the *road* into town.

track A path. The many footprints showed the *track* was still used.

trail A path. Karen followed the narrow *trail* along the lake.

strong *adj.* Powerful; not weak. The strong man lifted the bricks.

firm Strong; steady. Americans have *firm* ideas about freedom.

swim

forceful Strong. Washington
was a *forceful* leader.
mighty Very strong. A *mighty*
tractor pushed away the hills of
mud.
sturdy Strong. The *sturdy* house
did not shake in the wind.
tough Strong; rugged. Stuart wore
a *tough* pair of shoes on his
long hike.
ANTONYM: weak

swim *v.* To use your arms and legs
to move along in water. Carol
is learning to swim.
bathe To go into a body of water.
In summer, we *bathe* in the
river.
float To rest on top of water. The
raft can *float* on the lake.
paddle To move your hands and
feet in water. Most dogs will
paddle across water.

T

talk *v.* To say words. Myra will
talk to the class about her idea.
chat To talk in a relaxed way. My
grandmother likes to *chat* with
her friends.
discuss To talk over. The teacher
said tomorrow we will *discuss*
the meaning of the poem.
speak To say words. May I *speak* to
Nora, please?
teacher *n.* A person who helps
others learn. I am learning to
play the violin from a music
teacher

trim

coach A teacher or trainer, as for
pupils, athletes, or actors. The
coach taught the new player
how to throw the football.
trainer A person who trains. The
horse *trainer* pulled on the
reins, and the horse stopped.

trap *v.* To catch and hold. The
spider tries to trap a fly in
its web.
catch To take in a trap or by
means of a hook. Dad and I
didn't *catch* anything on our
fishing trip.
corner To force into a corner; to
trap. The riders want to *corner*
the wild horses in a valley.
snare To trap or catch with a rope
loop that jerks tight. The
farmers hope to *snare* the fox
tonight.

trim *v.* To cut to make neat. The
mother liked to trim the girl's
hair.
clip To trim. The vet came to *clip*
the poodle's hair for the
summer.
crop To trim. The man wants to
crop the dead limbs from the
trees.
shear To cut hair or fleece. We
shear the sheep for their wool,
which is used in clothing
and rugs.
See also **neat.**

turn

turn *v.* To move around. The wheels turn when a car moves.

spin To turn or whirl about. The child's pinwheel did not *spin* because there wasn't a breeze.

swirl To move or cause to move with a whirling or twisting motion. The fallen leaves *swirl* in the wind.

twirl To turn around quickly. Watch Lynn *twirl* her baton in the air.

whirl To spin or make spin around very fast. The dancers *whirl* across the floor.

wind To turn and twist. The ivy will soon *wind* up the tree trunk.

W

walk *v.* To go on foot. A baby learns to walk at about one year old.

hike To take a long walk. We should *hike* back to camp before we are too tired to walk.

want

march To walk with even steps. The high school band will *march* in the parade.

plod To walk heavily or with great effort. Martin must *plod* up a snowy hill to his home.

step To move by taking steps. Please *step* to the end of the line.

stroll To walk in a slow, easy way. Many people *stroll* in the park on Sunday.

tramp To walk with a heavy step. After the storm, we had to *tramp* through the mud.

want *v.* To wish for. Barney may want eggs for breakfast.

desire To want very badly. They all *desire* to become teachers.

hope To want and expect. I *hope* the weather will be warm tomorrow.

long To want greatly. I *long* to have a puppy.

wish To hope for something. We *wish* we were home now.

WRITER'S GUIDE

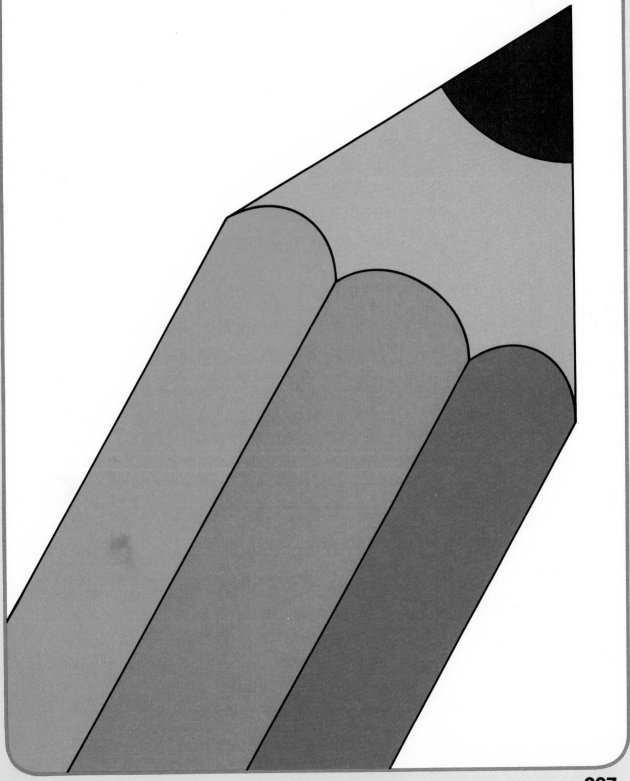

SPELLING RULES

Unit 1: Short Vowel Sounds

The short vowel sounds are usually spelled with one vowel letter.

- /a/ is spelled with **a**, as in <u>happy</u>.
- /e/ is spelled with **e**, as in <u>pen</u>.
- /i/ is spelled with **i**, as in <u>hid</u>.
- /o/ is spelled with **o**, as in <u>dot</u>.
- /u/ is spelled with **u**, as in <u>sunny</u>.

Unit 2: Double Letters

Some words end with a consonant sound that is spelled with double consonant letters after a short vowel sound.

- /l/ is spelled with **ll**, as in <u>drill</u>.
- /f/ is spelled with **ff**, as in <u>cliff</u>.
- /s/ is spelled with **ss**, as in <u>less</u>.
- /d/ is spelled with **dd**, as in <u>odd</u>.
- ☐ Some words do not have a short vowel sound but end with two consonant letters, as in <u>roll</u>.

Unit 3: Verbs

- If a verb ends with one vowel letter and one consonant letter, double the last letter before adding <u>ed</u>.
  chop—chopped   trip—tripped
- If a verb ends with one vowel letter and one consonant letter, double the last letter before adding <u>ing</u>.
  step—stepping   tap—tapping

Unit 4: **Consonant Clusters**

A **consonant cluster** is two or three consonant letters that are written together. All of the consonant sounds are heard.

- **cl** as in <u>cl</u>ose
- **dr** as in <u>dr</u>ive
- **fl** as in <u>fl</u>oor
- **pr** as in <u>pr</u>int
- **sn** as in <u>sn</u>ow

- **st** as in <u>st</u>ar
- **tr** as in <u>tr</u>ick
- **str** as in <u>str</u>ing
- **spr** as in <u>spr</u>ay

Unit 5: **More Consonant Clusters**

Consonant clusters often come at the end of words.

- **ct** as in <u>act</u>
- **st** as in <u>west</u>
- **ft** as in <u>lift</u>
- **nd** as in <u>grand</u>

- **ld** as in <u>child</u>
- **lk** as in <u>milk</u>
- **mp** as in <u>bump</u>

Unit 7: **More Letters Than Sounds**

Some consonant sounds are spelled with more than one letter.

- The first sound in <u>that</u> is spelled **th,** as in <u>weather</u>.
- The first sound in <u>child</u> is spelled **ch** or **tch,** as in <u>which</u> and <u>kitchen</u>.
- The first sound in <u>should</u> is spelled **sh,** as in <u>crash</u>.
- The last sound in <u>sing</u> is spelled **ng** or **n,** as in <u>strong</u> and <u>angry</u>.

Unit 8: **Plurals**

A word that names just one thing is **singular.** A word that names more than one thing is **plural.** Here are two ways to make a word plural.

- Add <u>s</u> to most words.
  robin—robins
- Add <u>es</u> to the words that end with <u>s</u>, <u>ss</u>, <u>sh</u>, or <u>ch</u>.
  circus—circuses
  guess—guesses
  bush—bushes
  ranch—ranches

Unit 9: **The Sound /j/**

Here are four ways to spell /j/.

- with **j** at the beginning of a word, as in <u>juice</u>
- with **g** before **e** or **i,** as in <u>gentle</u> and <u>giraffe</u>
- with **ge** at the end of a word, as in <u>cage</u>
- with **dge** after a short vowel sound, as in <u>bridge</u>

Unit 10: **The Sound /k/**

Here are three ways to spell /k/.

- with **c** or **k** at the beginning of a word, as in <u>cane</u> or <u>key</u>
- with **k** after a long vowel sound, as in <u>speak</u>
- with **ck** after a short vowel sound, as in <u>neck</u>

Unit 11: **The Sound /s/**

Here are four ways to spell /s/.

- with **s,** as in <u>s</u>uit
- with **c,** as in pen<u>c</u>il
- with **ce** at the end of a word, as in on<u>ce</u>
- with **ss,** as in mi<u>ss</u>

Unit 13: **Verbs That End with e**

- If a verb ends with <u>e</u>, drop the <u>e</u> before adding <u>ed</u>.
      skate—skated   hike—hiked
- If a verb ends with e, drop the e before adding <u>ing</u>.
      invite—inviting   live—living

Unit 14: **The Vowel Sound /ā/**

Here are five ways to spell /ā/.

- with **a**-consonant-**e,** as in br<u>a</u>v<u>e</u>
- with **ai,** as in p<u>ai</u>d
- with **ay** at the end of a word, as in cl<u>ay</u>
- □ with **ey** at the end of a word, as in ob<u>ey</u>
- □ with **eigh,** as in <u>eigh</u>t

Unit 15: **The Vowel Sound /ē/**

Here are four ways to spell /ē/.

- with **ea,** as in t<u>ea</u>m
- with **ee,** as in ch<u>ee</u>k
- with **e,** as in <u>e</u>ven
- with **y** at the end of a word with more than one syllable, as in reall<u>y</u>

Unit 16: **The Vowel Sound /ī/**

Here are five ways to spell /ī/.

- with **i**-consonant-**e,** as in <u>bite</u>
- with **igh,** as in <u>fight</u>
- with **i,** as in <u>lion</u>
- with **y** at the end of a syllable or word, as in <u>myself</u>
- □ with **uy,** as in <u>buy</u>

Unit 17: **The Vowel Sound /ō/**

Here are four ways to spell /ō/.

- with **o**-consonant-**e,** as in <u>rose</u>
- with **oa,** as in <u>load</u>
- with **o,** as in <u>both</u>
- with **ow,** as in <u>window</u>

Unit 19: **Compound Words**

- A **compound word** is formed by putting two smaller words together.

    bed + room = bedroom   foot + ball = football

Unit 20: **Contractions**

- A **contraction** is a short way of writing two words together. Some of the letters are left out. An **apostrophe** (') takes their place.

    I <u>do</u> <u>not</u> have to work today.
    I <u>don't</u> have to work today.

    I hope <u>we</u> <u>will</u> be invited.
    I hope <u>we'll</u> be invited.

Unit 21: **The Sounds /ô/ and /ôr/**

Here are three ways to spell /ô/.

- with **a,** as in <u>walk</u>
- with **aw,** as in <u>jaw</u>
- with **au,** as in <u>cause</u>

Here are two ways to spell /ôr/.

- with **or,** as in <u>short</u>
- with **our,** as in <u>course</u> and <u>four</u>

Unit 22: **The Sounds /ûr/**

Here are four ways to spell /ûr/.

- with **ir,** as in <u>skirt</u>
- with **ur,** as in <u>burn</u>
- with **ear,** as in <u>earth</u>
- with **or,** as in <u>world</u>

Unit 23: **The Sounds /är/ and /âr/**

Here are two ways to spell /är/.

- with **ar,** as in <u>barn</u>
- □ with **ear,** as in <u>heart</u>

Here are two ways to spell /âr/.

- with **air,** as in <u>fair</u>
- with **ear,** as in <u>pear</u>

Unit 25: **More Plurals**

A **plural noun** names more than one thing.

- To form the plural of most nouns, add s.
  grade—grades   wheel—wheels
- To form the plural of nouns ending with a consonant and y, change the y to i and add es.
  fairy—fairies   guppy—guppies

Unit 26: **"Silent" Letters**

- When the sound of a letter is not heard, we call it a "silent" letter.
  knock   lamb   wrote

Unit 27: **Words That End with y**

- To form the plural of nouns ending with a consonant and y, change the y to i and add es.
  library—libraries
- If a verb ends with a consonant and y, change the y to i before adding ed.
  carry—carried
- If a verb ends with a consonant and y, just add ing.
  cry—crying

Unit 28: **The Sounds /əl/ and /ər/**

Here are two ways to spell /əl/.

- with **le,** as in bottle
- with **el,** as in nickel

Here are two ways to spell /ər/.

- with **er,** as in <u>summer</u>
- with **ar,** as in <u>sugar</u>

Unit 29: **Homophones**

- Homophones are words that sound alike but are spelled differently and have different meanings.

  break   brake

Unit 31: **The Sounds /o͝o/ and /o͞o/**

Here is one way to spell /o͝o/.

- with **oo,** as in <u>shook</u>

Here are four ways to spell /o͞o/.

- with **oo,** as in <u>balloon</u>
- with **ou,** as in <u>soup</u>
- with **ew,** as in <u>grew</u>
- ☐ with **o,** as in <u>lose</u>

Unit 32: **The Sounds /ou/ and /oi/**

Here are two ways to spell /ou/.

- with **ou,** as in <u>cloud</u>
- with **ow,** as in <u>crown</u>

Here are two ways to spell /oi/.

- with **oi,** as in <u>point</u>
- with **oy,** as at the end of <u>joy</u>

Unit 33: **Words with <u>ou</u> and <u>ough</u>**

The letters <u>ou</u> stand for three different sounds.

- The letters **ou** sound like the **u** in <u>much</u>, as in <u>touch</u>.
- The letters **ou** sound like the **ou** in <u>round</u>.
- With **gh, ou** sounds like the end of <u>paw</u>, as in <u>bought</u>.

The letters <u>ough</u> stand for two sounds.

- The letters **ough** rhyme with **oh,** like the **ough** in <u>though</u>.
- The letters **ough** rhyme with **uf,** like the **ough** in <u>rough</u>.

Unit 34: **Syllable Patterns**

- When a word has the same two consonant letters in the middle, divide the word into syllables between the two consonant letters that are the same.

    cat·tle   din·ner   les·son
- Some words have two different consonant letters in the middle. Divide these words into syllables between the two consonant letters.

    for·got   per·haps   won·der

Unit 35: **Another Syllable Pattern**

- When a word has one consonant letter between the two vowel sounds, divide the word into syllables before the consonant.

    a·like   be·long   pa·per

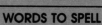
TROUBLESOME WORDS TO SPELL

again	friend	mother	Thanksgiving
always	from	Mrs.	that's
am	fun	much	the
and	good	name	their
aunt	had	nice	then
baby	Halloween	now	there
balloon	has	on	time
basketball	have	once	to
because	he	one	today
bought	here	our	tomorrow
boy	him	out	too
brother	his	party	train
brought	home	people	two
can	hope	play	vacation
children	house	please	very
cousin	I'm	pretty	we
day	in	said	were
didn't	it	saw	when
dog	know	sent	white
don't	like	snow	with
everybody	little	some	write
father	made	sometimes	writing
fine	make	store	you
football	me	teacher	your
for			

LANGUAGE: A Glossary of Terms and Examples

Grammar

Sentences

- A **sentence** is a group of words that tells a complete thought. Every sentence begins with a capital letter.
- The **subject** of the sentence is the part about which something is being said.

  The bicycle is here. Sally sees it.
- The **predicate** is all the words that tell something about the subject.

  The bicycle stopped. It is parked on the grass.
- A **statement** tells something. It ends with a period (.).

  I cut my finger.
- A **question** asks something. It ends with a question mark (**?**).

  Did you tell the secret?
- A **command** gives an order or a direction. It ends with a period (.).

  Go home.
- An **exclamation** shows strong feeling. It ends with an exclamation mark (**!**).

  What a great idea you have!

Nouns

- A **noun** is a word that names a person, place, or thing.
- A **common noun** names any person, place, or thing. It begins with a small letter.

  pumpkin sister floor cabin

- A **proper noun** names a special person, place, or thing. A proper noun begins with a capital letter.

    Mrs. Takara   California   Halloween

- A **singular noun** names one person, place, or thing.

- A **plural noun** names more than one person, place, or thing.

- To form the plural of most nouns, add <u>s</u>.

    dot—dots   pen—pens

- To form the plural of nouns ending in <u>s</u>, <u>ss</u>, <u>x</u>, <u>ch</u>, or <u>sh</u>, add <u>es</u>.

    circus—circuses   six—sixes   watch—watches
    class—classes   dish—dishes

- To form the plural of nouns ending with a consonant and <u>y</u>, change the <u>y</u> to i and add <u>es</u>.

    cherry—cherries   party—parties

Verbs

- An **action verb** is a word that shows an action. It is found in the predicate of a sentence.

    eat   scratch   dash   call

- A **linking verb** connects the subject with words in the predicate. It tells what the subject <u>is</u> or <u>is like</u>. The following forms of <u>be</u> are often used as linking verbs.

    am   is   are   was   were

- You add <u>ing</u> to make a verb that can be used with these linking verbs. These verbs tell what <u>is</u> or <u>was</u> happening.

    I <u>am carrying</u> it for her.
    We <u>were studying</u> together.
    I <u>am inviting</u> John to the party.
    They <u>are skating</u> at the lake.
    She <u>is hiking</u> up the mountain.

- A **helping verb** helps the main verb tell about an action. The following words are often used as helping verbs.

am	is	are	was
were	have	has	had

Verb Tenses

- **Present time verbs** tell about actions that are happening now.

  > The curtains <u>open</u>.
  > The people <u>clap</u> and <u>cheer</u>.

- **Past time verbs** tell about actions in the past. Most past time verbs end in <u>ed</u>.

  > Abby <u>walked</u> quickly. Her dog <u>raced</u> ahead.
  > The dog <u>hurried</u>. Abby <u>chased</u> it.

Irregular Verbs

- **Irregular verbs** are verbs that do not add <u>ed</u> to show past time. Some of these verbs are on the chart.

Verb	Present	Past
begin	begin(s)	began
choose	choose(es)	chose
grow	grow(s)	grew
shake	shake(s)	shook

Adjectives

- An **adjective** is a word that describes a noun.

  > I have an <u>old</u> wagon.

Vocabulary

Compound Words

- A **compound word** is formed by putting two smaller words together.

    newspaper   haircut   football

Contractions

- A **contraction** is a short way of writing two words together. Some of the letters are left out. An apostrophe (') takes their place.

    I <u>can not</u> go to the party.
    I <u>can't</u> go to the party.

Homophones

- **Homophones** are words that sound alike. They are spelled differently and have different meanings.

    knot—not   brake—break

Rhyming Words

- **Rhyming words** end in the same sound.

    bake—lake   girl—whirl

Time-Clue Words

- **Time-clue words** help readers put a story in order.

    once   soon   when   before   after   finally

DICTIONARY: A Glossary of Terms and Examples

Alphabetical Order

- The order of letters from <u>A</u> to <u>Z</u> is called **alphabetical** order. Words in a dictionary are listed in alphabetical order. These words are in alphabetical order.

>   bluebird
>   crayon
>   pirate
>   pocket
>   space
>   spider

Guide Words

- There are two **guide words** at the top of each dictionary page. The word on the left is the first word on the page. The word on the right is the last word. All the other words on the page are in alphabetical order between those words.

---

package		paw

pack·age /pak′ij/ *n.* **1** Something wrapped up or tied up: We mailed a *package* to my brother at camp. **2** The box that holds something: The directions are on the *package.*

pad·dle /pad′(ə)l/ *n.* A short oar. —*v.* **paddled, paddling** **1** To use a paddle to move a boat. **2** To move your hands and feet in water: The children *paddled* about in the lake.

par·ent /pâr′ənt/ *n.* A person's mother or father.

park /pärk/ *n.* Land with trees, grass, and playgrounds. —*v.* To put a car somewhere and leave it: *Park* the car over there.

part /pärt/ *n.* **1** A piece of a whole. **2** Share: We all must do our *part.* **3** A role in a play. **4** Where hair is divided after combing: The *part* in Lynn's hair is crooked.

Entry Word

- On a dictionary page, an **entry word** is a word in dark print that is followed by its meaning or meanings. Entry words appear in alphabetical order.

> **chew** /cho͞o/ *v.* To grind up with your teeth: Always *chew* your food well.
> **child** /chīld/ *n.*, *pl.* **children** A young boy or girl.
> **chin** /chin/ *n.* The part of your face below your mouth.

Pronunciation

- A **pronunciation** is given after each entry word in a dictionary. It is a special way of writing a word that shows how to say the word.

  an·y   /en'ē/

Definition

- A **definition** tells what a word means in the dictionary. Many words have more than one definition.

> **move** /mo͞ov/ *v.* **moved, moving**
> **1** To go from one place to another: The car *moved* down the street.
> **2** To change where you live: The Engels *moved* to Grant Street.
> **3** To change position: The sleeping child didn't *move*.

Pronunciation Key

- A **pronunciation key** shows how to read the pronunciation.

act, āte, câre, ärt;   egg, ēven;   if, īce;   on, ōver, ôr;   bŏŏk, fōōd;   up, tûrn;
ə = a in *ago,* e in *listen,* i in *giraffe,* o in *pilot,* u in *circus;*   yōō = u in *music;*   oil;   out;
chair;   sing;   shop;   thank;   that;   zh in *treasure.*

Syllables

- A word is made up of several parts called **syllables.** Each syllable has a vowel sound.
- In a word with two or more syllables in the dictionary, the **accent mark** (') in the pronunciation shows which syllable is said with the most force.
- The syllable with the accent mark is called the **accented syllable.**

COMPOSITION

Guides for the Writing Process

Prewriting

Use this checklist to plan your writing.

- Think about what you want to write.
- Think about why you are writing.
- Think about who will read your work.
- Ask yourself questions about your idea.
- Make a plan.
- Read over your plan.
- Add more ideas to your plan as you think of them.

Here are some prewriting plans.

LISTMAKING
Thinking of Words

Parade

bands   flags   balloons

clowns   music   jugglers

singing   animals   clapping

CLUSTERING
Planning Sentences

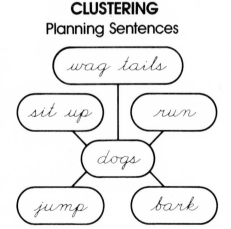

CHARTING
Sensory Details

See	Hear	Taste	Feel	Smell
beach	waves crashing	salty water	hot sand	fresh air
picnic	people talking	sour lemonade	cool grass	meat cooking

MAPPING
Drawing a Plan

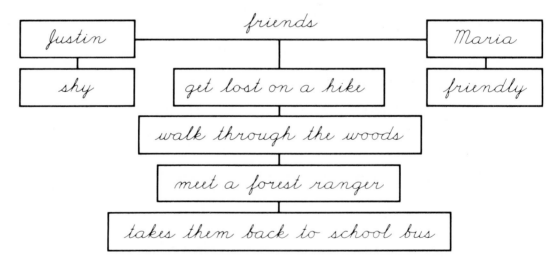

Composing

Use this checklist as you write.

- Read over your plan.
- Use your plan.
- Write quickly.
- Do not worry about mistakes.
- Remember that you may get more ideas as you write.
- Add new ideas as you think of them.
- Think about why you are writing.
- Think about who will read what you write.

Revising

Use this checklist when you edit and proofread your work.

Editing

- Read over your work.
- Be sure your sentences make sense.
- Check that each sentence is a complete thought.
- Be sure each paragraph has a clear topic sentence.
- Check that all the detail sentences support the main idea.
- Be sure the words are lively and interesting.

Proofreading

- Be sure you used capital letters correctly.
- Be sure you used periods, question marks, and exclamation points correctly.
- Check the spelling of each word.
- Be sure you used each word correctly.
- Be sure the first line of each paragraph is indented.
- Be sure your handwriting is neat and readable.

WRITER'S GUIDE

Editing and Proofreading Marks

- Use **editing and proofreading marks** when you revise your writing. These marks help you see the changes you want to make.
- Remember that you can go back and change words or sentences as many times as you want or need to.

Editing and Proofreading Marks

≡	capitalize
⊙	make a period
∧	add something
⌄,	add a comma
⌄⌄	add quotation marks
⌿	take something away
◯	spell correctly
⌿	indent the paragraph
/	make a lowercase letter
∼tr	transpose

The school fair will be held next tuesday afternoon. All students are going to attend⊙
            writing
There will be a∧contest and a crafts show.

Science projects will also be displayed. Teachers, families, and friends will be invited. The school band will play "The Star-Spangled Banner." Then the principal and the coach
        Prizes
will give a speech. (Prises) will be given for the best compositions and drawings. ⌿The fair has always been a highlight of the school year.

Plans are already being made for the fair next year. It will (place take) in April instead
                    tr
of in May.

248

A Glossary of Terms and Examples

Kinds of Sentences

- A **sentence** is a group of words that tells a complete thought. Every sentence begins with a capital letter.
- A **statement** tells something. It ends with a period (.).
    I cut my finger.
- A **question** asks something. It ends with a question mark (**?**).
    Did you tell the secret?
- A **command** gives an order or a direction. It ends with a period (.).
    Go home.
- An **exclamation** shows strong feeling. It ends with an exclamation mark (**!**).
    What a great idea you have!

Paragraph

- A **paragraph** is a group of sentences that tell about one main idea.
- The **topic sentence** tells the main idea of the paragraph.
- The first line of a paragraph is indented.

Descriptive Paragraph

- A paragraph that describes a person, place, or thing is called a **descriptive paragraph.**
- A descriptive paragraph begins with a topic sentence. This sentence tells what the paragraph is about.
- Other sentences in the paragraph are the **detail sentences.** These sentences use clear and colorful words to describe the topic.

An example of a descriptive paragraph is on the next page.

Here is an example of a descriptive paragraph.

> *It was the day after the big snowfall. Clean white snow glistened in the bright sunlight. Long, sparkling icicles hung from roofs. Laughing children ran out of their houses. The cold, crisp air stung their cheeks. They carried bright red sleds in their arms.*

How-to Paragraph

- A **how-to paragraph** gives directions on how to do something.
- The topic sentence tells what the paragraph is about.
- The paragraph tells what materials are needed.
- Detail sentences explain the steps of how to do something.
- **Time-clue words,** words that help the reader follow the correct order, are also used. <u>First</u> and <u>last</u> are some examples of time-clue words.

Here is an example of a how-to paragraph.

> *Making play dough is easy. You need a cup of water, some food coloring, a cup of salt, two cups of flour, two tablespoons of oil, a bowl, and a big spoon. First, put the water in the bowl. Second, add the food coloring to the water and stir with the spoon. Next, add the salt, the flour, and the oil to the water mixture. Last, stir the mixture with the spoon until it is smooth.*

Friendly Letter

- A **friendly letter** has five parts.

- The **heading** contains the letter writer's address and the date. A comma is used between the name of the city and the state and between the day and the year.

- The **greeting** welcomes the person who receives the letter. The greeting begins with a capital letter. The greeting is followed by a comma.

- The **body** of the letter contains the message.

- The **closing** is the end of the letter. The first word is capitalized. A comma follows the closing.

- The **signature** is the written name of the person who wrote the letter.

Here is an example of a friendly letter.

```
                        1508 N.E. 49th St.
                        Gladstone, Missouri 64118    Heading
                        September 28, 19—

Dear Mike,                                           Greeting
    Thanks for your letter. I'm glad you are
having fun with your grandparents. Dad               Body
and I went fishing yesterday. Wish you could
have been with us. See you soon.

                        Sincerely,                   Closing
                        Dave                         Signature
```

Journal

- A **journal** is something for you to write in every day. You can write about what happens to you each day.
- Each journal entry starts with the day and date.

Here is an example of a journal entry.

Saturday, October 13, 19——

  Today was my ninth birthday. Mom and Dad invited my friends over for a surprise party. I was happy to see my friends. I thought everyone had forgotten my birthday.

Story

- A **story beginning** sets the scene for the action in the story. It tells <u>who</u> the story is about. It tells <u>what</u> is happening. It tells <u>where</u> it is happening and <u>when</u> it is happening.
- The **middle of the story** tells what happens to the characters. Sentences in a story must be in order so that the story makes sense.
- The **ending of the story** should tell how the characters solve their problems. It should answer the question <u>why</u>. Make sure the ending finishes the story.
- A story has a title. The first word and each important word begin with a capital letter.

See the example of a story on page 253.

> ### A Ride in a Big Truck
>
> Last summer I was riding with Dad in his big truck. We came to a tunnel in the city. We drove into the tunnel, and suddenly we were stuck. The tunnel was too low for the truck! Dad didn't know what to do. Then I had a good idea. I told Dad that maybe he should let some air out of our tires. A big smile came onto Dad's face. He let some air out of each tire. Then we drove out of the tunnel. Dad was proud of me, and I was proud of myself too.

News Story

- A **news story** is written to give readers information.
- The most important information in a news story is presented first.
- The answers to the questions <u>who</u>, <u>what</u>, <u>when</u>, <u>where</u>, and <u>how</u> are included at the beginning of the news story.
- A **headline** is a title that gives a short statement of the content of the story. The first word and each important word begin with a capital letter.

Here is an example of the beginning of a news story.

> ### Bantam Circus Comes to Mayfield
>
> A crowd of more than 1,000 people enjoyed the opening of the Bantam Circus last night at the County Fairgrounds. The circus, which has shows daily at 7:00 P.M. through Saturday, donated the money from last night's performance to three Mayfield charities.

Report

- A **report** presents facts about a topic.
- Before writing a report, take notes.
- Use your notes to make an **outline.** An outline has a title and lists the most important ideas from the notes.
- Write a paragraph for each main topic of the outline.

Here is an example of a title and first paragraph from a report.

A Comparison of Spiders and Insects

People often call spiders insects, but spiders are different from insects in many ways. Spiders have eight legs. Insects have only six legs. A spider's body has two sections. An insect's body has three sections. Spiders have no wings. Most insects have two wings.

Rhyming Poem

- The last words in many lines of poetry end in the same sound. When words end in the same sounds, they rhyme.

Here is an example of a rhyming poem.

The falling snowflakes make no sound.
as they softly touch the ground.
Like a mother dressed in white.
come to kiss her babe goodnight.

MECHANICS: A Glossary of Rules

Capital Letters

Names and Titles of People and I

- Begin the name of a person with a capital letter.
  Douglas Dunn   Marsha Billings
- Begin titles of a person such as Ms., Mrs., Mr., and Dr. with a capital letter.
- Capitalize initials that take the place of names.
  Dorothy J. Arthur   Jackie E. Smith
- Always capitalize the word I.

Names of Places

- Begin each important word in the name of a town, city, state, or country with a capital letter.
  Enfield, New York
- Begin each important word in the name of a street and its abbreviation with a capital letter.
  Green St.

Names of Days, Months, and Holidays

- Begin the name of a day of the week or its abbreviation with a capital letter.
  Monday   Mon.   Wednesday   Wed.
- Begin the name of a month or its abbreviation with a capital letter.
  December   Dec.   August   Aug.
- Begin each important word in the name of a holiday with a capital letter.
  Washington's Birthday   Thanksgiving

Names of Books, Stories, Poems, and Television Shows

- Use a capital letter to begin the first, last, and all important words in the title of a book, story, poem, or television show.

    <u>The Wind in the Willows</u>   "Sleeping Beauty"

Sentences

- Use a capital letter to begin a sentence.

    That book is mine.

Punctuation

Period

- Use a period (.) at the end of a statement or command.

    I see you.   Go away.
- Use a period (.) after an abbreviation.

    Wed.   Ave.   A.M.   Dr.
- Use a period (.) after a numeral before the main topic in an outline.

    I. United States
    II. Mexico

Comma

- Use a comma (,) between the city and the state.

    Baton Rouge, Louisiana   Albany, New York
- Use a comma (,) between the day and the year.

    January 1, 1916
- Use a comma (,) after the greeting in a friendly letter and after the closing of any letter.

    Dear Sara,   Your friend,

Question Mark

- Use a question mark (**?**) at the end of a question.
    Did they stay long?

Exclamation Point

- Use an exclamation point (**!**) at the end of an exclamation.
    What a pretty child!

Quotation Marks and Underlines

- Use quotation marks (" ") before and after the title of a story or poem.
    "Cinderella"   "My Dog"
- Use quotation marks around a speaker's words when writing conversation.
    Marianne said, "I'm going home."
- Underline the title of a book or television show.
    Encyclopedia Brown   The Cosby Show

Apostrophe and Colon

- Use an apostrophe (**'**) to show that one or more letters have been left out in a contraction.
    he's   we'll
- Add an apostrophe (**'**) and an <u>s</u> to singular nouns to show possession.
    Fran's toy   student's book
- Add an apostrophe (**'**) to plural nouns that end in <u>s</u> to show possession.
    the boys' bicycles   the Smiths' house
- Use a colon (**:**) between the hour and the minutes in the time of day.
    4:00   6:45   11:30

HANDWRITING: Alphabet and Common Errors

Uppercase Manuscript Alphabet

Lowercase Manuscript Alphabet

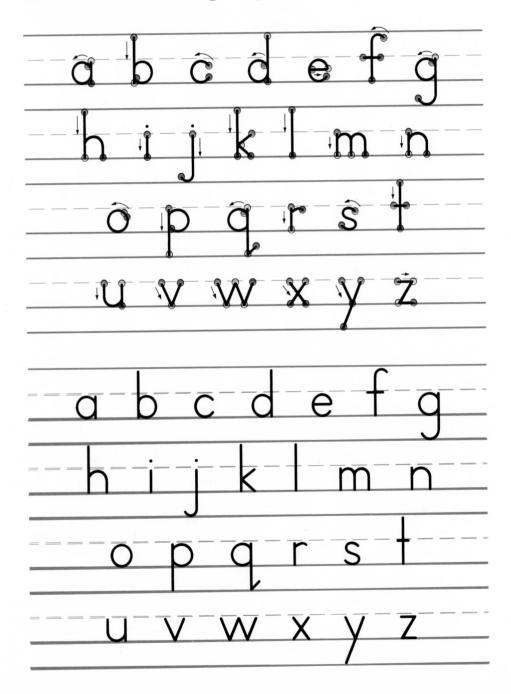

Uppercase Cursive Alphabet

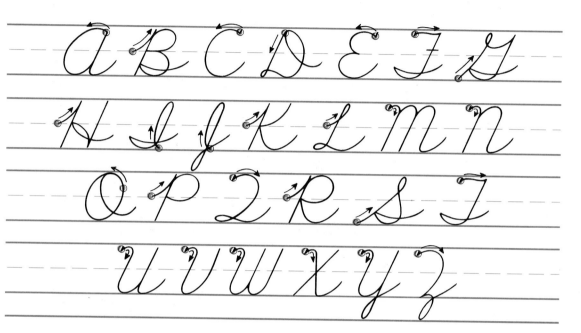

Lowercase Cursive Alphabet

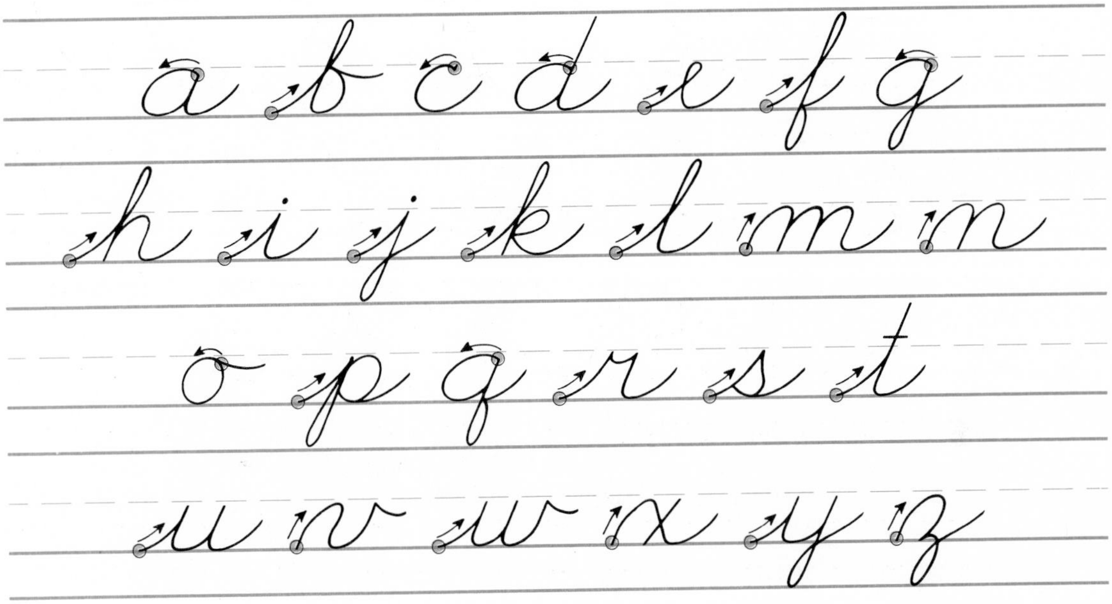

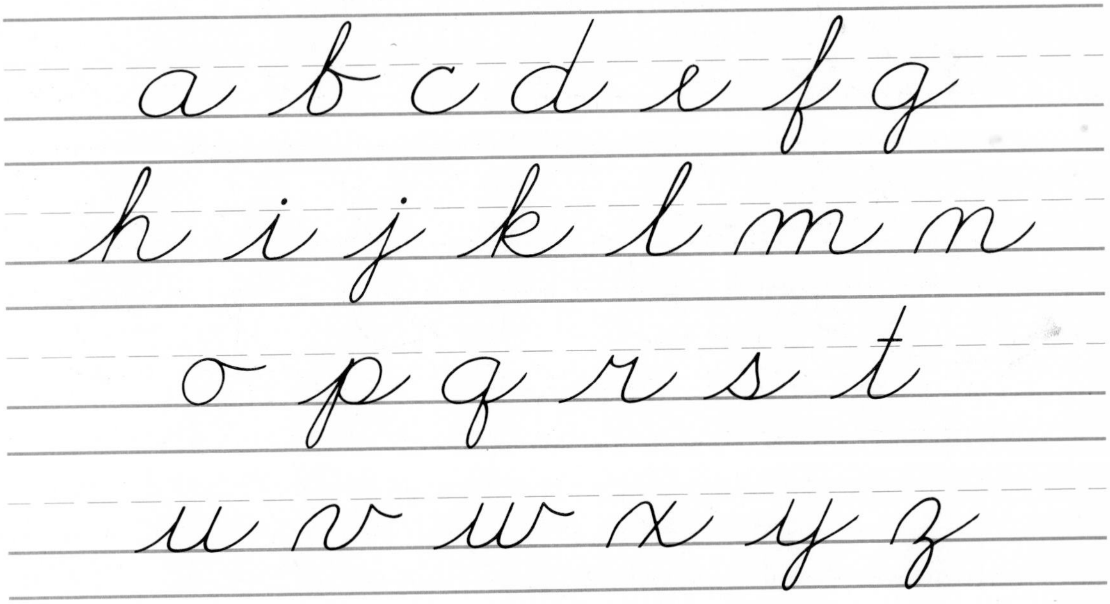

a b c d e f g

h i j k l m n

o p q r s t

u v w x y z

a b c d e f g

h i j k l m n

o p q r s t

u v w x y z

Common Errors–Manuscript Letters

• Write the letters correctly.

Wrong   Right

V   *r*   Be sure to retrace almost to the midline.
The **r** could look like **v.**

Wrong   Right

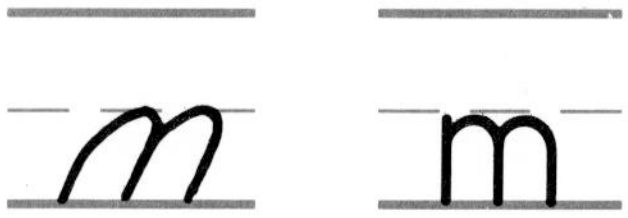

m   *m*   Be sure to start at the midline.
The **m** could look like cursive **n.**

Wrong   Right

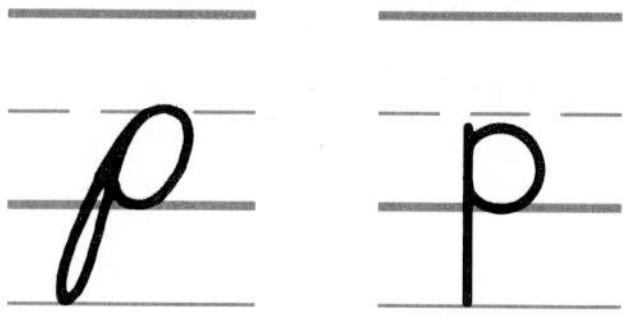

p   *p*   Be sure not to loop in the retrace.
The **p** could look like cursive **p.**

Wrong   Right

d   *d*   Be sure to close the circle and retrace.
The **d** could look like cursive **cl.**

Wrong   Right

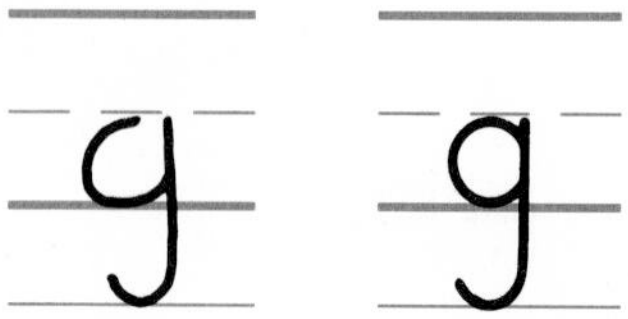

g   *g*   Be sure to close the circle.
The **g** could look like cursive **cj.**

Wrong   Right

Be sure to use the slant right stroke.
The **q** could look like **g**.

Wrong   Right

Be sure not to loop in the retrace stroke.
The **u** could look like cursive **ie**.

Wrong   Right

Be sure to start the second stroke at
the midline. The **k** could look like
uppercase **K**.

Wrong   Right

Be sure to use the across strokes.
The **I** could look like lowercase **l**.

Wrong   Right

Be sure to add the slant stroke.
The **Q** could look like **O**.

Wrong   Right

Be sure to use the across stroke at the midline. The **G** could look like **C.**

Wrong   Right

Be sure not to retrace. The **U** could look like cursive **U.**

Wrong   Right

Be sure to use a straight downstroke and retrace. The **D** could look like **O.**

Wrong   Right

Be sure to start at the top line.
The **W** could look like lowercase **w.**

Common Errors–Cursive Letters

● Write the letters correctly.

Wrong   Right

Be sure not to loop. The **i** could look like **e**.

Wrong   Right

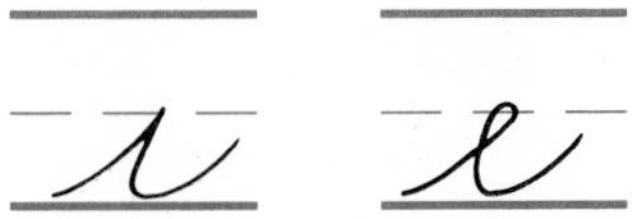

Be sure to make a loop. The **e** could look like **i**.

Wrong   Right

Be sure to touch the top line. The **l** could look like **e**.

Wrong   Right

Be sure the slant stroke returns to the bottom line. The **u** could look like **v**.

Wrong   Right

Be sure not to loop. The **u** could look like **ee**.

Wrong   Right

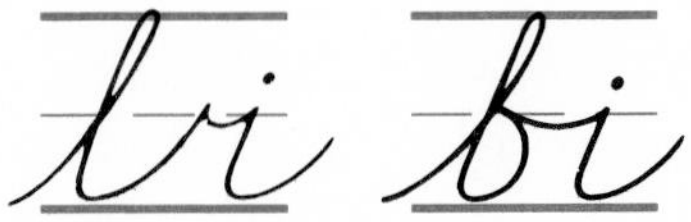

Be sure to close the circle stroke. The **bi** could look like **lr**.

Wrong	Right	
tr	*h*	Be sure to retrace with the overcurve. The **h** could look like **lr**.
jo	*p*	Be sure to retrace to the midline. The **p** could look like **jo**.
tri	*tri*	Be sure to touch the midline twice. The **tri** could look like **tu**.
a	*a*	Be sure to close the circle stroke. The **a** could look like **u**.
cl	*d*	Be sure to close the circle stroke. The **d** could look like **cl**.
q	*g*	Be sure to loop left. The **g** could look like **q**.

Wrong	Right	
mm	*m*	Be sure to make cursive **m** look like manuscript **m.**
ve	*ve*	Be sure to make the straight slant in the right direction. The **ve** could look like **re.**
Pe	*Pe*	Remember **P** does not join other letters. The **P** could look like **R.**
K	*K*	Be sure to touch the stem. The **K** could look like **H.**
n	*N*	Be sure to start at the top line. The **N** could look like lowercase **n.**
Ua	*Va*	Remember **V** has no joining stroke. The **V** could look like **U.**

Wrong   Right

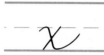 

Remember **W** only joins with **h**.
The **We** could look like **Ule**.

Wrong   Right

Be sure to start at the top line.
The **X** could look like lowercase **x**.

Wrong   Right

Be sure not to cross **T**.
The **T** could look like **F**.

Wrong   Right

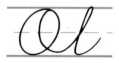 

Be sure to close the circle and not
loop. The **A** could look like **Cl**.

Wrong   Right

Be sure the joining stroke curves to
the midline. The **Ol** could look
like **Al**.

Wrong   Right

Be sure to start at the midline and
undercurve to the top line. The **L**
could look like **Q**.

Wrong   Right

Be sure to slant the first stroke.
The **S** could look like **G**.

Wrong   Right

Be sure to curve to the top line.
The **J** could look like **g**.

8
9
0
E 1
F 2
G 3
H 4
I 5
J 6